Legends and Life in Texas
Folklore from the Lone Star State, in Stories and Song

Legends and Life in Texas
Folklore from the Lone Star State, in Stories and Song

Edited by
Kenneth L. Untiedt

Publications of the Texas Folklore Society LXXII

University of North Texas Press
Denton, Texas

10 9 8 7 6 5 4 3 2 1

Permissions:
University of North Texas Press
1155 Union Circle #311336
Denton, TX 76203-5017

The paper used in this book meets the minimum requirements of the American National Standard for Permanence of Paper for Printed Library Materials, z39.48.1984. Binding materials have been chosen for durability.

Library of Congress Cataloging-in-Publication Data

Untiedt, Kenneth L., 1966- editor.
Legends and life in Texas : folklore from the Lone Star State, in stories and song / edited by Kenneth L. Untiedt.
Publications of the Texas Folklore Society ; no. 72.
Denton, Texas : University of North Texas Press, [2017] | Publications of the Texas Folklore Society ; lxxii | Includes bibliographical references and index.
LCCN 2017039500| ISBN 9781574416978 (cloth : alk. paper) | ISBN 9781574417081 (ebook)
LCSH: Folklore--Texas. | Texas--Biography. | Texas--Social life and customs. | Folk songs, English--Texas--History and criticism. | Folk music--Texas--History and criticism.
LCC GR110.T5 L43 2017 | DDC 398.209764--dc23
LC record available at https://lccn.loc.gov/2017039500

Legends and Life in Texas: Folklore from the Lone Star State, in Stories and Song is Number LXXII in the Publications of the Texas Folklore Society Series

The electronic edition of this book was made possible by the support of the Vick Family Foundation.

CONTENTS

PREFACE

When I first heard Jerry Young give his paper on Jacob Brodbeck at the 2016 TFS meeting in Austin, I knew I wanted to publish it. Here was a story of a man who built his own airship and had sustained flight, forty years before the Wright Brothers. He was truly someone who was a legendary Texan, someone who possessed the tenacity, strength, courage, and sheer determination that embody all that make this state unlike any other. Jerry's paper was just one of several that year that featured Texans whose stories were fascinating for one reason or another, yet many had been lost in the annals of Texas history. A rodeo star with a wooden leg who rode buffalo, female bullfighters, Cynthia Ann Parker, Sam Houston, Davy Crockett, and a mysterious hermit who inhabited a cavern that has become a tourist attraction—all of these people are what make Texas such a unique and amazing place, and these articles pick up where the history books left off.

Such began the framework for this, the 72nd volume in our regular PTFS series. I knew that I wanted to feature not only these larger-than-life characters, but also a few of our own. You'll find articles in this volume about Mody Boatright and John O. West. If you're part of the TFS family, these names are familiar; if you don't recognize them, this is your chance to learn more about the people who helped shape the Society, by learning about their origins, their personal lives, and the impact they had on others. Originally, I thought I'd do the entire volume on just these renowned Texans that history had seemed to have forgotten in some cases, but I didn't want to limit the focus too much. Well, I admit that I also had some papers in hand that I just couldn't resist—some on "times passed," that look back on what life was like in the days when people actually visited in person and appreciated simple luxuries, such as early automobiles and innovations that made cooking easier. I also couldn't wait to publish a few papers members had done in recent years on music. If you've been to a meeting, you know how important music is to our group, and although it's a short chapter, the papers in it provide insight into childhood songs, dance customs, and music from some pretty eclectic groups.

The Society has published full-length books on several special topics, as well as dozens of miscellanies. These books are generally comprised of papers presented at our annual meetings, although some come from independent submissions. These publications represent a wide array of folklore scholarship that is central to the mission of the Texas Folklore Society: to collect, present, and preserve the lore of Texas and the Southwest. This book does just that, focusing on what seems like three distinct areas—legendary characters, music, and remembering the "old days." However, readers should see the thread that runs through each of these papers. There is a story behind each unique character, behind every song, connected to each memory of days of our youth; these stories are shared among families, and passed on from generation to generation. Regardless of what history books tell us, these are tales that we keep alive because they are dear to our hearts.

I am thankful to the contributors whose works are included in this book. While I appreciated being able to call on some of the "faithful"—Jack Duncan, Jean Schnitz, and Charles Martin—I am also glad to be able to introduce some "rookies"—Erin Marissa Russell and Matt Gibson, Barbara Finlay, Jim Bridges, and John Meadows, whose works appear for the first time in a TFS publication (even though a few have been members for a long time). I trust they will continue to contribute for years to come.

I also want to share my appreciation of some other key people who help make these publications possible. At the risk of seeming too "automatic" since I always mention them, I thank all the folks at the UNT Press who help us put these books together each year; although I thank them each year, I really must emphasize what a great working relationship the TFS has with Karen DeVinney, Ron

Chrisman, and the entire UNT group. I also want to express my sincere gratitude to the people at Stephen F. Austin State University who continue to generously support the Society, including the Chair of the Department of English and Creative Writing, Mark Sanders, and Brian Murphy, the Dean of the College of Liberal and Applied Arts. There are, of course, other administrators, staff, and colleagues who help make SFA a pleasant place to work. At the very least, I give special thanks to Charlotte Blacksher, our Office Secretary and Treasurer.

Jerry Young's paper was the genesis of this publication, and he was among the first to rework his manuscript, sign the necessary forms, and complete the checklist we have for our contributors. Unfortunately, Jerry passed away before this book saw print. At the time of his death, he was still faithfully serving as a Councilor on the Texas Folklore Society Board, as well as entertaining thousands of people with his tales at storytelling events across this state and beyond. I dedicate this book to him, and I thank him for his service to the Texas Folklore Society, and his devotion to keeping the stories alive. Jerry, you're missed already.

Kenneth L. Untiedt
Stephen F. Austin State University
Nacogdoches, Texas
May 19, 2017

TENNESSEE
HERITAGE TRAIL
WELCOME
TO
SAM HOUSTON
SCHOOLHOUSE
1784

I. "Legendary" Texans

Jerry Young giving his paper on Jacob Brodbeck at the 2016 TFS Meeting.

JACOB BRODBECK: THE FIRST MAN TO FLY

by Jerry Young

Jacob Brodbeck and his younger brother George joined the German migration to Texas in 1847. The voyage aboard the ship *Element* was a stormy and blustery crossing. Brodbeck came to believe there had to be a safer and smoother way to cross the Atlantic.

Sitting on the deck of the ship, Brodbeck watched the way the ship's sails were trimmed to catch the wind and drive the ship. With special interest, he observed the flight of gulls, and the way they slipped and soared in the air above the ship.[1] Spending hours contemplating the movement of the ship and the flight of gulls, Brodbeck began to piece together in his mind an idea for a machine he called an air-ship that would launch mankind into the air to fly with the birds.

The idea gestated in Jacob Brodbeck's head for twenty years before he launched his air-ship in 1865, thirty-eight years before the Wright brothers' plane lifted off the sands of Kitty Hawk.[2]

Brodbeck's achievement is one of those events in Texas history that remains unknown, overlooked, or ignored. Although the evidence is murky at times, this paper proposes to establish that Texan Jacob Brodbeck was the first man to fly a heavier-than-air machine—not once but twice! Once was in Boerne in 1865 and once was in Luckenbach in 1875.

Jacob Brodbeck was born in Württemberg, Germany, in 1821. He attended university where he majored in mathematics and graduated at the age of eighteen. He taught school in his hometown for six years before he and his brother joined the German settlers on the frontier in New Braunfels and Fredricksburg.[3]

Brodbeck was something of a mechanical genius. Before he left Germany, he designed and built for the King of Prussia a self-winding clock that supposedly ran off perpetual motion.[4] Once in

Texas, he built rubber-band powered flying toys for his children. He designed and built an ice making machine for his close friend and financial backer, Dr. Ferdinand Herff of Boerne.[5] In the 1860s, Mrs. Brodbeck did her laundry with a washing machine that ran off a power takeoff wheel from the windmill, another of Brodbeck's inventions.[6]

Within a year of settling in Texas, Brodbeck was appointed teacher for Fredericksburg's Verne Kirche. The Kirche had little to offer as a place of learning. The building had only a sand floor, and there were no student desks, only crude benches made of rough sawed planks for the children to sit on. Brodbeck taught the children reading, writing, and mathematics. Apparently, he was as creative a teacher as he was an inventor. With no slates for the children, Brodbeck used sticks to teach the students to count, add, and subtract. He led the students in singing songs as a way to learn oral language skills. Brodbeck also told stories to keep the students involved in their school work, and he told them about his idea "to build an air craft and fly like a bird in the air."[7] Some folks thought this was a crazy idea for a teacher to hold.

Brodbeck married Maria Christiana Beherens in 1858, and the newlyweds moved to a farm on Grape Creek near Luckenbach. The first of their twelve children was born the following year. In 1860, Brodbeck organized and taught in the Grape Hill School. As it turned out, Maria did most of the farming while Jacob taught school and tinkered with his air-ship.[8]

By 1863, Brodbeck had built his air-ship, but like most visionaries, he lacked cash to make his vision a reality. The Union blockade of Texas during the Civil War created belt-tightening measures for business and private ventures.[9] There was certainly no money in the state for a far-fetched idea like a flying machine.

In order to attract investors for his air-craft, Brodbeck constructed small working models and demonstrated them at fairs around the state.[10] In April, 1863, he published a notice in *The Galveston Tri-Weekly* newspaper hoping to solicit investors for the air-ship.[11] In the notice, Brodbeck offered investors an opportunity to buy shares in his flying-ship at five dollars a share, "to be refunded together with a part of the proceeds of the sale of the patent right, or the sale of air-ships." In response to the notice, several prominent men invested in Brodbeck's idea, including the well-known physician and Brodbeck's friend Dr. Herff, a New Braunfels brewer named Karl H. Gunther, and the Rev. August Engel, a Methodist preacher and postmaster of Carnes Mill.[12]

No plans or blueprints of Brodbeck's air-ship have survived. Only two pictures of the air-craft exist: one was supposedly drawn by Brodbeck's daughter on the day of the first flight,[13] and the second one is a plate glass negative of the wrecked air-ship.[14] Brodbeck's notice in *The Galveston Tri-Weekly* provides the only description of the air-ship's design.

The air-ship was a bi-plane design with an enclosed gondola suspended beneath the wings. For Brodbeck, the enclosed gondola was an essential part of the air-ship to protect the aeronaut. Brodbeck anticipated the air-ship to attain speeds of forty to one hundred miles an hour, and he feared at those speeds, the aeronaut, as he tagged the pilot, would be unable to breathe.

The gondola was shaped like a ship with a prow and a stern. A propeller screw was attached at the stern of the gondola in the event the air-ship landed on water. The helicopter-like propeller blades above the wings were powered by two massive clock-spring engines. Brodbeck's thought was that as spring motor "A" ran down, the aeronaut would re-wind spring motor "B" to maintain a sustained flight.[15]

Within the gondola, the aeronaut had a compass in front of him to maintain a flight path and a barometer to determine altitude. Two handles allowed the aeronaut to steer the air-ship by adjusting the pitch of the wings. Also, there were cranks in front of the aeronaut with which to re-wind the spring motors.[16] The gondola would have been a very busy place for the aeronaut as he manipulated handles to keep the plane in the air and, at the same time, twisted cranks to re-wind the spring motors.

On September 20, 1865, Brodbeck and some of his neighbors hauled the air-ship to the top of a barn in a field on Dr. Herff's farm east of Boerne. (Part of Herff's farm is now the Cibolo Nature

Center.) The air-ship was anchored atop the barn with a rope, poised to take flight and fly with the birds. Or that was Jacob Brodbeck's anticipation.

Spectators crowded around the edge of the field waiting to see Brodbeck's contraption fly. Among the crowd were Brodbeck's financial backers. A successful flight meant financial profit for the investors. Brodbeck's wife Maria and their children, along with Brodbeck's brother George, held their breaths and crossed their fingers that the air-ship would take off and land safely. Curious onlookers among the crowd just wanted to see what all the hoopla was about. And skeptics among the crowd scoffed and declared, "If God had intended mankind to fly, He would have created men with wings."

At the starting moment, Brodbeck cut the anchor rope with a knife, and the air-ship slid down the barn roof. Powered by the giant spring motors, the overhead propellers made a whosh, whosh sound as the air-craft launched into the air. Jacob Brodbeck lived his dream. The air-ship flew above the field with the birds. Some years later, Brodbeck wrote the following account of his first flight:

> I wound up the massive coil spring and cut loose the rope as I released the lever for take-off. The take-off was a success and the "Air Ship" soared majestically (about 50 yards) over the tree-tops. As the coil spring unwound suddenly something happened with the mechanism and I was unable to rewind the spring fast enough to remain aloft. I found myself dashing towards the ground with my spirits shattered. I suffered only minor injuries, but my "pride and joy" suffered severe damage.[17]

Brodbeck surveyed the damage. Twenty years of dreaming, planning, and labor lay before him, a broken and crumpled pile of wood and fabric. What was he to do? For Jacob Brodbeck, there was only one option: haul the wrecked air-ship back to Dr. Herff's barn and start over.[18]

After the air-ship failed to fly, Brodbeck's investors lost faith in the project and withdrew their support. The men who bought shares in the air-ship do not mention Brodbeck nor the air-ship in their personal diaries or correspondence. Nor do they record their financial involvement in the project.[19] Neighbors wrote off Jacob Brodbeck as a "crack-pot" with a "hare-brained" idea that didn't work. It would be ten years before he made a second attempt to fly the air-ship.

Day to day necessities of a large family required Brodbeck to earn a living. He taught in the Grape Hill School for several years before Dr. Herff secured Brodbeck a position as Bexar County School Inspector. Brodbeck left his family in Luckenbach and moved to San Antonio. At the end of the term in 1870, Dr. Herff urged his friend to return to his family and to continue working on the air-ship.[20]

Brodbeck and his bother built a workshop with a high, steep roof as a launching pad on the farm three miles east of Luckenbach. They then hauled the wrecked air-ship from Dr. Herff's farm in Boerne to Luckenbach. Brodbeck and his brother worked on the air-ship through family crises such as a short-lived Indian scare, a lost herd of horses, and Brodbeck's bouts with arthritis. However, by the summer of 1875, the air-ship was repaired and ready for flight. Again, neighbors were enlisted to help hoist the air-ship to the top of the workshop. On August 7, 1875, Jacob Brodbeck cut the air-ship from the anchor rope, and the craft flew about one hundred feet at ten to twelve feet above the field before crashing once again.[21]

Evidence of a second flight is contradictory. Most sources cite the Luckenbach flight, assigning it either the 1865 or the 1875 date. In their book *Aviation in Texas*, Roger Bilstein and Jay Miller are flat out skeptical the flights ever took place, yet they go on to state the Luckenbach flight took place in 1865. Their analysis of Brodbeck's description of the air-ship leads Bilstein and Miller to conclude the machine's design was a type of ornithopeter and therefore a "dead end concept."[22] However, Anita Tatsch affirms in her memorial biography of Brodbeck that he did make two flights, the one on Herff's farm in Boerne in 1865, and the second flight on the Luckenbach farm in 1875. Brent Evans also confirms two flights in a pamphlet titled "The White Feather." [23]

Jacob Brodbeck, devastated by a sense of failure, never came to terms with his flawed vision. He showed his drawings and plans to anyone who would look at them, and he continued to seek financial backers for the project without success.[24] During his travels about the country to drum up financial support, Brodbeck's plans and drawings for the air-ship disappeared. One source reports the plans and drawings went missing while Brodbeck met with Octave Chanute in Michigan. (Chanute was known for his experiments with gliders,[25] and he was a close friend and financial supporter of Orville and Wilbur Wright.)[26] Another source suggests the plans were stolen when Brodbeck took them and a small working model of the air-ship to the 1900 Saint Louis World's Fair[27] A third account relates that Brodbeck's drawings were stolen while he was in Washington D.C., trying to secure a patent and raise money for the air-ship.[28]

One of two busts celebrating Jacob Brodbeck's achievements.

With the drawings and plans lost, a pall of failure fell about Brodbeck, and he returned to Texas, a man with a lost vision. He lived out his life on his farm in Luckenbach, where he died in 1910, seven years after the Wright brothers flew their airplane.[29] Over the years, Brodbeck's achievement faded into obscurity.

So what is Jacob Brodbeck's legacy? Two busts, one in Fredericksburg's City Park and a second one in San Antonio's San Pedro Park, recognize his achievement. In 1967, Governor John Connally named Brodbeck the Father of Aviation.[30] And while Brodbeck's name is not listed among the honor roll of pioneer flyers like the Wright brothers, Charles Lindbergh, John Glenn, and Sally Ride, this paper commemorates Jacob Brodbeck as a legendary Texan who was the first man to fly in a machine he called an air-ship.

Endnotes

1. Anita Tatsch. *Reached for the Sky.* Fredericksburg, TX. 1989. 24.
2. Ibid. 24.
3. "The Brodbeck Airship First Flight." www.texaslesstraveled.com/brodbeck.htm. July 23, 2015. 1.
4. Ibid 1.
5. "The Brodbeck Airship First Flight." 1.
6. C. F. Eckhardt. "First to Fly." www.texasescapes.com/CFEckhardt/First-to-Fly-Jacob-Brodbeck.htm. July 24, 2015. 1.
7. Tatsch. 33.
8. Ibid. 36 ff.
9. Ibid 35.
10. "The Brodbeck Airship First Flight." 2.
11. "Beyond the Gate." Daughters of the Republic of Texas (DRT). www.drtlibrary.wordpress.com/2009/09/30/was-a-texan-the-first-man-to-fly-in-an-airplane/. 2.
12. "Brodbeck, Jacob Fredrich." Texas State Historical Association (TSHA). www.texasaviationonline.com/2/category/jacob%20brodbeck/1.html. March 2015. 1.
13. "The Brodbeck Flight in Kendall County." *Explore Magazine.* www.hillcountryexplore.com/?p=2099. October 31, 2013. 2.
14. "Beyond the Gate." 1.
15. Roger Bilstein, and Jay Miller. *Aviation in Texas.* Austin, Texas. 1989. 8.
16. Ibid. 8.
17. "The Brodbeck Flight in Kendall County."
18. Tatsch. 42.
19. Ibid. 35, 36.
20. Ibid. 38.
21. Ibid. 45.
22. Bilstein and Miller. 8.
23. Brent Evans. "The White Feather." Boerne, TX: Cibolo Nature Center & Farm.

24. "Wings Over Luckenbach: Jacob Brodbeck and the Limits of History." www.madronoranch.com/?p=311. March 19, 2010. 2.
25. Tatsch. 46.
26. David McCullough. *The Wright Brothers.* New York: Simon & Schuster. 2015.
27. Eckhardt. 2.
28. "Wings Over Luckenbach." 2.
29. "Brodbeck, Joseph Fredrich." 2.
30. "The Brodbeck Flight in Kendall County."

Jo Virgil.

HUGH "HACKBERRY SLIM" JOHNSON, II

by Jo Virgil

Lots of folks and stories in Texas history are considered "legends," but few meet the true definition of the word more than Hugh "Hackberry Slim" Johnson and his tales.

The *Merriam-Webster Dictionary* defines a legend as "a story coming down from the past, especially one popularly regarded as historical although not verifiable, or a person that is a subject of such a story." That's Hackberry Slim to a T, the legendary Buffalo Rodeo master and genuine storyteller.

Hugh Allen Johnson II, who later came to be known as Hackberry Slim, was born in 1888 on Bull Branch in the southeast part of Bell County, Texas. His father had served as a Confederate soldier in Mississippi during the Civil War and came to Texas shortly after the war's end to work herding cattle, and he wound up marrying the trail boss's daughter. The two of them parented Hugh and twelve other children. Hugh Johnson II, aka Hackberry Slim, was the last survivor of the family and lived to be 91 years old.

His whole life, including the day he died, is quite a story—most of it verifiable, some of it just a mighty fine story, factual or not. Johnson's early years, before his Buffalo Rodeo, are sketchy at best, but he became known as "Hackberry Slim" Johnson sometime in the early 1900s.

"The story my dad heard," said Daniel Johnson, Hackberry's great-grandson, in a conversation we had recently, "was that Hugh was working for the railroad and had some awful accident that made him lose his leg."

Other versions, mostly told by Hackberry to various reporters, include his losing a wild tangle with a mean horse, or being thrown from a bull, or getting his leg caught while trying to rope a raunchy steer at a rodeo. During World War II, when Hackberry worked as a boiler tender at the Brown Shipyard in Houston, he spoke with an Associated Press reporter about his rodeo history. In the interview, published in 1944 in *The Evening Independent*, a St. Petersburg, Florida, newspaper, he refused to say exactly how he lost his leg, but simply claimed it had to do with being tossed from a bronc in Dalhart, in the Panhandle of Texas.[1]

Regardless of which of the stories was closest to the truth, once he had recuperated from the loss of his leg, the tale goes, Hugh carved himself a wooden leg from a hackberry tree. He began to introduce himself as Hackberry Johnson and, not surprisingly, the name stuck. It later evolved into "Hackberry Slim," a name befitting a cowboy of his stature, both literally and metaphorically.

Indeed, there are many media stories about Hackberry Slim Johnson and his quirky personality, but the facts can be a bit sketchy. Because Hackberry loved to spin tales, his life story evolved as time went along, and reporters often found it difficult to determine which elements of the tale were fact and which were simply exaggerated elements of good storytelling.

In discovering the tales of his great-grandfather, Daniel Johnson wasn't much concerned about some of Hackberry's embellishments. In his mind, that's just part of who Hackberry was. "Dad told me a lot of stories about Hackberry that I'm pretty sure are true," Daniel said. "He was one of the first to put together a big-time Buffalo Rodeo that toured all over, and he would ride a buffalo, peg leg and all. Dad said he was friends with Willie Nelson and had a small role in Willie's movie, *Honeysuckle Rose*."[2] In fact, Willie Nelson and that movie played a significant role in the dramatic finale to Hackberry's story. More on that later.

Daniel's father, Charles Johnson, was Hackberry's grandson and possibly his biggest fan. Although Daniel never got to actually meet his great-grandfather, he grew up hearing his father tell lots of Hackberry stories, trying to make them as entertaining and amazing as Hackberry must have done.

"Dad said Hackberry could just walk into any bar and start telling stories, and have everyone laughing and patting him on the back," Daniel said.

In fact, Daniel's father tried very hard to find a professional filmmaker who would be interested in producing a movie about

Hackberry's life. He envisioned Robert Duvall playing the part of Hackberry, and Willie Nelson himself involved in the filming. Daniel's father even wrote a theme song for the potential movie, titled *King of the Rodeo*.

Hugh "Hackberry Slim" Johnson.

The strongest and most verifiable tales of Hackberry Slim, though, were about his fame as one of the first creators of a Buffalo Rodeo. Over the course of his lifetime, he produced more than 100 buffalo rodeos in all parts of the Midwest and Southwest U.S. In a story in the San Antonio *Express News* in 1973, reporter George Carmack wrote about Hackberry's relationship with his buffaloes which traveled with him to an event in Skidmore, Texas, a little town between San Antonio and Corpus Christi:

> Hackberry is best known as the Buffalo Man. He's been raising buffalo for 50 years and putting on buffalo acts at rodeos. At 85, he is still doing it . . . . Hackberry has eight buffalo with him. Boss of the herd and allowing no nonsense is a young 3-year-old, thick-shouldered, big-necked bull. "He's been the boss since he was a calf. He's a tough one," Hackberry says. "I named him John Connally."

Carmack also described Hackberry's story of what he considered to be the greatest rodeo in which he performed—a rodeo specifically put together during World War II at McCloskey General Hospital in Temple, where many of the amputees from battle were treated: "You can imagine how gloomy a lot of those men who had lost arms or legs were," Hackberry said. "I decided I would bulldog a steer . . . Then I sat down in the ring there, took off my artificial leg and held it up. Those boys just went wild."[3]

Hackberry told several reporters that he became a rodeo cowboy out of necessity. When he lost his leg, ranchers wouldn't hire him. Money was tight at the time and the ranchers didn't feel they could take a chance with him, he said. So on Labor Day, 1911, in Arizona, Hackberry Slim Johnson, wearing his peg leg, entered his first rodeo and won top money. By 1934, he was a well-known rodeo cowboy and, he told reporter George Carmack, he won the Texas All-Round Cowboy Championship. Hackberry also told Rick Smith, a reporter for the *Sherman Democrat*, that he had been inducted into the Cowboy Hall of Fame in Oklahoma City.[4] (No verifiable record of either of these achievements could be found—but then, Hackberry was known for being quite a storyteller).

Hackberry traveled all over the U.S. with his Buffalo Rodeo. In an interview with Berneta Peeples of the *Belton Journal* in 1978, when Hackberry was almost 91 years old, he said he started his rodeo in 1920 with his own herd of buffalo, purchased originally from Native Americans. He told Peeples that his herd was one of only a few that had kept buffalo from becoming extinct. He described events such as his buffalo stampede shows and a buffalo chariot race, as well as his popular Junior Rodeo, with little kids riding the buffalo calves.

In the interview, Hackberry said one of his favorite stories was the time he "was doggin' a steer in a rodeo—and my leg came off. Like 'ta scared them people to death. They didn't know I had a peg leg."[5]

In a bit more embellished version of the story that same year, Hackberry told Rick Smith, the *Sherman Democrat* reporter:

> Now that leg, that was to my advantage sometimes. Pecos Pate taught me this trick, see. When I was about to ride a bronc, I'd loosen the leg. I'd start yellin' about halfway through the ride. Yell that I was gettin' bucked to pieces. Then I'd let the leg fly off. Strong men would scream and women'd faint. The tent'd be half empty by the time I clambered down.[6]

Hackberry had lots of tales about how he made good use of his wooden leg. One that he repeated often to laughing audiences came from a time that he had been working with a couple of cowboys who didn't know him well. The three of them came upon a large rattlesnake, and Hackberry jumped from his horse and stomped the snake to death. Because the other two cowboys didn't know about his artificial leg—it was not visible under his pants and boot—they were absolutely amazed at how he could stomp a rattlesnake to death and not get bit.[7]

Another frequent story he told was about how a friend of his once bet a cowboy that Hackberry was so tough that the cowboy could stab him in the leg with a knife and Hackberry wouldn't even flinch. That one, though, according to Hackberry, didn't go so well, because the cowboy wound up stabbing Hackberry in the wrong leg.[8] Many of Hackberry's stories in newspapers and magazines are hard to verify, but, as his great-grandson Daniel said, his stories may have been embellished and exaggerated in his own telling, but in some ways, that was the point; Hackberry was a storyteller.

In interviews, Hackberry frequently cited his lengthy list of good friends: Will Rogers, Wiley Post, Pawnee Bill, Buffalo Bill Cody II, Willie Nelson, and, according to Peeples' story in the *Belton Journal*, "a whole herd of presidents, governors, senators and congressmen, movie stars and some assorted outlaws, including some of the Dalton gang."[9]

Hackberry's love of attention and publicity from time to time led him down the trail of the film world. He claimed to have made a movie with a friend in the early 1920s, but it never hit the big screen. In the mid-1960s, Hackberry had a small role in *Motel Confidential*, a racy movie about the "instant sex market" played as comedy-drama, directed by Stephen C. Apostolof.[10]

But not all of Hackberry's personal history stories are verifiable. His claim to have been inducted into the Oklahoma Cowboy Hall of Fame was refuted when journalist Rick Smith tried to confirm it. And some of Hackberry's stories, such as the one about letting his peg leg fly off as he rode a bull or buffalo, changed shape and played with facts. But, of course, they all made good stories, and his audience—be it journalists, friends, strangers in the bar, or family—all loved to hear him tell them.

His final story, though, is painted with nothing but a factual brush. Hackberry didn't live to tell the dramatic ending, but it stands on its own as one dadgum heck of a tale, as he probably would have said.

Hackberry had signed on to play a bit part in Willie Nelson's movie, *Honeysuckle Rose*, filmed in 1979, when Hackberry was 91 years old. He loved the limelight and became buddies with most of the folks on the set. They often partied after work hours, with Willie and his band providing music and jokes—and, of course, Hackberry was most likely providing his own storytelling entertainment.

Record album cover for the soundtrack to Honeysuckle Rose.

On Monday evening, December 3, 1979, the cast and crew had wrapped up the day's filming and gathered at the Austin Opera House for an evening of celebrating and relaxing. Willie Nelson's band played some of his classic tunes, and the folks in the audience ate, drank, danced, and laughed.

Johnny Gimble, a fiddler performing with Willie's band that night, said in an interview with the Associated Press that he saw Hackberry in the audience, having a great time, so Gimble asked the band to play "Milk Cow Blues" and dedicated it to Hackberry. Hackberry got up and took turns dancing with several young women, loving the attention. At age 91, he was at the top of his game that night.

Hackberry had his eyes on one young lady in the crowd in her twenties. He asked her to dance with him towards the end of the song, and she agreed. They danced, laughed, and then, at the end of the song, the audience applauded.

Hackberry walked back over to his seat, sat down, put his head on the table, and died. Emergency responders were not able to resuscitate Hackberry. When it was clear that he had died, the band played "What a Friend We Have in Jesus" and then cancelled the rest of the party.[11]

"That's probably just exactly the way he would have wanted to go," said Daniel Johnson. "Hackberry told my dad once that he wanted to go with his boots on, but that he'd be satisfied to go with just one boot on."

Endnotes

1. "One-Legged Bronc Buster Quits to Go into War Work." Associated Press, *The Evening Independent Newspaper*, St. Petersburg FL, April 14, 1944.
2. Jerry Schatzberg, Producer. *Honeysuckle Rose*. Filmed in Austin, Texas, Release date July 18, 1980.
3. George Carmack. "Hackberry's a Living Legend, So Shake a Leg to Skidmore." *San Antonio Express News*, San Antonio, Texas, May 19, 1973.
4. Rick Smith. "Remembering the Old West with Hackberry Slim." *Sherman Democrat* (also published in the *Del Rio News Herald*), Sherman and Del Rio, Texas, March 25, 1988.
5. Bernetta Peeples. "Stalking the Wild Buffalo Rodeo." *Belton Journal*, Belton, Texas, September 14, 1978.
6. Smith.
7. Carmack.
8. Ibid.
9. Peeples.
10. Stephen C. Apostolof, Director. *Motel Confidential*. Release date 1967.
11. "Ol' Hackberry Had His Boots On." Combined UPI, Associated Press, *The Deseret News*, Salt Lake City, UT, December 5, 1979.

Jo Virgil at 2016 meeting.

Barbara Finlay.

THE GRAVE OF THE LONESOME COWBOY: MITCHELL CROSSING RANCH, MCCULLOCH COUNTY, TEXAS

by Barbara Finlay

> *O bury me not on the lone prairie,*
> *Where the coyotes howl, and the wind blows free.*

This familiar song, known variously as "The Dying Cowboy," "Bury Me Not on the Lone Prairie," "The Lonesome Cowboy," or simply "The Lone Prairie," is sung throughout the United States and around the world, a reminder of the days of trail drives and the cowboys who risked their lives riding herd over rough country to get the cattle to market. As Walter Prescott Webb notes in his classic study, *The Great Plains*:

> The cowboy found singing a part of his occupation, a necessary accomplishment of his trade. The singing soothed the cattle and distracted their attention from sudden noises that might have caused them to stampede, and who knows but it comforted them in other ways? Out of this necessity, this desire to sing, grew the cowboy ballads. The best-known of all these ballads is . . . "The Dying Cowboy."[1]

The song has a long history, seemingly having originated as an adaptation of an old English sea chanty called "Bury me not in the deep, deep sea."[2] There are multiple stories of the song's origin being about a cowboy who was buried out on the lonesome prairie, contrary to his dying wishes, whereupon someone familiar with the old ocean song wrote new words to honor the cowboy. Soon the song was being sung up and down the trail to eventually become known throughout the country.

A number of grave sites scattered around Texas and elsewhere are believed by locals to be the place where this very cowboy died and was buried, and about whom the song was written—or so the stories go. One such grave is found on a remote and nearly-abandoned ranch in northern McCulloch County, near the community of Fife.

Entry Marker to the Mitchell Crossing Ranch.

The grave is located on what is known as the Mitchell Crossing Ranch, property bordered by the Colorado River to the north, off the nearest paved road by about a mile. Completely isolated from any other grave or structure, it lies some ⅜ of a mile north of the abandoned home at the front of the place, and only around 300 yards from the river, on a rise that gradually slopes down to the river. Surrounded by dry grassy and rocky land, cactus, a few live oak trees, some mesquite, and plenty of yucca, the grave has been the topic of speculation and legend by locals for decades—at least since the early twentieth century, and probably before that.

Rubbing of the headstone, with letters outlined to make them clearer.

The burial is marked by a single limestone rock, with the inscription, roughly scratched into the stone, "J M Davis, Died Nov 4 1877." The letter *S* in Davis is written backward. The letters are almost unreadable now, worn with age and weathering, although I remember seeing them clearly many years ago when they were more distinct. On one visit I made a rubbing of the stone marker, and outlined the letters and numbers to make them clearer. A few years ago, limestone rocks were piled on the top of the grave to mark its location better, as an Eagle Scout project, but originally the only marker was the headstone. By now grass and a small *agarita* bush have grown up between the rocks, almost hiding them. At the head of the grave is a persimmon tree and a large *agarita*.

Grave almost covered with grass, with headstone and limestone rocks marking it.

But why is this grave in this remote location? There were cattle drives through this area in the late 1870s, the Western Trail running through on its path from South Texas to northern markets in Nebraska.[3] There is a nice river crossing on the perimeter of the ranch, still known as Mitchell Crossing. The land was not purchased and settled until a couple of years after the grave's date, when Scotsman Alexander G. Mitchell moved his family there and purchased it from the railroad. At the time, the general area was called Waldrip, which was a small town located a few miles to the west of the Mitchell ranch, but the nearest named place now is Fife, just three miles to the west. If Mr. Davis was part of a cattle drive, it is probable that he died on the way back from markets in the north, given the date of his death in November.

No one knows much about Davis or how the rumor started, but old timers believed that this was the cowboy about whom the Lonesome Cowboy song was written. Even J. Frank Dobie heard this story and alluded to it in the seventh volume of *Publications of the Texas Folklore Society* in 1927.[4] Dobie had heard the story from a former student of his who had been hired as a school teacher at nearby Lohn, a Mr. Hewitt. He told Dobie about a grave about twenty miles north of Brady that local folks said was the grave of the cowboy who "composed" the song, "The Lone Prairie." Hewitt had heard of an *unmarked* grave out on the prairie, but no one could tell him the name of the cowboy. He did say that many people in the area could sing the song and they always associated it with that grave.[5] According to information in the local museum in Lohn, Mr. Hewitt taught at Lohn School for only one year, 1922–23, so that must have been when he heard about the grave and its association with the song.

Another interesting item placing the origin of the song in northern McCulloch County is a letter to the editor of the *Uvalde Leader-News* (Uvalde, Texas), published in April 1928. Written by one Tom Kellum, the letter purports to tell the history of the song and the grave. Kellum writes that his parents, still living at the time of his letter, well remembered the circumstances surrounding the young man's death and the origin of the song. In this version, the young man was not a cowboy, but an Easterner who came to Texas around 1860 for his health, as he was suffering from tuberculosis. He stopped at a place called "Lohn's Prairie," about twenty miles north of Brady. Too late to be helped by the drier climate, he died, telling the people around him not to bury him there but to send his body back East. But, of course, they did bury him there. The letter writer gives the location of the grave as "between the town of Lohn and the town of Waldrip, on the Colorado River . . . . As a small boy, I remember his grave," writes Kellum. He also writes that the original song was "Bury me not on the LOHN prairie," as the area was known at the time as Lohn's Prairie.[6] The area is still called the Lohn Valley, with the main small town named Lohn. Although this is not the way the story is usually told, it is an intriguing variant.

Kellum's letter identifies the young man's name as Wilson, not Davis, so it might be a different grave. He also thought the grave was unmarked, whereas the one on the Mitchell ranch is marked by a limestone marker. Still, it is interesting that the story claims to identify the origin of the song as having been near the Colorado River in the Waldrip area. It seems probable that two graves and two stories got conflated over time. In addition to Kellum's letter and Dobie's story, another author, writing for the Abilene, Texas, McMurry College publication, *The Galleon*, was aware of the McCulloch County grave and its association with the song.[7]

Most of the stories one hears or reads tell of a young cowboy who was herding cattle, and who either was thrown from his horse or whose horse fell on him, causing his death out on the prairie, far from any city. In those circumstances, the usual procedure was to bury the person near where he fell. All of these stories about the local origins of "The Lonesome Cowboy" go back into the late 19th century, and they were still well known among old-timers when I was a girl growing up in Fife in the 1950s.

The song seems to have originated (as an adaptation of the ocean burial song) sometime in the 1870s or 1880s. The first published version was contributed in 1901 to the *Journal of the American Folklore Society* by another resident of Uvalde, Texas, a Mrs. Annie Laurie Ellis.[8] A few years later the cowboy song collector Howard Thorp identified the author of the song as H. Clemons of Deadwood, Dakota;[9] Dobie had serious doubts about this attribution.[10] The song seems likely to have come from Texas, and it was known to have been sung by cowboys as they herded their cattle along the trail northward. And through that means, the song became known throughout the Great Plains and then farther.

Regardless of the exact origin of the song, there are many stories in far-flung places that claim it. In Taylor County near Abilene, for example, it is thought by some that the origin of the song is in that place, on the old Hashknife ranch.[11] There are apparently three graves, one of which is supposed to be that of the cowboy who died when his horse stepped in a prairie dog hole and fell on the rider as they were working cattle. Archer County also has a grave that people claim to be the *one*.[12] Others can be discovered here and there. However, every native of northern McCulloch County "knows" that the true lonesome cowboy grave is right there, on the

Mitchell Crossing Ranch, just a quarter mile from the river crossing and only a few miles from the geographical center (the "heart") of Texas. What more fitting place could there be for this legend to continue on?

Endnotes

1. Walter Prescott Webb. *The Great Plains.* New York: Grosset & Dunlap, 1931. 459.
2. J. Frank Dobie. "Ballads and Songs of the Frontier Folk." *Texas and Southwestern Lore*, *Publications of the Texas Folklore* Society VII, Austin, 1927. 121–183; and Francis Edward Abernethy. *Singin' Texas.* Denton: University of North Texas Press, 1994. 152–53.
3. "Western Trail," Texas State Historical Association, *The Handbook of Texas Online*, https://tshaonline.org/handbook/ponline/articles/ayw02.
4. Dobie. 175.
5. Ibid.
6. "Writes History of 'The Lone Prairie,'" *Uvalde Leader-News*, April 10, 1928.
7. Lucille Gist. "The Dying Cowboy Did Not Die." *The Galleon*, Vol. 5 (2). Abilene: McMurry College, 1929. 11–13.
8. Annie Laurie Ellis. "O Bury Me Not on the Lone Prairie." *Journal of the American Folklore Society*, Vol 14, No. 54 (1901). 186.
9. Howard Thorp. *Songs of the Cowboys.* Boston: Houghton Mifflin Company, 1921. 62.
10. Dobie. 175.
11. Gist. 11–13.
12. Jack Loftin. *Trails through Archer: A Centennial History, 1880–1980.* Austin: Eakin Publications, 1979. 432–433.

Ms. Knowles accepts accolades from the crowd after a successful bullfight in the Plaza de Mexico arena in Mexico City (Photograph from the personal collection of Georgiana Knowles).

GEORGIANNA KNOWLES: BORDERLAND BULLFIGHTER

by Charlie T. McCormick

Texans love their athletes—especially those that are successful. This is what makes it all the more interesting that we have forgotten the tradition of Texas women bullfighters which flowered in the middle of the twentieth century. In the area between the American Southwest and northern Mexico (in places such as Ciudad Acuna, Juarez, and Tijuana), from about 1952 to about 1965, a group of American women bullfighters enjoyed brief, storied, and—now—largely forgotten careers as *toreras* and *rejoneadoras*. This cohort of women bullfighters included such talented athletes as Patricia McCormick, Bette Ford, Georgianna Knowles, and Patricia Hays. Given their collective and individual talents, it is not apparent why we have largely forgotten these women athletes, but it seems that this forgetting was not accidental; instead, it was an example of the erasure that takes place when things do not fit our conceptions of the way things should be.

Arguing that these women have been erased from our consciousness seems logical when you consider that there is a long, long history of women bullfighters, and the American women from the 1950s were not evidence of just an exceptional moment in time. For example, in the mythological tradition of the Cretes, Zeus seduced the Phoecian woman, Europa, by transforming himself into a white bull and mixing with her father's herd. Europa was gathering flowers among the herd and found herself next to the animal. She climbed onto its back, and Zeus promptly spirited her away, across the sea to Crete, where she became the first queen of Crete. Though there is no explicit reference to a bullfight in this account, the woman climbing on the bull's back denotes both a sexual and a physical encounter, and it is probably one of the earliest examples of the performative tradition of a woman bullfighter.

Beyond this oral tradition, the lived experience of women performing with bulls also is significantly old. Surviving Minoan artwork—dating from about 1,700 BC—seems to show that bull-wrestling and especially bull-jumping were popular sports that both men and women performed. Surviving fresco fragments from Knossos illustrate the ancient history of bull-jumping or leaping. Both men and women are shown performing the feat—jumping over the bull's horns and back, and dismounting in a backward somersault over the rear of a bull.[1]

Bullfighter historian Lyn Sherwood has traced the early history of women bullfighters who fought in the *torera*-style (our contemporary style of bullfighting). Sherwood notes that the first textual reference to a *torera* has been found in a Spanish document from 1654. In Mexico, around 1700, there is a record of a black woman *charra* (or Mexican cowgirl) who fought and killed bulls from horseback, and later in the eighteenth century, a nun, Dona Maria de Gaucin, left the convent and spent several successful seasons as a *torera*. And much more recently, Conchita Citron, "The Blonde Goddess," entranced most of the western world with her charismatic performances of *rejoneo*.[2]

To be sure, then, something powerful was permitted in these bullrings, especially for women who could enter and appropriate—in certain ways—this hyper-masculine world. Ironically, the freedom found within the borderland bullring was the primary obstacle to the memory of the performance outside of this liminal space. The borderland bullring was, then, as much containing and constraining as it was liberating.

Complicating all of this remembering, forgetting, and erasing is the fact that the borderland is a liminal space. The limen refers to thresholds—like doorways—in which you find yourself neither inside nor outside. It is a space between one world and the next. Borderlands are charged places, full of potentiality and equally filled with pitfall. They are places where the world is turned upside down and the normal rules do not apply. Our sensibilities—trained as they have been outside the borderland—are repulsed even as we are seduced by the rawness and sensuality of the place. Borderlands are precisely the type of location in which a woman could enter the hyper-masculine world of the bullfight without being turned away. It is also precisely the sort of location that outsiders erase once they leave the space because it is unseemly and irrelevant, and it does not fit into our conception of the way things are supposed to be.

Sarah Pink, in her book on women and bullfighting in Spain (a work which, interestingly enough, never acknowledges the existence of our American women bullfighters), suggests that women in the bullrings were not considered natural and therefore "classified as curious oddities: exceptions to be marveled at rather than revolutionary or change-producing phenomena. From such a perspective women bullfighters may be regarded as harmless."[3]

Certainly, comments from American women bullfighters of the 1950s support Pink's argument: they note that they felt like curious oddities. Joy Marie Price, for example, was quoted as saying that women bullfighters "want to show the world that women bullfighters are more than novelties."[4] Patricia McCormick was concerned that she was becoming "a side show freak" because of the offers for personal appearances she received.[5] Carla Lee, a bullfighter from the late 1950s, reflecting back on her career said, "I never mention to anyone in the States that I was once a bullfighter... because people just don't understand. They tend to think it is worse than being a bank robber or a criminal, and you get more disapproving looks than if you were about to light a cigarette in a no-smoking area."[6]

The Borderland was liminal for American audiences; the bullring was liminal, too; unsurprisingly, these women—as liminal figures themselves—could perform in these spaces. But the very space which liberated them by allowing them to pursue an activity that they could not get away with in conventional society and conventional spaces was also that space which made them seem ultimately irrelevant and just plain odd. Since their borderland identities did not conform to a conventional identity either inside the bullring or outside the bullring, then they were either forced into conventional conceptions of who they were supposed to be or they were forgotten all together—either way their authentic self ended up being erased.

This is not to suggest that these women bullfighters wanted to be erased. Georgianna Knowles, at age seventy-five, told me one hot afternoon in El Paso that "[i]f a bullfighter wants to be completely safe all she has to do is stand perfectly still. If she stands still, the bull will lose track of her and be distracted by something else. As long as you don't move, the bull will run all over the arena and not see you standing right there in the middle of the ring." Safety is not the primary concern of a bullfighter, though. The glory of a good fight is the primary concern. An effective bullfighter has to be noticed. These were women who were trying to be noticed. Borderland arenas allowed these women to be noticed, but only in a limited way.

The borderland—as a liminal space for bullfighting outside the conventional world of bullfighting—allowed these women to own their otherness and unconventionality by controlling this otherness in ways that did not liberate the women from the power of expectation, but rather allowed them to creatively determine their performances within the borderland. For example, El Paso native Ms. Georgianna Knowles could determine the contours of her otherness as a borderland bullfighter. Like some of the other women bullfighters at this time, Georgianna fell in love with bullfighting in the movies she saw. During a weekend party in Juarez with the El Paso Tauromachia Club, she literally fell in love with Tabaquito (David Siquierous) who was a bullfighter and trainer.

As a young woman who wanted to make a mark on the bullfighting world, Georgianna, with the support of Tabaquito, originally planned to fight bulls in the conventional way—on foot. Georgianna never felt comfortable fighting from the ground. She remembered that the cape was too heavy and her small frame too weak to successfully manipulate it in a way that would draw the bull's attention or the judge's favor to her. One of the first ways that this liminal space of the borderland bullring provided her creative possibility was through her development of an unconventional fighting style.

Tabaquito loved horses, and he quickly learned that Georgianna shared his affection. She had grown up on horseback. Her earliest horse was Redwing, a horse she broke herself because she fell in love with it as a colt and wanted to have the experience of riding it. She believed she could ride any horse. So, she and Tabaquito made the decision that she would be a *rejoneadora*, or a lady bullfighter on horseback.

Having settled on *rejoneo* as Georgianna's best opportunity for success in the bullring, she and Tabaquito had to find her an appropriate horse. Tabaquito was fond of a horse that was owned by the mayor of Juarez, but he did not know if the stallion would be too much for Georgianna. The mayor's horse, Tony, appeared to be past his prime and so infrequently ridden that he had become, basically, wild. Tony had already lived a storied life. He grew up a palomino stallion on the King Ranch; later, he became comfortable in front of crowds as the horse used by B-list movie star, Gilbert Rowland. By 1951, when Tony had become the mayor of Juarez's horse, he remained a beautiful—if overweight—horse that was, in a word, mean. So mean, in fact, that the mayor would ride him only once a year if he would ride him at all. It took the mayor's men weeks of work before the horse would let the mayor on his back. Tabaquito suspected the mayor would be willing to part with the horse if Tony did not scare off Georgianna.

Tony acted predictably when Tabaquito and Georgianna first met him. He charged at them, teeth bared, threatening to bite them, kick them, or do whatever it took to run them off. Georgianna stood her ground. $400 later, she owned Tony. Tabaquito and Georgianna took Tony to a recently plowed field to sweat the wild out of him. Georgianna rode him day after day through the soft clay until his wild energy was exhausted. Then she fed him sugar. Every day they returned to the field until he learned to have confidence in Georgianna, and she in him. Tony became, quite simply, perfect.

It took six months to complete Tony's training: teaching him to walk sideways, to back up, to turn on a dime. In the first exhibition match with a live bull in which Georgianna and Tony performed, Tony played his part perfectly and fearlessly. Georgianna took a nasty fall on her head. She was satisfied with her own performance, but she and Tabaquito knew they had something special with Tony.

Most *rejoneadors* fight in what is known as "Portuguese-style," a reference to the huge, tooled leather saddles and decorative and protective stirrup leather that enclose and protect the *rejoneadors*, lifting them up above the danger of the bull's horns. The *rejoneador*'s horse was in danger of being gored, but there was little chance of harm befalling the *rejoneador* himself. Georgianna owned her otherness by manipulating the performance of the conventional *rejoneador*. Georgianna's skill in the saddle led her to adopt what she describes as a "Mexican-style" or "*Charro*-style" of *rejoneo*, less of a nod to the art's aristocratic roots and more of an homage to the indigenous rodeo and horseman tradition of Mexico—the *charro*. Georgianna rode bareback, being held in place only by a leather strap wrapped around the horse in which she placed her knees. Never a slave to tradition, Georgianna added a modified cape to her routine so that she alone, among all those who practiced *rejeneo*, worked a bull with the cape from horseback before placing the *banderilleros* and the *rejone*.

Ms. Knowles, riding on her palomino stallion (Tony), places the banderilleros in the bull in the Plaza de Mexico arena in Mexico City (Photograph from the personal collection of Georgiana Knowles).

Georgianna controlled the contours of her otherness in this liminal space, too, by the logic through which she could deeply love Tony and, without hesitation, kill bulls. It is not that she loved some animals and hated others. She loved the bulls, too. She remembers that, initially, she was repulsed when she saw the bull killed by the matador in the arena. The more of an aficionado she became, though, the more she saw that the bullfight provided a way for the bull to become transformed, to transcend itself and its base existence as a bull. In the arena, facing death, the bull became a creature of significance, beauty, and portent. It mattered in a way that it simply could not if death were not circling around. I think it was as true for bullfighters as it was for the bulls.

As a final example of how the borderland enabled women bullfighters such as Georgianna to control their otherness, consider her costume. Remember that, incredibly, these women were able to be women bullfighters in the arena, not simply male impersonators. That is the power of the borderlands. They did not dress in the form-fitting "suit of lights" as the men did. Bette Ford was the occasional exception, but most of the other women bullfighters were able to confirm their otherness by their dress and own this otherness, too. Georgianna, for example, pushed her *charro*-style performance into her dress, too, all of which she made herself. While these outfits did not accentuate and call attention to the contours of her body, they did reference the *charro* traditions of sombrero and embroidered jacket. Still, this outfit did not really "fit" within the world of bullfighting or outside the world of bullfighting.

Outside of the bullring, conventional expectations applied to Georgianna's dress and her lifestyle. If she didn't want to be erased in this area, she had to conform to expectations and perform conventional activities such as cooking, crocheting, and playing dolls with children. As a conventional woman, though, Georgianna was not that memorable. Here again, she ends up not fitting into the story of what should be, and she becomes written out of the story. To be sure, women bullfighters needed a liminal space to express themselves. In order to find a place where they could own their identity, they inhabited the borderlands. Georgianna, for example, had the opportunity to fully express her skills and abilities as a bullfighter when she exploited her differences, thereby enabling people to see her for who she was instead of who they thought she should be. But ultimately, this location and performance wasn't liberating. It was as restrictive as conventional society in terms of organizing memory.

From inauspicious beginnings in a borderland area between the U.S. and Mexico throughout the 1950s and early 1960s, several American women decided to become bullfighters. Their motivations for doing so and their experiences in the borderland arenas remain largely erased. Outside the borderlands, their performance was never appreciated. Conventional expectations for these women in American culture could not accommodate their borderland identities. Ultimately, conventional expectations of bullfighting could not accommodate their borderland performances, either. They simply did not fit. Importantly, though, their borderland identifies did not simply disappear. Erasure is never complete. A trace remains, and it reappears when we least expect it, shaping the present in ways no one can fully anticipate or expect. Take, for example, your reading of this article.

[Elements of this article appeared in an earlier publication for *Heritage* magazine (Volume 4: 8–13, 2009) entitled "Of Matadoras and Taurine Glory."—*McCormick*]

Endnotes

1. Hannah Velton. *Cow*. London: Reaktion Books, 2007.
2. Lyn Sherwood. *Yankees in the Afternoon: An Illustrated History of American Bullfighters.* Jefferson, North Carolina: McFarland and Company, 2002. 173, 176.
3. Sarah Pink. *Women and Bullfighting: Gender, Sex, and the Consumption of Tradition.* New York: Berg, 1997. 167.
4. Haldeen Braddy. "Queens of the Bullring." *Southern Folklore Quarterly*, 26, 1962. 107–121.
5. Patricia McCormick. *Lady Bullfighter: The Autobiography of the North American Matador.* New York: Henry Holt and Company, 1954.
6. Muriel Feiner. *Women and the Bullring.* Gainesville, FL: University of Press of Florida, 2003.

Vicky J. Rose.

SAM HOUSTON WAS NOT BORN IN TEXAS, AND OTHER DISTURBING FACTS

by Vicky J. Rose

In my late fifties, I experienced a shocking epiphany about what it means to be a Texan. Examining the past made it plain to me that being a Texan doesn't have anything to do with where a person was born, who their parents were, or how they got here.

My father's side of the family loved Texas history and talked about it all the time. Although my grandmother was not much of a conversationalist, she liked to tell stories about her ancestors. Her favorite, repeated to me often, was about a grandmother who lost a shoe during a wild ride in the Runaway Scrape. In their frantic efforts to escape Santa Anna's approaching army, she was not allowed to stop long enough to get off her horse and pick up the shoe. In today's world, that would be no major catastrophe, since there is a store on almost every corner, but in those days it was almost the equivalent of losing one's cell phone today.

After I repeated this tale to a friend one day, she said, "You really need to join DRT—The Daughters of the Republic of Texas." Heeding her advice, I sallied off to my first meeting. I discovered that no matter how much I think I know about history, there is always a little white-haired lady in the corner (who may or may not have graduated from high school) who knows a heck of a lot more than I do. In order to join DRT, a woman must prove direct lineage to an ancestor who was in Texas before statehood. Luckily, I found besides that one great-great-grandmother who lost her shoe fleeing from Santa Anna's army, I had nineteen more ancestors I could prove had been in the Republic, much to the ecstatic joy of our chapter registrar.

The chapter I joined is The Baron de Bastrop Chapter, situated in Stephen F. Austin's second "Little Colony." Bastrop is touted as the most historical small town in Texas. Most DRT chapter members conduct their meetings with decorum and proper parliamentary procedures. The Bastrop Chapter, however, was so full of avid historians, it was impossible for any of us to keep our mouths shut during the meetings.

Renee Tiroff lambasted Moses Austin for trying to steal her ancestor's mining land in Missouri and then rubbing salt into the wound by talking the man's Indian wife into accompanying him to Texas. Vice-President Alyce Ferguson laughed about what a dancing fool William B. Travis was. President Mariann Laughlin told how Davy Crockett got liquored up in Bastrop on his way to the Alamo. We heard the story of Texas Vice-President and Bastrop resident Edward Burleson and his wife, who pleaded with him to chop kindling before he left to fight Indians. Edward, who would rather fight Indians than farm, couldn't be bothered. When he got home, instead of calling out to his wife in a laughing, teasing tone, "Old lady, how many hogs you got? What sort of crop you got?" he looked at his house in shock. Most of his roof was missing—his wife had the wooden shingles torn off one by one and used them for kindling in retaliation. Edward didn't fight all Indians, and his friend, Tonkawa Chief Placido, probably got a good laugh out of that story.

As much as we liked to talk about everything pertaining to Texas history, the liveliest discussions often centered on Sam Houston. Member Undine Judy Sien said Houston used to sit on a log eating ginger cakes, drinking cider, and discussing affairs of the Republic in front of her ancestor, Joseph Beitel's bakery in Harrisburg.

One of my ancestors, Titus H. Mundine, was Vice-President at the San Jacinto Battle Ground Assembly in 1860, and he nominated his good friend Sam Houston for president. Titus also served in the Texas Legislature, and he was one of the few men who stood with Sam Houston in opposing secession. Later, Titus sent shock waves throughout the 1868 assembly when he proposed that women and blacks should have the right to vote. He was a big, fat man, topping 300 pounds, and the press was always making fun of him, writing that "his views have much WEIGHT."[1]

Besides shaking things up in the Texas legislature, Titus Mundine founded the Masonic Lodge in Lexington, Texas (Courtesy of Texas State Library and Archives Commission).

Sam Houston often visited the Mundine family. When my great-great-grandmother had just delivered yet another healthy boy while the Houstons were visiting, Sam, never bashful, said, "Why don't you name him after me?" Despite having a famous Texas legislator for a father and being named after another even more illustrious statesman, according to my father, Sam Houston Mundine turned outlaw, robbing a store in the small community of Fedor with a cousin by the name of Will Mundine. Will, a fiery redhead with a pronounced mean streak, shot the German storekeeper while Sam held the reins on the horses.

Later, a deputy sheriff came to McDade looking for the Mundines. Will hid in an alley and shot him as he walked by. Sam went on the run, hiding out in the Mississippi canebrakes. Will was found not guilty of the murder of the storekeeper by a non-German jury who was terrified of him. The wife of the sheriff he killed raised her son to hate Will Mundine, and as soon as he got old enough he stabbed him. As Will lay dying, my great-grandfather and

Sam Houston Mundine's brother, Charley, told him, "Will, you're dying. Why don't you take all the blame for the robbery in Fedor so Sam can come home?" Another relative interrupted and growled, "No Will, you've lived like a man, now die like one and keep your mouth shut." So Will did, and Sam Houston Mundine had to wait until the statute of limitations was up before he could come back. He lived an uneventful, law-abiding life after that, except his grandchildren said he was a grouchy old man who would whop them with his cane if they aggravated him too much. The moral of the story is: It's not a good idea to name your child Elvis hoping he will become a great singer.

The Mundines weren't my only ancestors who were friends with Houston. So were the Millicans, an Old Three Hundred family who settled in the Brazos Valley. The Millicans were educated, but were so rough they made the Hatfields and McCoys look like a pack of sissies.[2] They were renowned Indian fighters, they fought one another, they sued people constantly—including their own family members—and even shot one another.[3] When I told a group of women who were active in the Old Three Hundred club that my ancestors were the Millicans, one of them said, "Oh, yes. We've heard about *them*."

The patriarch of the family, Robert Hemphill Millican, supposedly stood seven feet tall and was seventy years old when he came to Texas.[4] Robert caused a minor sensation when he struck a Mexican soldier at Fort Tenoxtitlan for stealing one of his cows.[5] The family swore he was put on the Mexican "wanted dead or alive" list, but no proof of this has ever been found. However, Colonel José Francisco Ruiz, the presiding officer over Fort Tenoxtitlan, did call for the Anglos to bring Robert in. They, in turn, played the Mexican political game of politely agreeing to everything Ruiz said, assuring him of their cooperation and then doing nothing. He, on the other hand, was sympathetic to the colonists but was tired of being stuck out in the boondocks so far away from Mexico City. He finally threw up his hands figuratively and more or less said, "To hell with it," and dropped the matter.

Sam Houston often visited an inn owned by one of Robert's sons, Elliot Millican, a doctor, legislator, and fearless fighter.[6] Once, Elliot and two other men were attacked by a large band of Indians. Taking shelter in a thicket, the other two men reloaded rifles, letting Elliot, who was a crack shot, pick off the attacking Indians one by one.

One evening while sitting by the fire at Elliot's inn, Sam Houston took aim, and instead of hitting the flame, he accidentally spit tobacco in the ear of one of Elliot's little boys. When the boy got angry, Sam laughed and said, "Sonny, one of these days you will brag that Sam Houston spit in your ear."[7] (As you can see, Houston had a high opinion of himself.) That little boy, Leander "L. R." Millican, nicknamed "Lallie" by his family, grew up to become a rather famous circuit riding minister in West Texas, founding the Paisano Baptist Encampment, an annual cowboy camp meeting held yearly in the Davis Mountains. Lallie spearheaded the campaign to keep the illegal Fitzsimmons-Maher Prizefight out of El Paso in 1896. Judge Roy Bean circumvented Lallie and the law by holding the prizefight on a sandbar on the Mexican side of the Rio Grande.[8] Lallie, however, remained proud of his family's association with Sam Houston.[9]

Leander Randon "Lallie" Millican never considered himself anything except a cowboy preacher, traveling all over West Texas to spread the word.

So, I have two different sets of ancestors who were good friends of Houston, which may or may not be a good thing, depending on how you look at it. He had his good side and his bad side.

Mariann Laughlin related a story that has circulated around Bastrop for years. Supposedly, Sam Houston went to Bastrop to visit his son, Sam Jr., who was then a student at the Bastrop Military Institute. Sam climbed up to the second floor to give a speech, but he was so drunk, he fell off the balcony.

Sam really did make friends at Bastrop, swapping stories late into the night and regaling his admirers with his exploits. One old ranger named Ham White, though, had repeatedly threatened to kill Houston. During the so-called "Archives War" when Sam desperately wanted the state capital to be in Houston, not Austin, he had made a few disparaging off-the-cuff remarks suggesting that people living on the Upper Colorado were horse thieves. Ham White took offense at this, and one night in Bastrop when he found himself seated across the table from Houston, he made a highly insulting remark intended for Sam. Houston put down his knife and fork, straightened up in his chair, and stared at Ham until the latter had to drop his eyes back to his plate and forget all about following through with his death threats.[10]

Kay Valenta, our DRT chapter treasurer, also related a story about Sam being the object of hatred from a former soldier. Mary Turner Billingsley, whose father fought in the battles of Gonzales and Salado, told of visiting her husband's uncle, Capt. Jesse Billingsley, in McDade. Jesse commanded a company of volunteers from the Bastrop area at the Battle of San Jacinto; he later served as a legislator and senator, in between fighting Indians. J. Frank Dobie claimed he was the first man to yell "Remember the Alamo!" As far as being a Texan goes, the captain's credentials are impeccable. However, Mary said every time Sam Houston's name was mentioned, Jesse would begin to curse. He despised Houston until the day he died, calling him a coward for retreating all the way to San Jacinto before fighting the Mexican army.

There is a lot of speculation surrounding Sam's decision to retreat to San Jacinto. To be fair, the Mexican army was considered one of the best armies in the world at the time, far better trained and equipped than Houston's volunteers. Houston did use the time to drill his men in the fundamentals of linear combat. Others suggest Houston was trying to get as close to General Andrew Jackson's troops in Louisiana as he could.

All these reasons add up, but one of the best explanations goes back to an incident that happened when Houston was a young officer in the U.S. Army. According to Houston biographer and author James L. Haley, Houston led a charge only to look behind him and realize his undisciplined Tennessee volunteers were not following him into battle.[11] Taking a wound in his shoulder and arm, he limped back to safety. General Edward Burleson's biographer, Bastrop historian Ken Kesselus, states that at San Jacinto, Houston insulted Capt. Billingsley and Burleson by repeatedly asking them if their men would fight. Given how hemmed in the Texas troops were at San Jacinto, it appears that Sam was not willing to be caught with his pants down again. He made sure he was so positioned that his raw Texas recruits would have to fight or die.[12]

Houston carried on a love/hate relationship with the widely popular Burleson. Edward was a rough frontiersman of almost unparalleled courage on the field of battle who, unlike Houston, never let himself be caught unawares. Off the battlefield, he and Houston were almost the exact opposites in personality. Houston was full of personal ambition, showy and prone to push himself forward on every occasion, while Edward was willing to let others take the limelight. It is safe to say that if Edward Burleson had had a good publicist, he could have easily outshined Houston in the annals of history. Despite being jealous of Edward and undermining him every chance he got, Houston knew he needed Burleson for the sake of Texas. In 1842, he wrote a letter to Burleson who was acting general of a group of volunteers, encouraging him not to give up the pursuit of invading Mexican troops.

"Texas must be saved!" and he signed it, "Truly your friend, Sam Houston."[13]

Other stories about Houston abound. Once while eating at a friend's house, Sam took a mouthful of rice pudding that was too hot, and he promptly spit it out, spewing it everywhere. He looked at his shocked hostess and growled, "Many a damn fool would have swallowed that."[14] Houston, who was an inveterate tobacco chewer, upset many a hostess with his careless spitting habits. He infuriated Eliza Lockhart for spitting on her freshly cleaned porch when he could, Eliza said, "just have easily spit over the rail."[15] But Houston was so kind to her son, John, that Eliza could forgive Houston even of his erratic spittle.

Although the names Stephen F. Austin, Juan Seguín, and Lorenzo de Zavala are remembered with hazy reverence, it is Sam Houston who dominates the minds of those thinking about Texas history. He could always inspire either hatred or love—nothing in between. Houston embodies all that is Texas, bold brashness, an over-the-top largeness, a love of splash and color, wily and cunning native intelligence, a sort of uncouth George Washington.

As much as we Texans claim Houston as our own, we vaguely remembered those stories about him in Tennessee. . . .

Before serving under Andrew Jackson, before becoming a congressman and later governor of Tennessee, Houston built a schoolhouse in Maryville, Tennessee, teaching there for a year. It's a little hard to understand this, since Houston detested regular schooling, although he memorized Greek poets. However, he only did it for a year to make some sort of income in order to court the ladies and give gifts to his Indian friends. Years later, a set of metal knuckles with the initials S. H. were found tucked above the schoolhouse doorframe, so we can surmise that teaching school in Houston's day was no easier than it is now.[16] The metal knuckles above the doorframe are easier for us to accept about Houston than being a teacher of the ABCs.

The Sam Houston Schoolhouse in Maryville, Tennessee. Metal knuckles with his initials were found inside on top of the doorframe.

People may forget that Houston was a protégé of Andrew Jackson and once the governor of Tennessee; but almost all remember the stories of his disastrous first marriage. It ended when his young bride confessed she really loved another man and had been pushed into marrying Governor Houston by her ambitious parents. Either that or she was disgusted by his oozing war wounds. Then there is the gossip that she was repelled by Houston's excessive body hair. Whatever the reason, days after the wedding, while standing at a window and watching her new husband engaged in a snowball fight with children, Houston's new bride is purported to have muttered to her hostess, "I wish from the bottom of my heart that they would kill him."[17] That is not a good way for any man to start off a marriage, but one most Texans can philosophically empathize with.

However, something of equal, but little known, importance happened to Sam Houston earlier, when he was a young congressman. Mary Parke Custis, an heiress and great-granddaughter of Martha Washington, jilted Houston in favor of a bashful young cadet named Robert E. Lee.[18] Houston, full of sour grapes, could hardly believe that Mary chose a long engagement with a shy underclassman at West Point when she could have become his bride and the belle of Washington society.

It's almost impossible to imagine Robert E. Lee as ever being anything but a general for his beloved Virginia, no matter who he was married to, but it is easy to speculate that if Sam Houston had married the wealthy and well-connected Mary, he never would have come to Texas, and then where would we be? Therefore, we Texans owe much more of a debt to Robert E. Lee than most of us could ever realize. Although one of his friends once commented that Houston was the worst candidate for marriage he had ever seen, Houston did eventually find love. Margaret, a pretty and deeply religious young woman, saw Houston as someone who needed saving. Margaret overlooked Houston's age, his spitting, excessive body hair, and oozing war wounds, and with a staying power unrivaled by very few women, managed to get Houston baptized. A friend later remarked, "Well, General, I hear your sins were washed away." To which Houston replied, "I hope so, but if they were all washed away, the Lord help the fish down below."[19]

It's hard enough for us Texans to believe that Sam Houston came from somewhere else, that he wasn't born right here. If we have to, we can force ourselves to accept that the roughhewn Houston came from that rustic pioneer state of Tennessee. You will imagine my surprise when, while making plans for a camping trip in Virginia, I made a shocking discovery. Sam Houston was born outside of Lexington, Virginia. Virginia! That cultured epitome of the gracious Old South, a place of gentility and refinement. That Houston originally sprang from Virginia is almost too much to accept.

When I made this discovery and finally digested it, it forced me to take a giant leap in logic—something quite foreign to my nature.

We native Texans are extremely proud of being so. We have native Texan birth certificates; we have native Texan bumper stickers; we have native Texan license plates. But Sam Houston was not a native Texan! All those twenty ancestors I claimed in DRT—they weren't native Texans either. My lord, one of them even came from New York, of all places.

My foray into the strange land of deductive reasoning carried me one step further. Being a native Texan is really just an accident of birth, and therefore really doesn't mean a heck of a whole lot. But being from Texas is an important thing to people—so what makes a person a Texan?

Maybe to find out, it's a good idea to look at Houston. When things go wrong, we cut our losses and start over again. Even with rejection after rejection, fighting against insurmountable odds, we don't give up. We learn from our mistakes, using them to turn us into wily foxes that live to fight another day. We stand up for what we believe in, even when it means we might be standing all alone. We love the soil and the people that is Texas.

Sam Houston's dying words were, "Texas! Texas!" And then he spoke the name of his beloved wife, "Margaret."[20]

I'd like to end this story with another incident that happened to me in Virginia. Before leaving home, I bought my Golden Retriever a new dog tag. On one side was the Texas flag, on the other, just my name and phone number. At a Virginia state park, I tied Buddy to a post and went into the restroom. When I came out, a group of children had gathered around Buddy and were petting him. A little boy looked up at me and said, "You're from Texas, aren't you?" I said yes, and asked how he knew. "I saw it on your dog's tag." He had recognized the Lone Star flag, because that's how legendary we are.

You don't have to be a native Texan to become a Texan. Sam Houston wasn't, my twenty ancestors weren't. They turned themselves into Texans by being of service to their adopted land, and by the power of their love for it. So, no matter where you were born, if you have made Texas your home and someone asks, "You're from Texas, aren't you?" stick out your chest, lift up your chin, smile and say, "Yes, I am." Just like good old Sam Houston.

ENDNOTES

1. Randolph B. Campbell. "Mundine, Titus Howard." *Handbook of Texas Online*, accessed February 22, 2017, http://www.tshaonline.org/handbook/online/articles/fmuvf.
2. Malcolm Dallas McLean. *Papers Concerning Robertson's Colony in Texas Volume 6*. Fort Worth: Texas Christian University Press, 1974. 345.
3. SHH III: 21 MILLICAN, ELLOT M. (1808–1860). Document signed (Washington County), c. 1837. Statement regarding the estate of Robert Millican. Accessed December 5, 2009, http://tides.sfasu.edu:2006/cdm4/results.php?CISOOP1=any&CISOFIELD1=CISOSEARCHALL&CISOROOT=/Newton&CISOBOX1=21.
4. "Millican Families Celebrate 175th Year of the Connection with the State of Texas." *The Observer/Enterprise*, October 22, 1999.
5. Austin American. "Plight of Burleson County Fort Told." *Frontier Times Vol. 12 No 4*. Jan. 1935: 148–149.
6. Mary Downs Hayes. *Millican, Texas*. Bryan: Privately Published, 1984. 25.
7. Mike Cox. "President Houston and Millican Tales." *Bryan-College Station Eagle*, January 3, 1987.
8. "Austin: The Texas State Historical Association, 1996." *The New Handbook of Texas Vol. 4*. 746.
9. Cox.
10. A. W. Terrell. "Recollections of General Sam Houston." *The Southwestern Historical Quarterly Vol XVI No 2*. Oct. 1912. 130.
11. James L. Haley. *Sam Houston*. Norman: University of Oklahoma Press, 2002. 15.
12. John H. Jenkins and Kenneth Kesselus. *Edward Burleson: Texas Frontier Leader*. Austin: Jenkins Publishing Company, 1990. 109.
13. Houston letter: Gilder Lehrman Collection #: GLC01170.
    Place Written: City of Houston
    Type: Autograph letter signed
    Date: 10 April 1842
    Pagination: 4 p. ; 29 × 24 cm.
    https://www.gilderlehrman.org/collections/5c8653c2-2ecd-424c-93eb-323785684110 collected 2/22/2017.
14. "Life Goes to a Tall Tales Session in Texas." *Life* June 1, 1942: 81.
15. Haley. 253.

16. Sam Houston Schoolhouse Museum, Maryville, Tennessee.
17. Haley. 51.
18. Ibid. 42.
19. Ibid. 333.
20. Ibid. 415.

Dining room of the Stagecoach Inn.

DID DAVID CROCKETT REALLY STOP IN BASTROP? SOME FACTS AND FOLKLORE

by Mariann Fisk Laughlin

It is a well-known fact that David Crockett left Tennessee after a resounding defeat in his second race for Congress. His words, "You may all go to Hell, and I will go to Texas," have been made famous in books and movies. Crockett started South, visiting friends and family and hunting along the way. It was his intention, according to Crockett historian Joy Bland, to look for land. "David never liked the name Davy," she told me. "He went to Texas to look for land," she stated, "and just got caught up in the Texas Revolution."[1] We were conversing because I had sent her my family folktale about Davy Crockett. In it, Davy Crockett stops at the stagecoach inn of Greenleaf and Mary Ann Manlove Fisk in Bastrop, Texas, in late January of 1836, shortly before traveling on to the Alamo.[2]

Bland went on to state, "David must have enjoyed his trip South, because there is a story about his trip through Memphis, that is almost like the one that you tell of him in Texas. I have a copy of a bill from a West Tennessee store, where he still owed for all of the liquor. He was quite entertaining, however."[3] Thus began my journey to see if there was a grain of truth in our family folktale. I found that a few historians did not believe that Crockett stopped in Bastrop. So, I set out to see if he really did.

I first established that Greenleaf Fisk did indeed own the Stagecoach Inn at 1005 Hill Street in Bastrop from 1835 to 1837.[4] I also found that the house had been listed on the National Historic Register.[5] Next, I looked at marriage records. Oral history from my Fisk family said that Mary Ann was the daughter of Colonel Bartholomew Manlove, and that she had married Greenleaf Fisk in 1835 at the Manlove farm house at 502 Elm Street in Bastrop, Texas.[6, 7]

A further search for marriage records led me to look for documents that would prove the marriage of Greenleaf and Mary Ann, whose records appear to have been burned in the Runaway Scrape. Using the birth of their first born, William Augustus Fisk, I worked back to several documents which placed the approximate date of the marriage between April 23, 1835, and July 20, 1835.[8,9,10,11,12,13]

Having established that the residence and the marriage fit the timeline, I next moved on to David Crockett's journey to Texas. I first picked him up in Little Rock, Arkansas, on November 12, 1835, where the local newspapers reported that hundreds of people came into town to see him. A group of leading citizens had a dinner for him at the Jeffries Hotel and Crockett spoke about Texan independence and Washington politics.[14]

Later, a man named Eldridge E. Click of Cooper, Texas, is cited in the *Bastrop Advertiser* as placing Crockett at his home in 1835:

> Davy Crockett and my father, Matthias Click, went hunting and killed five bears. My father kept his bear meat up in the attic, said Eldridge. One day Davy Crockett got a ladder and climbed up to where the bear meat was, cut off a slab with his Bowie knife, and ate the raw meat. David Crockett's big Long rifle was broken at the breech. In Bastrop, there was an excellent gunsmith by the name of John Berry, who had come to Bastrop from Kentucky in 1834. Someone told Crockett, "Take it to John Berry; he can fix it for you." And he did.[15]

A quick online search of the Click family revealed that some members believed that Crockett was related to them through family member Temprance Hawkins Click (Crockett's mother was Rebecca Hawkins Crockett), and that Crockett was actually visiting with family members that he knew in Tennessee. But there was no formal proof offered of this.[16]

Crockett was placed in the area, now called Honey Grove, and named by others after his beautiful description of the place and its "wild bees."[17] In his last letter to his children, dated January 9, 1836, at San Augustine, Texas, Crockett praises Texas, says every man is entitled to more than 4,000 acres, and writes that he expects to settle near the northeast Texas town of Bonham. Crockett also mentions that he has "taken an oath of the new government and signed up for a six-month stint as a volunteer," saying that he is heading in a few days toward the Rio Grande with other volunteers, "and believes that he will be elected to office in Texas in the future."[18] However, author Stephen Hardin says that Crockett and sixty-five others signed the oath before Judge John Forbes, being promised 4,600 acres of land, on January 14, 1836.[19] His evidence suggests a discrepancy in dates with Crockett's last letter.

Meanwhile, on October 18, 1835, Noah Smithwick had been fighting in the Battle of Concepcion. Smithwick mentions in his *Evolution of a State*, that after the battle he left to "winter" in Bastrop, citing the lack of firm leadership, dissatisfaction with the delay in pursuing the Mexicans, and a "lack of robust health" as his reasons. That winter, he states that he had come down with a fever in Bastrop, but was convalescent when "Crockett came on." He says that he wanted to return with him to San Antonio, "but seeing that I was not in condition to do so, he (Crockett) persuaded me to wait for another party to arrive a few days later."[20]

In late January of 1836, according to Fisk and Manlove oral history, Crockett and four men arrived in Bastrop, and rented an upstairs room at the inn of Greenleaf Fisk. Crockett asked permission for others who would follow to camp outside the Stagecoach Inn, inquired about land and surveyors in the area, and then took his gun to be repaired. He and his men got drunk later and went on a shooting rampage in town, and were brought back to the inn by Bartholomew Manlove to "sleep it off" on the kitchen floor.[21]

Another story is later told by Hannah Berry, widow of John Berry, Bastrop gunsmith, and is written down in A. J. Sowell's book, entitled *Early Settlers and Indian Fighters of Southwest Texas*. Her story goes like this: "Colonel Crockett came to John Berry's gun shop in company with John McGhee and brought the gun with him. Mr. Berry examined it, and saying he could fix it all right, at once set about the work. A large, silver band was placed around the broken place, and so securely fashioned that it was as strong as ever and very ornamental when polished and flowered off. Colonel Crockett was well pleased and said it was now better than it was at first." Sowell says that mention was made several times of Crockett's beautiful silver mounted rifle, which was taken by the Mexican Army to Mexico when the war was over. Hannah Berry further states, "I would know the gun now if I could see it, by the silver band I watched my husband put there. I remember well how Colonel Crockett looked. He did not wear a cap while at Bastrop."[22]

In reading through Bill Moore's book, *Bastrop County 1691–1900*, I found a map drawn by early pioneer, John Holland Jenkins, of Bastrop in 1837. There, to my surprise, were Greenleaf Fisk and John Berry, both neighbors on this map. The El Camino Real ran through Fisk's land and underneath the trail drawn by Jenkins, which read "to Nacogdoches."[23] That, I thought, is why the Stagecoach Inn is the only house turned sideways on Hill Street. The El Camino Real ran right in front of it! The Fisk and Manlove account of the story also says that the townspeople wanted to throw Crockett and his friends in the stockade.[24] I found that there was a fort of the stockade type in early Bastrop.[25]

So, there you have it. Dates of Crockett sightings in Texas, the account of three eyewitnesses that Crockett was in Bastrop before going on to San Antonio, a deed record placing Greenleaf and Mary Ann Fisk on lot 32 in Bastrop between 1835–1837, and a map of 1837 Bastrop, drawn by John Holland Jenkins, which shows Greenleaf Fisk and John Berry, the gunsmith, as neighbors. I believe there is enough hard *and* circumstantial evidence here to say that Davy Crockett did indeed stop in Bastrop.

The family story about Crockett's stay at the inn in Bastrop was told to the children of Judge Greenleaf and Mary Ann Fisk, and has been passed down through every generation until today through the descendants of James Bartholomew Fisk and Ann Elizabeth Fisk Cashion Faubion. Mama and Papa Manlove in the story are

Bat and Avarilla, the children's grandparents.[26, 27] The story is as follows:

> One day in late January of 1836, Mr. David Crockett and some friends arrived at your father and mother, Greenleaf and Mary Ann Fisk's stagecoach inn along the old El Camino Real in Bastrop. Mr. Crockett had been looking for land in Texas and in general having a mighty good time while he was here.
>
> Mr. Crockett, you see, had broken his bear hunting gun while passing through East Texas. He inquired around and was told that a Mr. John Berry in Bastrop was a fine and well known gunsmith and that there was a stagecoach inn nearby. This inn, he was told, was on the old El Camino Real and was on the way to San Antonio. Its owner, Greenleaf Fisk, was a lawyer and a surveyor, and had land for sale. So, Mr. Crockett thought Bastrop might be a good stopping place to get his gun repaired and find out about available land in Texas.
>
> When arriving in Bastrop, Mr. Crockett and his friends rented beds upstairs and asked permission from your mother, Mary Ann, for those joining them to camp outside the inn, which was often the custom for settlers and large parties traveling together. Mr. Crockett inquired about land for sale. He asked directions to John Berry's house and took his rifle to be repaired.
>
> One night while staying there, Mr. Crockett and three friends became inebriated. "That means they got drunk!" Mama Manlove said. "It was cold and there weren't just a passel of things to do in Bastrop. Well, they started

shootin' off their guns, fightin,' and in general, disturbin' everyone's sleep. They rode their horses down into town and raised a ruckus."

Colonel James Bartholomew Manlove.

Your grandfather, Captain Bartholomew Manlove, raised some of the Bastrop militia and rounded up Mr. Crockett and his friends. Most of the militia and the townspeople wanted to throw them in the stockade. But Captain Manlove took pity on them on this cold night. He settled the men down and reasoned with Mr. Crockett. Then he made the decision to take them back to the inn. The militia loaded them in a wagon, collected their guns and horses, and escorted them back to your father, Greenleaf's inn. There, they put the horses in a livestock pen and went to the house.

Papa Manlove knocked on the door and called out to your mother, Mary Ann, who was six months with child. This was to be her first child, your brother, William Augustus Fisk. Your mother peered through the window, and seeing that it was Papa Manlove, lit the lamp and came to the door. Upon opening the door, she saw your grandfather standing there and more men behind him armed with rifles and pistols. Papa Manlove addressed her saying, "Daughter, Mr. Crockett and his friends have had too much to drink and it is cold. I pray Thee let them sleep here on the floor by the fire in the inn, for they have come to fight for our cause."

Now your mother did not know what to do. She had been awakened from her sleep. She could not refuse her father, who after all, had addressed her in the Quaker. But she did not want them in the parlor and she did not want them in the dining room, which needed to be clean for other guests. Well, it just needed to be clean, and they smelled of sweat and corn liquor. Suddenly, she said, "I will light the big fire in the kitchen and you can lay them there. But, Papa, you must stay with them here tonight." Papa Manlove nodded and collected their guns. The matter was settled.

Less than two months later, Mr. Crockett and his friends lost their lives at the Alamo, fighting for our cause of liberty. There was to be no free land or political office for these brave friends who gave their lives to make Texas free. We children were never told whether Mr. Crockett collected his bear gun or not, but we were told always to remember the sacrifices made for our freedom and pass them on to our children.[28]

And, indeed, they did pass them on to their children. The girl who could have cared less became the keeper of the family stories, as so many of us do when our children are ready to move on and we become the older generation. Texas "sings in my blood" because the stories were passed on of indomitable spirit, courage, friendship, and sacrifice. I want Texas to continue to sing in the blood of my children, grandchildren, and the generations to come.

ENDNOTES

1. Joy Bland, official Crockett family historian. Phone interview, April 5, 2011.
2. Oral history, Greenleaf Fisk and Bartholomew Manlove families, as told to Mariann Fisk Dyer by her cousin, Tom Cashion, Jr., and her mother, Norma Fisk. See DRT #025709 for genealogical proof.
3. Bland.
4. Bastrop County Clerk's Office Records. Vol. A, p. 254. Bastrop, Texas.
5. National Register Information System #78003353, Record #376798. Keywords: Greenlief Fisk, 1836; Place: Texas, Bastrop County, Bastrop.
6. Oral history, Greenleaf Fisk and Bartholomew Manlove families.
7. National Register Information System #78003311. Bartholomew Manlove House, 1835; Place: Texas Bastrop County, Bastrop.
8. Annie Walker Burns. *Records of Marriages, Bourbon County, Paris, Kentucky*. Frankfort, KY: Kentucky Vital Statistics, 1931. 57.
9. TGLO, Milan Colony Map. Vol. 3, p. 79. Still shows Mary Ann Lindsay as the widow of Ezekial Lindsay.
10. TGLO, Vol. 22, p. 481; deed record lists Mary Ann Fisk as "late" Mrs. Mary Ann Lindsay.
11. Miss Jane Summer (abstracted and compiled by). *Some Early Travis County Texas Records*. Williamson County, Texas, 1979. DC#444. 145–146.
12. 1850 Williamson County, Texas Census (Greenleaf Fisk family).
13. Frederick Clifton Pierce. *Fiske and Fisk family: being the record of the descendants of Sir Symond Fiske, lord of the manor of Stadhaugh, Suffolk County, England*. Chicago: F. C. Pierce, 1896. 518.
14. Manley F. Cobia, Jr. *Journey into the Land of Trials: The Story of Davy Crockett's Expedition to the Alamo*. Franklin, TN: Hillsboro Press, 2003. 40–44.
15. O. W. Summerlin. "From Out of the Past." *Bastrop Advertiser*, 1956. Bastrop Historical Museum.

16. Carolyn Whitaker. http://wc.rootsweb.ancestry.com/cgibin/igm.cgi?op=GET&db=carolynwhitaker.
17. Inscription, Crockett Park Monument, Honey Grove, Texas.
18. Polly Ross Hughes. "Davy Crockett's Last Letter in Texas' Hands." *Houston Chronicle*, Austin Bureau, September 5, 2007.
19. Stephen, L. Hardin. *Texian Illiad.* Austin: University of Texas Press, 1994. 117.
20. Noah Smithwick. Evolution of a State. Austin: University of Texas Press, 1983. 81.
21. Oral history, Greenleaf Fisk and Bartholomew Manlove families.
22. A. J. Sowell. Early Settlers and Indian Fighters of Southwest Texas. Reprint. Memphis, TN: General Books, 2010. 31.
23. Bill Moore. Bastrop County, 1691–1900. Wichita Falls, Texas: Nortex Press, 1977. 50.
24. Oral history, Greenleaf Fisk and Bartholomew Manlove families.
25. Ken Kesselus. History of Bastrop County Before Statehood; and, History of Bastrop County, Texas 1846–1865. (Revised Editions). Bastrop, Texas: Wash Jones Press, 2005. 63.
26. 1850 Bastrop County Census, Bartholomew and "Aberilla" Manlove.
27. Sumner.
28. Oral history, Greenleaf Fisk and Bartholomew Manlove families.

Cynthia Ann Parker and child in photo album (Courtesy: Southwest Collection/Special Collections Library, Texas Tech University).

MYTH, FOLKLORE, AND MISCONCEPTION IN THE 1860 CAPTURE OF CYNTHIA ANN PARKER

by Paul H. Carlson

Former Pope John Paul II once said something to the effect that majority opinion and truth are not always the same. Such certainly is the case with the 1860 capture of Cynthia Ann Parker, the death or non-death of her husband during the occurring skirmish, and several other aspects of the brief but tragic fight in the battle of Pease River, an event that has made its way into the myth and folklore of Texas.[1]

The basic facts are simple enough. Against her will, Comanche warriors captured Cynthia Ann Parker in May 1836 when she was nine years old. For the next twenty-five years—a quarter of a century—Parker, known as Naduah among Comanches, lived with the Indians. In time, she married a Comanche warrior, gave birth to three Comanche children, and acquired the ways, ethos, ethics, language, and spiritual beliefs of her Indian relatives and friends. Then, in 1860, against her will, Federal troops in the battle of Pease River captured her from Comanches. Although only thirty-four years old, Naduah sadly never again saw her husband or her two young boys.[2]

Stories, retold tales, folklore, histories, and other accounts of the 1860 capture are numerous. Some of them are old, dating back to the day of her capture. Some are contemporary, dating only to the most recent books or articles on Texas Comanches and Texas Rangers. Some represent good history, of course, and some—those full of misconceptions and errors—represent myth. Some represent romantic, but wonderful folklore.

Indeed, folklore, myth, and legend dominate stories associated with the 1860 capture of Naduah—Cynthia Ann Parker. Over and over again, for example, myth and folklore suggest that Parker's husband Peta Nocona was a Comanche chief. They suggest that Peta Nocona died in the 1860 fight. They often suggest that Cynthia Ann was Peta Nocona's only wife. They often suggest that Quanah Parker was at the battle but escaped with his younger brother. Myth and folklore also suggest that Texas Rangers captured Cynthia Ann Parker, that Texas Rangers achieved a great victory over Comanche warriors at Pease River, and that during the fight Ranger captain Lawrence Sullivan "Sul" Ross fought an individual battle with Peta Nocona.

None of the above is true, as it turns out, but all of it makes for a good story. Indeed, the so-called battle of Pease River was not a fight between a company of Texas Rangers and a band of Comanche warriors. It was a swift, early morning attack by Federal troops and Texas Rangers on a small Comanche hunting camp, one populated mainly by women and children.

In short, myth, folklore, and misconceptions abound in the story of the 1860 capture of Cynthia Ann Parker. In 1929, for example, nearly seventy years after the massacre, a member of the large Parker family of Texas complained about what she saw as errors in the history of the half-battle/half-massacre and Parker's capture.[3] And, just a few years ago a new book covering the conjoined events—a *New York Times* bestseller by the by—appeared. As with several other books and articles, the bestseller continues to perpetuate myth, misconceptions, and folklore associated with the fight near Pease River.[4]

In brief, here is what happened: On December 19, 1860, along Mule Creek just upstream from its junction with the Pease River in modern Foard County, twenty Federal troops and not more than twenty Texas Rangers surprised and struck a small Comanche hunting camp. The camp contained nine "grass tents" and approximately fifteen people. Most people in the camp were women and children who, having packed their provisions, were beginning to leave.

The fight, or massacre if you will, was over in twenty or so minutes. The Texas Rangers and Federal troops killed seven Indians: four women and three men. The Rangers captured a boy whom Sul Ross brought home and named Pease Ross. Federal cavalrymen captured two Comanches: Cynthia Ann Parker and her infant daughter. About six Indians got away, either because of the cavalrymen's jaded horses or because the soldiers were reluctant to kill women and children who were offering no resistance and trying to escape. The Anglo attackers suffered no injuries, not even minor ones.[5]

That's pretty much it. But, over time the story changed. Participants themselves mainly, but later writers, some historians, and a few other folks transformed the event and reinterpreted what happened. Collectively, they turned the brief, one-sided attack on the small hunting camp into a major Texas Ranger victory against a superior force of Comanche warriors. In 1886, for example, James T. DeShields, a writer and friend of Sul Ross, concluded about the so-called battle: "So single a victory had never before been gained over the fierce and war-like Comanches; . . . The great Comanche confederacy was forever broken."[6]

As a second example, former Texas Ranger Benjamin Franklin "Uncle Frank" Gholson, who was not at the battle of Pease River and the capture of Cynthia Ann but claimed he was, left us with a couple of interviews. In one of them, dated 1931, he said the Comanche village contained between 500 and 600 Indians, 150 to 200 of them warriors. He also said that he and eleven other Rangers chased fleeing Indians for twelve miles. At the end of the chase, he said, they counted seventy Comanches on horseback carrying thirty-two dead or wounded companions. Upon returning from the chase, Gholson and the other Rangers, Gholson stated, carried seven Comanche scalps.[7]

In other words, Gholson wanted us to believe that twelve Texas Rangers on tired and worn horses chased 109 Indians for twelve miles, killing or wounding thirty-nine of them—while at the same time suffering no casualties themselves.

Texas Ranger Hiram B. Rogers came closer to the truth. He was at the Mule Creek fight. In 1928, about seventy years after the event, he said, "I was in the Pease river fight, but I am not very proud of it. That was not a battle at all, but just a killing of [women]. One or two [men] and sixteen [women] were killed."[8]

Thus, there is much folklore and a lot of myth associated with the Pease River battle. That it was fought on December 18 is a misconception. The fight occurred on a very cold December 19 morning. The wrong date first appeared in 1875, when Sul Ross in a letter wrote the fight occurred on the eighteenth.[9] The date stuck. It is now carved into a granite historical marker erected near the battle site; it is the date cited at least twice in the *New Handbook of Texas*, and it is the date used in some well-respected books related to Cynthia Ann Parker.[10]

That Ben "Uncle Frank" Gholson was at Pease River is a myth. He made up his stories, and in 1928 and 1931 used them to bamboozle interviewers, amuse his family, and entertain his friends. They are the stuff of tall tales. Unfortunately, to tell their stories several writers use his faulty reminiscences, including the author of the 2010 *New York Times* bestseller.

That Peta Nocona, or Putauck, was a Comanche chief is a myth. He was a warrior, he was the husband of Naduah, and he was the father of Quanah, but he was not a Comanche chief. Horace Jones, an army scout and interpreter who knew him, said, "Peta Nocona was not one of the big men among the Indians." Charles Goodnight, the Panhandle rancher and acquaintance of Quanah Parker and other Comanches, also said that Peta Nocona was not a chief. Sul Ross, who wrongly claimed he shot the man, said Peta Nocona was "a noted warrior of great repute." Most of all, Peta Nocona's name does not appear among contemporary, nineteenth century lists of Comanche chiefs.[11] That Peta Nocona died at Pease River is a myth. He was not there.

That Texas Rangers captured Cynthia Ann Parker is folklore. In fact, Federal troops, perhaps a soldier named Charles D. A. Loeffler, captured the mother of three children. At least Loeffler claimed he was responsible for her capture, and in 1893, Sul Ross, while president of a little agricultural and mechanical school at College Station, Texas, finally admitted Federal troops and not any of the Texas Rangers captured Parker and her baby daughter.[12]

Quanah Parker (Courtesy: Southwest Collection/Special Collections Library, Texas Tech University).

That Quanah Parker was at the battle of Pease River is a myth. He was not there. Between nine and twelve years old in 1860, he was with his father some seventy or more miles away.

That Cynthia Ann Parker was her husband's only wife is a misconception. Her husband, the father of Quanah, had at least three wives, possibly four. Nor was Naduah his favorite wife. She was, like many Anglo woman captives, a "chore wife." And with one of the other wives at Mule Creek, she was responsible for butchering game, preparing hides, and packing meat. It was a tough, dirty job.

Such myth and folklore arose from the many accounts the Anglo participants left us. Nine people who were, or in Gholson's case, claimed to have been, participants left some eighteen reports, diaries, reminiscences, statements, or other documents describing their role in the affair.

Sul Ross, the "lying four-flusher," as Charles Goodnight called him, gave several accounts; the more significant ones were in 1861, 1875, and 1884—the latter published in 1886.[13] They are not always the same. Which are we to believe?

Sergeant John Spangler of the Federal troops gave two "official" reports. Why two "official" reports?

Jonathan Baker left a diary—one in which he wrote daily during the march to and from the battle ground along Mule Creek. But, an explanation seems needed. On the Anglo side of this sorry affair, three separate groups of men were part of the larger expedition. Captain Ross led forty Texas Rangers. Sergeant Spangler led twenty Federal troops. Captain J. J. "Jack" Cureton led the third group. It included seventy-two or more militiamen (citizen soldiers). Because half the Rangers' horses, however, and nearly all the citizens' horses were in poor condition made worse by inadequate forage, the citizens and at least half of the Rangers fell behind—by December 19, the morning of the battle, some four or five miles behind. Consequently, they did not participate in the attack on the Comanche hunting camp. Yet, not having participated did not keep some of them from reporting on what they did not see.

Jonathan Baker, a school teacher in Palo Pinto, was one of the militiamen under Captain Jack Cureton. As noted, he kept a diary. As he did not witness the battle, he did not write about it in his diary. Nonetheless, his description of the battlefield, which he reached a few hours after the fight, is the best and most reliable one available. At least such is the case if one reads and relies on his original diary. Many writers do not. Instead, they use an altered copy of the diary—thus perpetuating more of the myth and misconceptions.

Baker's original diary consists of several boxes of both tablets and loose papers on which the diary is handwritten.[14] There is a typed document alleged to be a copy of the original. Baker's daughter, Elizabeth Baker, seems to have typed the document. The typed version, which many writers have used, is not an exact copy of the handwritten original. Elizabeth made some notable additions to the diary, especially for the battle of Pease River.

One of the additions is part of the December 19 entry. It reads: "Tonight as we sat about the campfire, a discussion arose as to [the woman's] identity, and in the course of the talk, someone remarked that years ago a family by the name of Parker had been killed where Parker is now, and a child, Cynthia Ann Parker, had been carried off. At once the woman spoke up and said, 'Me Cynthia Ann.'"[15]

It did not happen. Parker was not identified until the Federal troops brought her to their home station at Camp Cooper in Throckmorten County. And, the "Me Cynthia Ann" story is not in Baker's original diary—the handwritten one.

Another addition in the typed version not found in the original account has to do with a moccasin. It is a bit romantic but apocryphal. It reads: "As we sat about the camp fire I [Baker] picked up a tiny moccasin, and after looking at it decided to keep it as it was a beautiful one." But, on "glancing round I noticed the woman looking at me intently. I looked at her and the little child, and noticed [the child] had on only one moccasin, so I held up the one I had picked up, [the woman] nodded her head, and I held it out and the child came over and got it and the mother put it [on] her."[16]

The event could not and did not happen. Cynthia Ann Parker and her daughter were with the Federal troops camped some distance away and not in the camp of Baker's militiamen. Again, the story is not in the original handwritten diary.

In the end, although myth and folklore associated with the 1860 capture of Cynthia Ann Parker remain, a few things at least seem clear. Seven Indians died in the brief encounter, three were captured, and Sul Ross became a hero. In fact, a contemporary of Ross apparently claimed it was "this Pease River fight and the capture of Cynthia Ann Parker that made Sul Ross governor of Texas."[17]

Cynthia Ann Parker gained nothing from the retelling or from the battle and her capture. Neither did her husband, Peta Nocona, or their two sons, Quanah and Pecos. Truth be told, the family suffered immeasurably from Naduah's 1860 capture.

Clearly, the brief fight along Mule Creek demonstrates again how myth and legend remain difficult to alter. Indeed, most of us object when our majority opinion about the past does not reflect the truth as we know it, or as the reporter said in the movie *The Man Who Shot Liberty Valance:* "When legend becomes fact, print the legend." For the time being, then, we are compelled to live with myths and misconceptions associated with the 1860 capture of Cynthia Ann Parker.

Endnotes

1. See Paul H. Carlson and Tom Crum. *Myth Memory and Massacre: The 1860 Capture of Cynthia Ann Parker.* Lubbock: Texas Tech University Press, 2010. 61–140.
2. Jack K Selden. *Return: The Parker Story.* Palestine, Texas: Clacton Press, 2006. 167–72; Tom Crum and Paul H. Carlson. "Did Quanah Parker Lie?" *The Chronicles of Oklahoma* 93, No 3 (Fall 2015): 328–41; and, Paul H. Carlson and Tom Crum, "The 'Battle' of Pease River and the Question of Reliable Sources in the Recapture of Cynthia Ann Parker," *Southwestern Historical Quarterly* 113, No. 1 (July 2009): 32–52.
3. Araminta McClellan Taulman. "The Capture of Cynthia Ann Parker." *Frontier Times* 6, No. 8 (May 1929): 311.
4. See, for example, S. C. Gwynne's flawed *Empire of the Summer Moon: Quanah Parker and the Rise and Fall of the Comanches, the Most Powerful Indian Tribe in American History.* New York: Scribner, 2010; see also the error-filled article by Robert H. Williams titled "The Case for Peta Nocona," *Texana* 10, No. 1 (1972): 55–72.
5. John W. Spangler, First Sergeant, Company H, to Nathan G. Evans, Captain, Second Cavalry, Camp Cooper, December 24, 1860, photocopy in possession of Judge Tom Crum; "From the Frontier," *Dallas Herald*, January 2, 1861; Captain L. S. Ross to Governor Sam Houston, January 4, 1861, as it appeared in "More about the Capture of Woman Prisoner," *San Antonio Express*, February 23, 1908; and in "Cynthia Ann Parker Again," *Beeville Bee*, February 28, 1908. A copy of the report is also in Eric C. Caren, comp., *Texas Extra: A Newspaper History of the Lone Star State, 1838–1935.* Edison, N. J.: Castle Books, 1999. 103; and, "Indian News," *Galveston Civilian*, January 15, 1861. For a recent secondary account of substance see Tom Crum, "Folklorization of the Battle on Pease River," *West Texas Historical Association Year Book* 72 (1996): 69–85.
6. James T. DeShields. *Cynthia Ann Parker.* Saint Louis: n. p., 1886; reprint, with foreword by John Graves, Dallas: Chama Press, 1991. 41–44; see also J. W. Wilbarger. *Indian Depredations in Texas.*

Austin: Hutchings Printing House 1889; facsimile reprint, Austin: The Steck Company, 1935. 335–38.

7. Benjamin Franklin Gholson interview with Felix Williams and Harvey Chelsey, August 26, 1931, in Rupert N. Richardson, ed., "The Death of Nocona and the Recovery of Cynthia Ann Parker," *Southwestern Historical Quarterly* 46 (July 1942): 15–42.
8. Hiram B. Rogers. "Recollections of Ranger H. B. Rogers of the Capture of Cynthia Ann Parker," as told to J. A. Rickard, n.d., filed with Benjamin Franklin Gholson, "Recollections of B. F. Gholson," as told to J. A. Rickard, August 1928, in Dolph Briscoe Center for American History, University of Texas at Austin.
9. "The Parker Captives." *Galveston News*, June 3, 1875.
10. "Parker, Cynthia Ann." *The New Handbook of Texas* 5: 58; "Parker, Isaac," Ibid., 5: 59; T. R. Fehrenbach. *Comanches: The Destruction of a People*. New York: Alfred A. Knopf, 1974. 439–41; William T. Hagan. *Quanah Parker, Comanche Chief*. Norman: University of Oklahoma Press, 1993. 6; Gerald Betty. *Comanche Society before the Reservation*. College Station: Texas A & M University Press, 2002. 4; and, Margaret Schmidt Hacker. *Cynthia Ann Parker: The Life and The Legend*. El Paso: Texas Western Press, 1990. 24.
11. The Horace Jones quote is in C. Richard King, ed., *Marion T. Brown: Letters from Fort Sill, 1886–1887*. Austin: Encino Press, 1970. 78; Goodnight's comments are in several sources (see, for example, Charles Goodnight, "My Recollections and Memories of the Capture of Cynthia Ann Parker," as told to J. Evetts Haley, Charles Goodnight, Papers, Panhandle-Plains Historical Museum, Canyon); the Ross statement is in DeShields' *Cynthia Ann Parker*, 41–42; see also Betty's *Comanche Society before the Reservation*. 4.
12. Susan Parker St. John, cousin of Cynthia Ann, interview with L. S. Ross, President of Texas A&M College, 1894, in Joseph Taulman Papers, Dolph Briscoe Center for American History, University of Texas at Austin.
13. See Carlson and Crum, *Myth Memory and Massacre*. 30–32, 69, 71–72, 75, and 81–82.
14. Jonathan Hamilton Baker. Diary of Jonathan Hamilton Baker, manuscript, private collection, Tarrant County Historical Commission, Fort Worth; Diary of Jonathan [James] Hamilton Baker, 1858–1918, typescript, Dolph Briscoe Center for American History, University of Texas at Austin, hereafter cited as Baker, Diary—second, typescript; see also Carlson and Crum, *Myth Memory and Massacre*. 42–48.
15. Baker, Diary—second, typescript; see also Carlson and Crum, *Myth Memory and Massacre*. 45, 159 notes 11 and 12.
16. Baker, Diary—second, typescript.
17. Ibid.

Michael Collins.

THE LEGEND OF OLD CASUSE AND HIS PAINT HORSE GALLOWS

by Michael Collins

In the border city of Matamoros, local legend has it that in the spring of 1875 an enigmatic blind woman walked the cobblestone streets and crowded markets. Some said that, despite the cataracts that clouded her eyes, the wizened old lady could see things that others could not. Many claimed that she had the gift of prophecy. Whether or not she could actually look into the future and predict events to come, they believed that she possessed some unexplained mystical power. Some feared her. Most avoided her. But others heeded her message of impending doom.

Like a modern-day Jeremiah, the aged woman with gnarled fingers and white hair stringing to her shoulders presented a striking if not strange figure on street corners and in public squares. No matter if bystanders paused to listen to her warn of the coming of the end days, the self-proclaimed seer still spoke of an impending apocalypse—the final judgment that was at hand. All must repent of their sins and prepare now, she warned her listeners, for the time foretold in *The Revelation of John* was upon them. The Almighty had allowed her a glimpse of hell's fury, or so she claimed. And she had seen the dreaded reaper of Satan. Death was coming, and coming soon, she cried, and he was riding alongside the Devil on a pale horse. And as the scripture proclaimed, "hell followed with him."[1]

Every spring thunderstorms roll in from the Gulf of Mexico. But in May of 1875, as Captain Leander H. McNelly led his column of Rangers southward toward the border, the tempests seemed to be especially violent. During the second week in May, McNelly and his Rangers skirted the "Big Sands" of the Wild Horse Desert, which sprawl along the Texas Gulf Coastal Plain for more than seventy-five miles. Along their route they observed daily evidence of the recent range wars that had ravaged the region: an occasional burned out and abandoned cabin, cattle wandering unclaimed, Tejanos with all their worldly belongings piled into mule-drawn carts and wagons heading north to some point of safety. Most disturbing, however, was the grisly sight of a Mexican vaquero dangling from a lone mesquite tree, a noose still tied tightly around his neck. No doubt, Captain McNelly knew, the young man had been a victim of vigilante vengeance, just like the two poor souls he and his troops had seen left hanging from the railroad trestle near the crossroads village of Banquete several days earlier.[2]

Heavy spring rains continued to turn the coastal plains into a quagmire, slowing McNelly's advance. Not until May 14 did Company A, Washington County Volunteers—McNelly's Special Force of Rangers—ride into the village of Edinburg. Tired, drenched, his boots covered with mud, McNelly dashed off a letter to Texas Adjutant General William Steele that afternoon, informing him that the company was now camped within ten miles of the Rio Grande. "I met [Ranger] Captain [Neal] Coldwell yesterday," McNelly began, "but think he is disinclined to take chances in crossing the river (which is not a ten foot rise). [General Juan] Cortina was on the opposite side yesterday and hung an alcalde and another Mexican for killing one of his cattle thieves. Can't say anything yet about the conditions of affairs here," he continued. "Everyone says that stealing is going on constantly, but Captain Coldwell thinks most of the reports are false."[3]

As it turned out Coldwell, commander of Company F of the Frontier Battalion of state Rangers, was the one who was wrong. Perhaps McNelly was the only one who sensed that at first. But soon, every one of his young Rangers would as well. Each day McNelly's scouting parties returned to camp with more reports of rustlers crossing the river into Mexico, trailing entire herds of cattle bearing Texas brands. Allegedly these thieves were in the employ of General Juan Cortina, the same "Red Robber of the Rio Grande" who had long been the chief nemesis of Anglo Texans on the border.

"Cattle Raid on the Texas Border," by William de la Montagne Cary, 1874.

By mid-May McNelly had bivouacked at Rancho Las Rucias in Cameron County, a few miles upriver from Brownsville. For the next two weeks he worked to establish a spy network, one that would bring him all the reliable information he needed. During the first week in June, acting on information gathered by his spies operating above and below the river, the Captain ordered seventeen of his Rangers to ride off to La Parra, below Brownsville. The next day McNelly's scouts picked up the tracks of a small party of raiders herding cattle southward to the banks of the Rio Grande. Within forty-eight hours the Rangers had trailed two of the alleged bandits to the river banks.[4]

When captured, both prisoners suffered the misfortune of being turned over to Jesus Sandoval, one of McNelly's spies recruited for his prowess as a tracker, his knowledge of the river, and his resolve to kill bandits. It soon became apparent that the ranchero turned man hunter was skilled in torturing captives into confessions, and that he enjoyed his work. The cattle thieves could not have had a more terrifying enemy. "Old Casuse," as the Rangers called him, was a rangy, brooding figure, with shoulder-length auburn hair and a matching beard streaked with gray. According to Ranger George Durham, Casuse (pronounced "Casoose") was "what you would call spooky" in appearance. "He looked like a crazy man," Durham remembered—a man who lived only to kill and to have his revenge against Cortina's rustlers, who had reportedly raided his rancho Estero Grande, some fifteen miles upriver from Brownsville, the previous year.

By some accounts, during Sandoval's absence raiders had raped his fifteen-year-old daughter and his wife, burned his barn and ranch house to the ground, and stolen his livestock, all the time threatening that they would soon return to kill him and his family if they continued to cooperate with "Gringo" officials. His "fierce, glittering eyes," as Ranger Napoleon Jennings recalled, revealed the hatred that he harbored and the terrible vengeance he sought. It was rumored that, just days before joining up with McNelly, Sandoval had hanged two alleged thieves from the same tree near the river, leaving their corpses swinging in the wind as a ghoulish reminder to other bandits who crossed the border.[5]

Now Old Casuse used the same gruesome method to extract information from the two captives taken near La Parra, one reportedly named Rafael Salinas. Sandoval took each to an isolated tree, tied a rope around his neck, tossed it over a limb, then hoisted the man two to three feet into the air, strangling him for several moments before lowering him back to ground. Casuse repeated the grisly ritual several times until the suspected bandit had apparently told all that he knew. "As far as we knew," Ranger William Callicott speculated, "this treatment always brought out the truth."[6]

After Captain McNelly was satisfied with the confessions, he left the captives with Casuse, who then tied a hangman's noose, looped it over each prisoner's head, and one at a time forced them to stand in the saddle of his tall paint horse. Then Sandoval walked behind the animal and switched him on the backside, causing him to dash away, thus leaving the victim swinging, thrashing and twisting until the life had left him. "Captain McNelly didn't like this kind of killing," Callicott insisted, "but Casuse did." As Callicott remembered further, "we caught several spies on that scout . . . and Casuse dealt with all of them alike, showing no partiality—he always made them a present of six feet of rope." [7]

Years later Ranger S. N. Hardy, who also served under Captain McNelly, confirmed stories of the "paint horse gallows" for famed folklorist J. Frank Dobie. "One night while we were camped on the Rio Grande, I was in charge of the guard," Hardy recalled. "Sandoval was keeping watch, and along about midnight I heard him cursing a blue streak in both Mexican and English. I went down to see what the trouble was." What Hardy described next was a horrific scene. "When I got near the river," Hardy recollected, "I saw an empty skiff, which had come over from the Mexican side. Also I saw Sandoval on a horse riding against a taut rope that was hitched to his saddle horn. The other end of the rope was tied to the neck of a Mexican . . . [whose] feet were tied to a mesquite bush. After he got through pulling, he dismounted and showed me another Mexican whose throat had been cut to the bone." Before young Hardy could inquire about their crimes, Old Casuse "explained that these two victims were the last of the gang who had burned his home and ruined his wife and daughter. I did not say anything to Captain McNelly until months later. Lots of things happened on the Rio Grande that never got into the ranger reports," Hardy admitted.[8]

The well-dressed and fair-complexioned Sandoval spoke with a kind voice, one befitting a priest, not a killer. But what little English he knew revealed the truth behind his mild manner. Bill Callicott insisted that, other than a few choice phrases like "damn 'em," "son of a bitch" and "kill 'em all," Sandoval stuck to his native Spanish. Jokingly, some of the boys insisted that Casuse could speak two languages—Spanish and profanity. [9]

No wonder. Sandoval may have mangled the *Gringos'* language, but the Rangers mangled his name as well, calling him "Casuse" rather than Jesus. The ranchero would come to call his fellow Rangers, most of whom he knew only by name, simply "*muy bravos hombres.*" Of the scraggly-looking Sandoval, Durham wrote, "His skin was dry and parched, and his light blue eyes seem to throw off sparks." Napoleon Jennings later described Casuse as a thin, angular figure in a panther skin vest, as "sinewy and strong and as active as any man I ever saw." An "extremely graceful rider and a daring one," according to Jennings, Sandoval "did not differ from hundreds of Mexicans on that border, except he was rather taller." He carried a "haughty bearing," Jennings observed, as if he somehow believed himself to be better than others of his nationality. No one knew how old he was, and no one dared to ask.[10]

What was well known was that the seemingly meek "Old Casuse" had a score to settle with the border bandits. Ironically named for the Prince of Peace, he earned his reputation as McNelly's "hangman." One Mexican newspaper from the border state of Tamaulipas carried a chilling account of Sandoval's method of executing prisoners. *Voz del Pueblo* ("the people's voice") of Matamoros published a report accusing McNelly's Rangers of summarily lynching captives "with impunity." The article even singled out Jesus Sandoval by name as McNelly's chief executioner. Based on accounts from purported eyewitnesses, the newspaper offered in graphic detail how Sandoval "enjoyed his work." The article described how Sandoval would tie the hands and feet of a captive, then placing a noose around the vaquero's neck, he would remove his hat, drop to his knees, and make the sign of the cross. Offering then a few words from the scriptures and a short prayer, he would call the victim by name, pronounce him guilty, then grasp his hand and whisper, "*adios* my good friend, goodbye." With that short ritual, the newspaper claimed, Sandoval conducted his executions with the knowledge and approval of his captain, also identified in the article by name—McNelly.[11]

Perhaps General Edward O. C. Ord, then commander of the Department of Texas headquartered in San Antonio, stated it most succinctly. Obviously with some knowledge of such lynchings conducted by Texas state troops, he confessed that McNelly "had a big advantage" over the United States Army, "mainly because he employed means of getting information . . . that was denied the military. His prisoners would talk. Ours wouldn't."[12]

The historical record regarding the life of Old Casuse leaves few documents but little doubt of Sandoval's short career as Captain McNelly's enforcer. Muster rolls in the Texas State Archives only offer dates for his service; federal census reports merely confirm his presence, his presumed age, and birth in Mexico—nothing more. A deposition submitted to the United States District Court and signed by the hand of the same Jesus Sandoval on May 3, 1875, offers a few fragments but fewer clues about his identity and character; yet one paragraph in his testimony stands out. Translated for the court, the text reads: "I have been a peaceable citizen of the United States since eighteen hundred fifty-three and . . . for that reason I have many enemies in Mexico; they say I am Americanized and consequently . . . a traitor to Mexico; they have persecuted me, threatened my life, and attempted to assassinate me. For seven months I have not slept in my house," he claimed, "I have slept in the chaparral—a solitary sentinel over my own home."[13]

Today along the lower Rio Grande, *corridos,* or border ballads sung along both banks of the river, still tell of the time when death was as common as dirt in the brush country of South Texas. After all these years the folk songs speak of the day when men were all too willing to kill for any cause, noble or otherwise. And as the lyrics proclaim, through the center of it all runs a crooked river, a timeless, slow moving and unpredictable current that bisects the blood-stained ranges of the border. These ballads also give voice to the old blind oracle's lamentations that the horsemen of the apocalypse would soon descend on this troubled country and bring wrath and judgment.

Prophecy, Providence or otherwise, in the spring of 1875 some of the more superstitious people on both sides of the border must have wondered. For when Captain Leander McNelly and his Rangers reached the Rio Grande, word quickly spread of the presence of *los Rinches*, the Rangers. Within days of his arrival in the border county of Cameron, Captain McNelly left his camp at Las Rucias with a small escort of Rangers by his side and traveled into Brownsville to interview local authorities about the ongoing contagion of cattle theft and violence. No doubt, when he rode through the streets of Brownsville astride a tall, spirited bay named Segal, the news had already preceded him: "*Los Diablos Tejanos*," the Texas Devils, had returned to the border. And with them rode a sullen, ghostly looking figure on a large paint horse, a well-dressed vaquero who still rides somewhere on the borders between Anglo-Texan myth and Mexican lore. The Rangers called him "Old Casuse." But to the bandits he hunted the quiet rider might as well have been *El Diablo*—the devil himself.

ENDNOTES

1. Rev. 6: 7–8 (ESV). The legend of the "she preacher" was related to the author by local residents during a visit to Brownsville and Matamoros on February 11–12, 1994. See Michael Collins, "The Texas Devils: McNelly's Rangers and the Palo Alto Fight," *Papers of the Second Annual Palo Alto Conference*. Brownsville, Texas: National Park Service, United States Department of the Interior, Palo Alto National Historic Site, 1997. 128–134.
2. Walter Prescott Webb. *The Texas Rangers: A Century of Frontier Defense*. Austin: University of Texas Press, 1935. 238–241.
3. George Durham. *Taming the Nueces Strip: The Story of McNelly's Rangers*. Austin: University of Texas Press, 1962. 40–42.
4. Chuck A. Parsons and Marianne E. Hall Little. *Captain L. H. McNelly, Texas Ranger: The Life and Times of a Fighting Man*. Austin: State House Press, 2001. 176–179.
5. Durham. 40, 44, 53–55; and Napoleon A. Jennings, *A Texas Ranger*. Norman: University of Oklahoma Press, 1997. 74–75, 78–79.
6. William Callicott, "Memoirs of William Callicott: As Told to Walter Prescott Webb," Dolph Briscoe Center for American History, University of Texas, Austin. 9–11; hereafter cited as Callicott, "Memoirs"; "Reminiscences of William Callicott of Houston," Dolph Briscoe Center for American History, University of Texas, Austin. 3–6.
7. Ibid.
8. J. Frank Dobie. "Foreword," in Jennings, *A Texas Ranger*, viii.
9. Callicott. "Memoirs." 9–11.
10. Jennings. 74–75, 78.

11. *Voz del Pueblo* (Matamoros), undated, in Consular Dispatches, Matamoros, Mexico, Records of the United States Department of State, Record Group 59, Microfilm edition.
12. Durham. 55.
13. U.S. Congress. House Committee on Foreign Affairs. 45th Congress. 2nd. Sess. Report No. 701. *Texas Frontier Troubles: Testimony Taken Before the Committee on Foreign Affairs.* 87–88.

The Cathedral Room at the end of Cascade Caverns is split through the ceiling by the Balcones Fault line. Church choirs used to sing in the Cathedral Room (Courtesy: Amy Ashcraft).

THE HERMIT: A STUDY OF THE LEGEND CENTRAL TO CASCADE CAVERNS IN BOERNE, TEXAS

by Erin Marissa Russell and Matt Gibson

> "Oftentimes we encounter truths, which, if presented as fiction, would be far too absurd for our human minds to accept, let alone digest. Such is true of the amazing coincidences which have woven themselves around this narrative and the cave which plays so prominent a part therein."—*Hermit of the Cavern* Introduction (by Frank E. Nicholson)[1]

In the 1840s, a German medical student boarded a desolate train, then a drafty, barnacle-clad boat to America, all for the sake of a lost love. He came aground again in modern-day Boerne, Texas. Some say he was heartbroken after a refusal from the woman he was courting; another version of the legend claims he caught his beloved with another man, murdered him, and was forced to flee his homeland. In another, less well-known derivative, the student leaves Germany after killing his brother.

The student set up a clinic in Texas, but his services were often unreliable. The young man took long walks as a respite, immersing himself in silence and the landscape. These nature walks grew longer and longer, until patients found him out more often than in. On one such walk, the German encountered an injured member of the Lipan Apache tribe and used his medical knowledge to treat the man's wounds. This began a friendship of mutual exchange. The young man provided curative treatments, and the Lipan acquainted him with the landscape and its resources, including a cave they used for shelter, meetings, and rituals.

The young man began spending more and more time with the Lipan and in the cavern itself. Our reluctant hero soon became enchanted by the cavern and obsessed with it. He began sleeping there, on a ledge in a sixty-foot vertical passage—the only entrance to the cave at that time. After being given the cave and the land around it by a Lipan chief, the medical student boarded his clinic's doors and took up full-time residency in the cavern, shunning society altogether. The cave was his constant companion, and like many hermits before him, the Boerne hermit found contentment in its meditative darkness and the muffled, perpetual dripping that shaped its passages. The German told his Lipan friends and wrote in his journal that he wanted to be buried in his subterranean home, but in a twist of fate, he was killed by a stray bullet in a gunfight above ground. After his death, the hermit's body was returned to the ledge where he had slept so many nights, along with his possessions (a journal and his gun). Until future landowner Alfred Gray explored the cavern, the legend goes, the hermit remained there undiscovered.

The first recorded version of the narrative was a winning entry in a writing contest for the *Volksblatt*, an early German newspaper published in Cincinnati, Ohio. The 96-page novella, titled *Ein Verfehltes Leben*, which translates in English to "a wasted life" or "a misspent life," was written by August Siemering in 1876. Siemering was a German himself, and "like many other well-educated men, he left his homeland for the United States with the 'Forty-Eighters' after the failed revolutions of 1848 in Europe."[2] According to the Texas State Historical Association, the Forty-Eighters supported European Revolution and managed the settlement of Fredericksburg, New Braunfels, and other liberal Texas colonies.[3] Local to Boerne was the Sisterdale settlement in Kendall County.[4] Like many of the Forty-Eighters, Siemering opposed slavery, and in 1853, he began authoring articles for a German anti-slavery San Antonio newspaper, *Zeitung*. When the abolitionist organization "*Die Freie Verein*" (The Free Society, in English) organized later that year, Siemering was elected to one of three secretary positions.[5] According to a thesis by Kathryn Adams of Texas Women's University,

"This group felt that the social injustices of slavery, capital punishment, speculation in land, and income and inheritance taxes should be abolished."[6] Siemering would go on to serve as Chief Justice of Bexar County.[7]

Fifty-six years later, in 1932, politician and educator May E. Francis published a translation and adaptation of Siemering's novella, this one titled *The Hermit of the Cavern*.[8] Francis's cave-dwelling hermit character, "Uncle Brown," calls a meeting to instate a secret organization of Unionist German settlers. In attempting to save a friend (Jackson) who is captured and about to be burned alive by Diego Escalante, an officer of the Mexican army, Brown is hit by a stray bullet. He dies under a doctor's watch, and his friend Jackson says, "I shall go tonight to the cave of Uncle Brown, to bury my friend where he lived." Although Francis's version of the story has largely shaped the hermit's legend, it remains unclear how much of it is based in fact.

An unpublished revision of *The Hermit of the Cavern*, titled War Clouds Over Texas, is housed in the May E. Francis Collection at the University of Northern Iowa's Rod Library. The title and some character names were changed, and writing was polished and edited. There are not many major changes to the parts of the story that concern the hermit's legend. In the revision, when the hermit (Uncle Cooper instead of Brown) relates the story of how he was given the cave, he quotes a Lipan chief:

> My son, tonight our hearts are heavy. You have lived for many moons with our people. We have bound your heart to ours with the silver thong of friendship. Now we must leave you. Our White Father in Washington says we must go from this land which has been the hunting grounds of our fathers. We go, but we give you this cavern and all of the land lying in front of it. It has been the sacred council house of the Lipon [*sic*] people. The spirits of our ancestors return to these rooms. Keep this cavern as the

> free gift of a Lipon chief, to his honored, and
> well-loved son![9]

The addition of this passage is a bit of romanticism on Francis's part. The Lipan had specific rituals they used to claim dominion over territory, and the tribe certainly would not have referred to a U.S. leader as their "White Father in Washington."[10] Other than this passage, and a few name changes, there is no major event or important addition in the revision that alters the story of the hermit from the original.

According to the 1932 book's introduction by speleologist Frank Ernest Nicholson, "Early in 1932, a frayed copy of the [Siemering] story fell from obscurity into the hands of the translator. At precisely the same time this speleologist chanced to wander upon the cave. . . . Eventually, their paths met. Notes were compared, and the connection between the narrative and the cavern were definitely established."[11] Were it not for the connection Nicholson and Francis found between Cascade Caverns and Siemering's story, it is unlikely the cavern would have been developed for public tours. However, physical copies of *The Hermit of the Cavern* are now quite rare; only six public libraries registered with WorldCat, a global library catalog, hold copies.[12]

An article by Nicholson, the aforementioned speleologist, gained investor attention for the cavern and funding was secured to open it to the public. Elizabeth Gray Hudson, the landowner's daughter, wrote that "immediately, blasting, washing with giant fire hoses, huge electrical cables, cement, gravel, and flagstones were to be seen everywhere. The place was as busy as a giant ant colony."[13] The majority of the cave system was, in the 1930s, filled by an underground lake, so it had to be drained before it could be developed. Groundwater still flowed through the strata, though, and a series of seven waterfalls gave the cavern its name (though the waterfalls are no longer active due to drought).[14] In 1932, the cave system was christened Cascade Caverns. Registers rang, cashiers tore tickets, and the footsteps of visitors echoed through the cave's passageways.[15]

The Hermit's Landing (Courtesy: Amy Ashcraft).

Today, the legend lives on through the tales of tour guides, who stop at the bottom of the Peep in the Deep—the sixty-foot vertical passage that was once the cavern's only entrance—and shine their flashlights hourly onto the Hermit's Landing. They tell an abbreviated and, depending on the employee's experience, perhaps improvised version of the narrative. The right tour guide in the right mood might tell you that he believes the hermit's ghost still haunts the cavern. During a personal tour, we were asked not to address the spirit by name or attempt to communicate. One tour guide said the hermit was "this brokenhearted, angry spirit that wanted to be away from people completely, and you've got people down here asking him what's up. He doesn't want to talk to you."[16] Yet just off the Cascade Caverns exit on Interstate I-10, an orange billboard stamped with white letters reads: "Straight ahead to see the hermit." The billboard piqued our interest, but it was the hermit's story that inspired this research.

One of our first research steps was reaching out to the Lipan Apache tribe of Texas to find out whether their lore included the cavern or our hermit. We reached Jaime Geronimo Vela, the tribe historian, who recommended books by Nancy Minor, a member of the Lipan tribe, that would inform our research on the native American element of the legend. Studies of the Lipan from an outsider's perspective lack the nuanced understanding that members of the Lipan tribe possess. These books were instrumental in understanding how Lipan beliefs regarding the land itself played into customs, such as raiding or stealing horses, that caused many native groups to be categorized as warlike or dangerous.[17, 18]

The first time we toured Cascade and heard the hermit's story, a cavern employee said his name was most likely Julius Bayard.[19] A San Antonio radio personality for MIX 96.1 FM had included the cave system in his "Haunted Tours" series and, after some research at the Patrick Heath Public Library, had linked Bayard's name to the legend.[20]

Julius Bayard shows many traits of the archetypal hermit. Bayard's *New York Times* obituary explains that he made his home in a desolate spot in Kendall County, seeing people only when their sickness required it, and concocting curative treatments from the local botanical resources:

> When forced to talk he conversed in monosyllables, and preferred to use a child as interpreter between himself and the persons with whom he conversed. He built a little log hut with his own hands, felling the trees himself, and in front of the door of his house he dug a cave 50 feet deep, in the entrance of which he

> would sun himself. In this cave he was buried according to a provision of his will.[21]

Several parts of Bayard's character appeared to align with our hermit, but a few nagging details seemed imprecise. Records such as Bayard's will and anecdotal family histories show him having married. We felt it unlikely that our heartbroken protagonist would marry so soon and that his wife would set up house in a cavern. In one census record, Bayard lists his country of origin as France, not Germany. And although he was known as the "Boerne hermit," if the story of our hero's death in *The Hermit of the Cavern* is rooted in reality, Julius Bayard died too late—in December of 1890—to have been a Civil War casualty.

While Francis's hermit dies as result of a conflict with the Mexican army, two alternative scenarios are more historically likely. The German Forty-Eighters were targeted by a militia troop they called "*Die Hangerbande*," or "The Hanging Bandits" in English.[22] The Hanging Bandits snatched those Germans who resisted conscription to the Confederate army out of their beds and hung them from the Texas oaks, along with their families. Many German Union sympathizers preferred sleeping in the woods to being found at home and meeting this fate. However, the involvement of Mexican army officers in Francis's version, especially in the gunfight leading to the hermit's death, negates a direct historical correlation between her narrative and *Die Hangerbande*. Another likely scenario that does not quite fit with Francis's tale is The Battle of the Nueces. Occurring at about the right time period in 1862, it was the result of sixty-eight German immigrants making for the Mexican border, which they found a better option than conscription in the Confederate army. Again, neither of these scenarios can be reinforced by Francis's book, however nicely they may fit with the legend.

Francis's hermit also calls a meeting for a secret anti-Confederate organization, and although the novel adaptation gives no real leads as to the organization's identity, a couple of historical societies could be a good fit. German settlers were often liberal intellectuals, supporters of the revolutions of 1848–49, who almost unanimously opposed slavery.[23] The author of the original German novella, Siemering, had his own group, *Die Freie Verein*, which would seem a likely candidate for inclusion in the legend.[24] Another group, The Union League, also known simply as "The Organization," formed before the war ended, in 1863.[25] After the Civil War, the Union League continued its political influence, sending campaigners to office in the election of 1866. The Organization worked to mobilize black voters for the Republican Party (which at that time espoused similar values to the modern Democratic Party). The liberal political leanings of many German settlers make pinning down the hermit's specific organizational affiliations almost impossible.

The first owner of the land above Cascade Caverns who was likely to have actually set foot there was Dr. Benjamin Hester, who purchased it in 1875.[26] Although some versions of the legend call the hermit "Dr. Hester," this date makes it impossible for Hester to have been the hermit (again, assuming the character's Civil War death is genuine). The cavern took on his name and was known as Hester's Cave until 1932, when it was rechristened as Cascade Caverns under the ownership of Alfred Gray.

In the 1930s, land owner Alfred Gray and Bernard Cartwright, cave explorer and bluegrass musician, pulled on waders and looped coils of rope over their arms, preparing to descend the cavern. Turbulent waters had ravaged the sixty-foot drop that was once the cave's only entrance, leaving behind a mass of boulders that ended at "The Giant Molar," a tooth-shaped stalactite submerged in water. Gray and Cartwright found to their relief that they could wade past and they pressed farther. Carrying flashlights in gallon molasses buckets to illuminate the stark beauty of the passageways, the men lighted candles at intervals, watching the flames closely. They were testing the air for black damp—carbon monoxide poisoning, a deadly hazard of cavern exploration. Hudson writes, "Their breath began to come in shorter gasps, as they worked their way over the rocks and around the formations. Their head sensations warned them of the danger. They did, however, reach the large room at the end of the current cave."[27] Two months later, Gray had found an investor—a Canadian named E. A. Drake—to fund draining and other alterations that opening the cave to the public required, but Cartwright would not benefit from this arrangement.

The Peep in the Deep is the 60-foot vertical passage that was once the only entrance to the cave. A ledge about 10 feet into the mouth is said to have been the landing where the hermit slept (Courtesy: Amy Ashcraft).

Instead, Frank Ernest Nicholson (whom we quoted in the epigram) would be Gray's business partner. "Newly released from employment at Carlsbad Caverns,"[28] Nicholson had read Cartwright's report in a San Antonio newspaper, and it sparked his interest. He re-imagined the article's findings—inserting himself as the explorer and leaving Cartwright out entirely—and published it in the *Philadelphia Public Ledger* and the *Literary Digest.* Nicholson took such liberty with the facts that the National Speleological Society found it necessary to compare his statements with those of some of their members in a 1948 NSS bulletin.[29]

Editorial commentary in that bulletin reveals inaccuracies such as a "great vaulted tunnel" measuring eight feet high and six feet wide and a "bottomless pit" ending at eighteen inches. Nicholson had written that he observed an estimated fifty "Spanish Oak and hackberry trees defying the laws of nature. More than a mile from daylight, in excess of 600 feet below the surface, denied sun and rain, this growth has carried on for years." The editors wryly remark that the fifty "trees" were in fact seedlings whose acorns floated in with flood waters, and that the botanist Nicholson claimed had dated their age at fifteen years, when questioned, staunchly denied it.

Nicholson was more than a master of hyperbole; he was a bit of a con man on the cavern circuit. In fact, he was fired from Cascade Caverns for pocketing the money from ticket sales. A 1976 article by William Halliday in the *Journal of Spelean History* calls him "the mystery man of American speleology."[30] Nicholson was a central player in several caverns developed during this era: Carlsbad Caverns, Cascade itself, Longhorn Caverns, and the Devil's Sinkhole. Halliday notes, "Suddenly he was the mainstream of American speleology. Equally suddenly he vanished, and few indeed are the clues to his passing [after 1932]."[31] Halliday chased Nicholson's trail to his hometown and Carlsbad Caverns, finding only a 1960s men's magazine that names him as leader of a caving expedition. And for all Nicholson's wild aggrandizement when relating his expeditions, he failed to mention finding human remains, a notebook, or even an antique weapon in the cavern to corroborate the legend.

The crux of the matter (the matter being the factual basis of this legend) is how closely the original recorded narrative, *Ein Verfehltes Leben*, aligns with historical events. While cavern tour guides first informed us that Siemering's story was based on the hermit's actual journal, according to our own translation, Siemering's foreword reads that concerning "the most interesting events and the people involved that the amendment of reality has taken place, that the work can thus be regarded as a time and a character painting and considered no less than a landscape."[32] In short, Siemering left no definitive clues as to the hermit's historical authenticity.

So far, we have been unable to link the legend to an actual historical figure. The hermit's death in the Francis story fails to align with any military records or obituaries. Those historical figures whose names have been connected with the hermit all died too late to support the Francis narrative. Historians from the Lipan Apache tribe have not verified the legend as part of their own history. And there is no record of a skeleton, journal, or antique weapons ever being excavated from the cavern (although one tour guide said the items had been sent to the University of Texas at Austin). However, our research has also failed to prove any parts are definitely *untrue*. Some of the data leads us to believe that the story could be an amalgamation of several historical figures, although the political leanings and affiliations of the hermit are strikingly similar to Siemering's own.

Folklore, however, considers the value of a specimen as more than simply its accuracy. Carl Jung writes, "The special significance of a true work of art resides in the fact that it has escaped from the limitations of the personal and has soared beyond the personal concerns of its creator."[33] Using this assessment, the hermit's legend has long since overrun whatever limitations Siemering, Francis, or any of those who have perpetuated the tale had in mind. The legend exists more as local mythology than history, intuitively true regardless of factual verity.

With oral transmission comes constant revision. Storytellers tend to forget parts of a plot that fail to resonate with the audience and remember sections that have listeners hanging on every word. Jung describes "the meaning and individual quality of a work of art" as "a living being that uses man only as a nutrient medium, employing his capacities according to its own laws and shaping itself to the fulfillment of its own creative purpose."[34] With this understanding, the hermit's folklore has unfolded naturally and spontaneously—it has inherent meaning apart from its historical truth. Whether fact or fiction, we believe that the legend is something that needs to be preserved for future generations of folklore enthusiasts and those who find themselves enthralled by the folklore that surrounds the caves of Texas.

This paper details the story as transmitted by multiple sources and presents the historical data compiled during research. We also plan to turn the narrative into a novel, combining historical evidence, the legend, and our own fictional interpretation. Because the last fictional version of the legend was published in 1932 and is now out of print, we hope this work will help the story become a widely known piece of Texas folklore for generations to come. The legend itself has been preserved through a series of coincidences, and it seems a shame to leave it in a book so rare that we cannot find a copy of our own to purchase.

Endnotes

1. Frank E. Nicholson. "Introduction" to *The Hermit of the Cavern*, by May E. Francis. San Antonio: Naylor Print Co., 1932.
2. Richard L. Puglisi, Jr. "Bexar County Chief Justice August Siemering, 1830–1883." *Journal of the Life and Culture of San Antonio.* http://www.uiw.edu/sanantonio/AugustSiemerling.html.
3. Glen E. Lich. "Forty-Eighters." *Handbook of Texas Online.* https://tshaonline.org/handbook/online/articles/pnf01.
4. Garland A. Perry. *Historic Images of Boerne, Texas.* San Antonio: Econ-o-Print, 1982.
5. Puglisi.
6. Kathryn L. Adams. *Foreign Visionaries of the Texas Hill Country: Early German Settlers in the Kendall County Area 1847–1900.* Master's thesis, Texas Woman's University: 1979.
7. Puglisi.
8. May E. Francis. *The Hermit of the Cavern.* San Antonio: Naylor Print Co., 1932.
9. May E. Francis. War Clouds over Texas. University of Northern Iowa Rod Library, unpublished.
10. Nancy McGown Minor. *The Light Gray People: An Ethno-History of the Lipan Apaches of Texas and Northern Mexico.* Lanham, Maryland, University Press of America, 2009.
11. Nicholson.
12. "The Hermit of the Cavern," WorldCat.org, accessed June 24, 2014, http://www.worldcat.org/title/hermit-of-the-cavern-a-novel-of-the-early-sixties-abounding-in-dramatic-situations-the-struggle-

of-those-early-german-settlers-in-southwest-texas-to-maintain-their-neutrality-in-a-nation-torn-asunder-by-internal-strife/oclc/54217479.

13. Elizabeth Gray Hudson. "Cascade Cavern." Cascade Caverns, 1984, http://www.cascadecaverns.com/wp-content/uploads/2009/08/Cascade_Caverns_Hudson.pdf.
14. Jeremy Collins (manager of Cascade Caverns) in discussion with the author, April 11, 2014.
15. Hudson.
16. Sam [LNU] (tour guide at Cascade Caverns) in discussion with the author, April 11, 2014.
17. Minor. *The Light Gray People.*
18. Nancy McGown Minor. *Turning Adversity to Advantage: A History of the Lipan Apaches of Texas and Northern Mexico, 1700–1900.* Lanham, Maryland, University Press of America, 2009.
19. Colllins.
20. "Investigation: Cascade Caverns." The Russell Rush Haunted Tour. Accessed April 28, 2014. http://www.mix961.com/pages/hauntedtour/cascadecaverns.html.
21. "Hermit Bayard Dead." *New York Times*, Dec. 19, 1890.
22. Robert G. Schulz, Jr. "*The Nueces Massacre, also known as the Battle of the Nueces*," contributed to Shon Powers' Civil War Blog. http://fspowerscw.blogspot.com/2006/08/nueces-massacre-also-known-as-battle.html.
23. Lich.
24. Puglisi.
25. Carl H. Moneyhon, "Union League." *Handbook of Texas Online.* https://tshaonline.org/handbook/online/articles/wau01.
26. Hudson.
27. Ibid.
28. Ibid.
29. Frank E. Nicholson. "A Celebrated Cave Exploration." *Bulletin of the National Speleological Society, 10*, No. 1 (1948).
30. William Halliday. "Frank Ernest Nicholson . . . The Mystery Man of American Speleology." *Journal of Spelean History* No. 4, 1976.
31. Ibid.
32. August Siemering. *Ein Verfehltes Leben: Preis Novelle.* San Antonio, Freie Presse, 1876.
33. Jung, Carl, "Relation of Analytical Psychology to Poetry," in *The Portable Jung*, ed. Joseph Campbell. New York, Viking Penguin, 1971.
34. Ibid.

Susanna Knight (Courtesy: The Walmsley Collection).

A BRITISH ADVENTURE IN THE YEAR OF THE TEXAS CENTENNIAL

by Adam Cree

Susannah Knight was a determined uncertified teacher who battled insularism, religious prejudice, and patriarchal chauvinism to create a uniquely printed memorial to the men of Chorley in Lancashire, England, who had died in the Great War. From 1919–1921, she recorded the images and biographies of over 750 victims of the conflict in a uniquely printed album. She then took the album on incredible journeys across Europe and North America, where it was viewed and signed by pontiffs, presidents, prime ministers, politicians, monarchs, and military commanders who had a hand in the peace and recovery. Her determination to fight the cause of "Allied friendship" with minimal means and no personal connections led her to present the album to the delegates at the Washington Arms Limitation Conference of 1921. In just over four weeks she had also recorded the signatures of President Warren Harding, his cabinet, many members of the Senate and the House of Representatives, General Pershing, and Admiral Coontz.

Susannah returned to the United States in November 1935, and remained there for twelve months. She continued to seek out signatures for the *Memorial Album*, particularly those who had been touched by war, but she recorded a much wider breadth of individuals. Whilst she was bold enough to berate Eleanor Roosevelt in June of 1936 to gain her autograph, she was most keen to meet veterans from wars in which Americans were engaged, from the Indian Wars onwards.

Susannah sought the ordinary as well as the "great and the good." The experiences of the ex-servicemen that she met on her travels emerge through the signatures. Susannah's story is about the consequences of war and the quest for peace: for nations, for the victims of war, and for a restless woman. This is an account of her American adventure in the year of the Texas Centennial.

Susannah boarded the *RMS Laconia* at Liverpool on 26 October, 1935. The Cunard liner docked in New York on 4 November. Susannah would have caught up with the members of her family that were still living in the city when on her arrival. Annie O'Connell, her now widowed cousin, was still at 2374 Amsterdam Avenue, and Susannah did return for a later visit as a consequence of her cousin's ailing health in 1936.

Susannah didn't stay long in New York, and the blast of noise and activity of the city was a jarring contrast to life in Chorley. She had an intriguing friend who provided a base for the next twelve months. Her New York family vouched that she had an address and a purpose on the paperwork that accompanied her previous visits. On this occasion a man called Bob Barker was named as her host on the passenger list of *Laconia*. This is the first time that Barker's name appears in the evidence that remains of Susannah's life, and yet she seems to have already had a very strong connection with him and his family. Within a fortnight of her arrival in America she was with his family at 2249 Sixth Avenue in Fort Worth, Texas. The city, relatively close to Dallas, is located in the centre of the state and seems to have been the place to which she periodically returned over the next year.

Bob Barker was the Secretary to the Senate of Texas, the clerk who made sure that the documents prepared for the state's Senate were in order. He was seven years younger than Susannah, and his wife, Nora Jones Barker, was nine years his junior. Neither the Barkers nor Texas had ever featured in Susannah's life up to this point. He was really too old to have been a veteran of the Great War, and yet he registered for service in September 1918, four days after he reached the age of 44. He was unlikely to have seen action. He seems to have been independent of mind, and the fact that he was a self-employed farmer in 1918 was a surprising preparation for a career in state government.

Somehow, Susannah had struck up a friendship with Barker and made his home state the focal point of her visit. Barker, respected but not necessarily celebrated by his contemporaries, had influential connections that put Susannah at the heart of Texas political, civic, and cultural life. Naturally, Barker and his wife are recorded with their signatures in the third volume. Susannah's interest in including civic, political, spiritual, and medical representatives in the *Album* remained at the core of this later work. She continued to record the names of the key figures, the great and the good who held communities together in the difficult years after the Great War.

Texas appears to have gripped Susannah, and if she had a little knowledge of the state before she arrived, she certainly gained a deeper understanding of its essence by the time she returned home. There are more than seventy pages in the *Album* devoted to the people of Texas, and there is strong evidence to suggest that she had been drawn by the dream of America when she saw Buffalo Bill Cody's performance in Liverpool in 1891. Buffalo Bill's show even passed though Chorley, where she was residing, in September 1904, and though there is no direct evidence, it is almost certain that she made the effort to see the parade through the town. The figure of the cowboy continued to fascinate her on this final journey, and may have represented the adventurous spirit of the West that she had tried to recapture throughout her life.

The significant event that spanned the full period of Susannah's visit was the Texas Centennial, celebrating a century of the state's independence from Mexico. A carefully choreographed series of events had been the germ of an idea in a speech presented by former Texas Governor James Stephen Hogg in 1900. This idea became an active venture as early as 1923. A permanent Centennial Commission was formed in July 1934, and Dallas was chosen as the venue for a spectacular exposition—a world fair in all but name. Susannah gave her full attention to these events, and the Centennial can be associated with many of the signatures that form the third volume of the *Album*.[1] The celebrations dominated her movements, but did not hold her attention exclusively. Susannah did not lose sight of her underlying mission, and she shared many encounters with American veterans of not only the Great War, but other conflicts in which America had engaged.

It is possible to track most of her adventures by following the chronology of the signatures. It is a trail that throws her into the company of a fascinating array of people who are representative of many different walks of life. On 20 November 1935, Susannah recorded her first dated signature of the American adventure. She had not stayed in Fort Worth for long and was in the city of Austin in the south of the state. Charles Lockhart, the Treasurer to the State of Texas, at 45 inches in height, had the notoriety of being the smallest treasurer to have held office for an American state. His photograph appears with his scratched signature. The autograph of Claude D. Teer was made on the same day, just beneath that of Lockhart. Teer worked closely with the State Treasurer, as he was the Chairman of the Board of Control, purchasing supplies for state departments, maintaining its properties, and preparing the budget. The official stamps of Teer's office were embossed upon the page, and three other officials from the state administration signed the *Album*.[2] Susannah also added the management and staff of the *Austin Dispatch* and the *Tyler Daily Courier-Times* on one of the occasions that she was in Austin.

Susannah established herself in Austin. She took a keen interest in meeting members of the University of Texas from 11 December onwards, perhaps through connections Bob Barker had opened up. Harry Yandell Benedict was a surprisingly remarkable individual and already had a long career to look back upon when Susannah met him, having led the development of mathematical astronomy at the university. He oversaw an extensive building programme in his long presidency of the university and was responsible for the McDonald Observatory. On that same day she met: Edward Jackson Mathews, the Registrar and Dean of Admissions; Hanson Tufts Parlin, Professor of English and Dean of the College of Arts and Sciences; and Benjamin Floyd Pittenger, Dean of the School of Education. They are all recorded together, with gold seals of the University of Texas alongside their names. The following page of the *Album* confirms that Susannah continued her tour of the University later that day. She recorded the names of: John William Calhoun from the Mathematics Department; Albert P. Brogan, the Dean of the Graduate

School; Victor Ivan Moore, Dean of Student Life; and J. Anderson Fitzgerald, the Dean of the School of Business Administration.

The connection between business and academic studies was no accident, as one of the aims of the Centennial Committee was to promote the state's canny commercial acumen. The remaining six signatures on this page were connected to engineering, geology, and petroleum. The University of Texas was providing the academic credentials for a post-Depression revival for the state. Susannah visited the Physics Department, which also played a part in the economic transformation of Texas. She met key individuals who had been instrumental in forming this department and driving its research. Though they are undated, the signatures must come from this period of Susannah's journey—either in December or January. She met Lucien LaCoste, who invented the gravity meter—perhaps not the most widely-known innovation to most people, but a fundamentally important piece of equipment which is still used today in surveying for oil. She also met physicists John Jaimison "J Squared" Miller, Olan Harvey Hamilton, and Renna Bonner Walker. Walker went on to see service in the Second World War in the Women's Army Corps.

Susannah made a point of acquainting herself within the Physics and Mathematics departments. The work of these departments was intrinsically connected with the activities of the department of Petroleum Engineering. Physics and Mathematics made the link between theory and practical reality to power the development of the industry. In mid-December and mid-January Susannah met a number of academics whose work blurred into the commercial world of the oil industry. These men and women gave their autographs as well as adding their achievements and publications. The names of Frederick Byron Plummer, E. C. Sargent, Helen Jeanne Plummer, George H. Fancher, and Thomas Ulvan Taylor are placed together in the *Album*, representing an essential source of expertise on which the oil industry depended. Mel Oakes, a former member of the department acting as its historian and archivist, described Taylor as "a very special faculty member at the University of Texas," stating that "he founded the engineering program here."[3]

Susannah had arrived in Texas at an exciting time, when science had the opportunity to drive the recovery. The physicists, geologists, engineers, and mathematicians led the way in providing the science and technology behind the revival of the economy, and the Centennial Exposition was as much a celebration of the spirit and culture of Texas as it was a driving force to attract commerce. Though Henry Ford's automotive company occupied one of the most dominant of the Art Deco structures in the Fair Park in Dallas, it was the oil industry of Texas that was enabling Ford's vehicles to become metaphors for freedom through capitalist endeavour. Oil was, quite literally, fuelling the future of the state.

There are also academics of the University of Texas in the *Album* who represented the cultural and historical character of the state. Caleb Perry Patterson was a particularly distinguished figure on the staff, and he placed his name at the head of a representative group of staff drawn from the History faculty. He had an influential background in history and political science, something he emphasised by including a list of his publications and editorships beneath his autograph. Susannah was thus given a very personal summary of his career and an appreciation of a time spent in London. This personal element suggests a strength of the connection that Susannah made with Patterson when she met him.

It is impossible to reconstruct what passed between Susannah and the people that she met, though the fact that many contributors gave more than their name suggests an underlying conversation which Susan had refined over time. The fact that Patterson was a firm believer that the USA should become a member of the League of Nations does add a certain interest that links him to other names that can be found in the *Album*. Susannah recorded the signatures of several senators and congressmen on her journey who had similar desires, and it is likely that she sympathised with the aims of the League. Men such as Thaddeus H. Caraway, also a cheerleader for the League, had been sought out in 1921. The United States, of course, had never pursued President Woodrow Wilson's desire for America to be a keystone in the promotion of world peace following the Great War. The profile of the signatures collected by Susannah suggests she had a strong sympathy with the efforts of individuals who sought to secure a post-war recovery.

Susannah wanted to absorb the culture of Texas and was keen to include representative figures in the *Album*. Milton Rietow Gutsch was a specialist in Medieval British history and had occupied senior roles in the department and faculty at the University of Texas from 1916. He placed his name on the same page as Patterson and annotated his entry in the *Album* with a reference to his book on the Crusades. He had a strong interest in British history and had previously been an editor of the *Texas History Teachers' Bulletin*. He made a note of this, too, beneath his name, though this referred to work that had kept him busy between 1912 and 1920. Above all, however, Susannah was drawn to Gutsch because he was responsible for compiling the Texas War Records Collection. This included enlistment, casualty, and personnel records of the men of Texas who had enlisted 1916–1919, an archive that expanded throughout the 20th century.[4] Gutsch and Susannah had a shared interest in recording those who had served and suffered in the Great War. Frank Burr Marsh was another History professor at the University of Texas to add his name to the *Album*, noting his specialism in Roman history and drawing attention to this with a summary of his main publications. Charles William Ramsdell is the final historian to be included on this page, regarded as the "Dean" of Southern historians, as someone who specialised in the Old South. He was about to take up the presidency of the Southern Historical Association when he met Susannah.

Susannah continued to engage with the history of Texas, a state which has a unique history of which it remains proud. A significant cultural connection that Susannah made was with Rev. Paul Foik, a Roman Catholic priest with a deep academic grounding. He had helped shape the development of librarianship in the USA, and began the collation of material that became the Catholic Archives of Texas. More pertinently, he was also a key member of the Texas Centennial Committee and, together with J. Frank Dobie and Louis Wiltz Kemp, selected the historical sites to be featured in the celebrations of 1935–1936.[5] Dobie, an artillery veteran of the

Great War, contributed a full-page expression of his thoughts about Texas history to the *Album*. He was the leading spokesperson for the state on cultural and literary matters during the Centennial.[6] His wife, Bertha, recorded a moving piece of historical prose in the *Album*, quoting from her "Women of the Salt Marshes."[7] They were both folklorists and gave a context to the sense of the depth of faith and feeling Texans had invested in the Centennial.

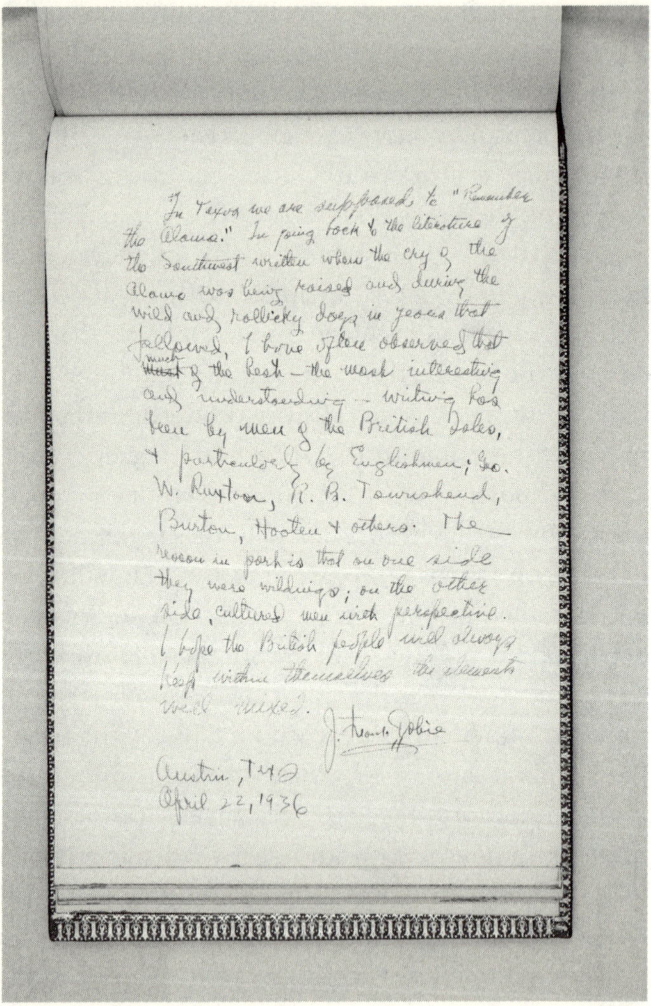

In Texas we are supposed to "Remember the Alamo." In going back to the literature of the Southwest written when the cry of the Alamo was being raised and during the wild and rollicky days in years that followed, I have often observed that much of the best – the most interesting and understanding – writing has been by men of the British Isles, & particularly by Englishmen; Geo. W. Ruxton, R. B. Townshend, Burton, Hooten & others. The reason in part is that on one side they were wildings; on the other side, cultured men with perspective. I hope the British people will always keep within themselves the elements well mixed.

J. Frank Dobie

Austin, Texas
April 22, 1936

J. Frank Dobie's page (Courtesy: Astley Hall Museum and Art Gallery).

Susannah also met Theresa M. Hunter, who was an active poet in the 1920s and 1930s. Hunter filled a full page of the *Album* with her poem entitled "At Dusk" from her collection *Panorama*, which told the story of three women kneeling as the sun dipped into twilight: "Like radiant stars, three virtues shone, Faith, Hope, and Charity!" Faith, hope, and charity have a great resonance, as these might well be virtues one could ascribe to Susannah. It seems that Hunter had a good measure of Susannah's interests and activities, and she chose the poem well. Foik, Dobie and Kemp were the architects of the spirit of the Centennial, and Susannah had got to the very heart of the event. It seems that Texas had got to the very heart of Susannah, too.

Susannah was a linguist, and so it is no surprise that she acquainted herself with academics who studied languages. She included the signature of Professor Robert Adger Law of the English Department, who had edited several editions of Shakespeare. Members of the Classics Department were also represented. Professor William James Battle added to his signature, describing himself as "an apostle of Greek and Roman culture for more than 40 years." Harry J. Leon, Professor of Classical Language and also President of the Texas Classical Association, gave his autograph. Aaron Schaffer, Professor of Romance Languages, went so far as to give his signature twice. Schaffer had written and signed a half-page account of his published work with his other achievements, and wrote his name again on the reverse of the page. The state's history represented a meeting point of cultures and languages which Susannah might well have recognised in connection with her own project. Texas was a meld of Native American, Spanish, French, and American cultures, now unified under a single star.

Susannah pursued an historian called Carlo E. Castenada, who was given the liberty of a whole page of the *Album* with what was effectively a bibliography of Texan history. Castenada was known to Foik, who had edited his *Our Catholic Heritage in Texas, 1519–1936*, which he had begun in 1936. The Catholic bias within the choice of texts listed suggests that Susannah had shared her interests and purpose with Castenada, and that he had time to make a considered response. There is no personal touch or a message of greeting in his entry, and it may be that this was one of those entries gained through a written request. There is just his signature, followed by a list of publications. He clearly felt that he was giving the detailed guidance that Susannah had sought. What Castenada did, however, was to provide Susannah with a bibliography which could help her to understand the course of Texan history between the 16th and the end of the 19th centuries from a Catholic perspective. It cannot be shown whether or not she read more deeply into the history of Texas, but she returned to the subject of the state's past on several occasions during her visit.

These custodians of the essence of Texas were joined in the *Album* by Mary Jourdan Atkinson, who included a passage from her recently published *The Texas Indians.*[8] Alongside an extended quotation summarising an invasive process of discovery, colonisation, conflict, and nation-building, Atkinson sketched the roughest of maps of Texas. It gives the locations of the Native American tribes of the region, and her text records the brave but futile resistance of the Comanche and the guileless hospitality of the Tiguas. She saw the tide of European migration as an historical inevitability.

Mary Jourdan Atkinson's unsettling account may have influenced Susannah to learn a little more about the experience of Native Americans and about the adventure of frontier life in the 19th century. European settlement had excluded Native Americans from the lands they had been accustomed to roam and hunt upon, and one of Susannah's encounters casts the status of Native Americans into sharp relief. Several "exhibition" features of the Centennial reflected on the life of Native Americans as defeated enemies or cultural curiosities. A Sioux man, Two Eagles, a descendant of Sitting Bull of the Battle of Little Big Horn, seems to have been a participant in a display at the Dallas Centennial. There is even an ambiguity of punctuation that could possibly place Two Eagles at the great battle himself. Susannah met him and must have made enough of an impression for him to present her with a signed photograph and a full page recounting his history. To Susannah, Two

Eagles was as much a victim of war as any veteran, stripped of his pride and nationhood and left to make his way living out a parody of the proud Sioux way.

Susannah was given an extensive monograph in this period by Rev. John M. Riach, the Chaplain of the Newman Club at the University of Texas. He was also a member of the Missionary Society of Saint Paul the Apostle, which was a Catholic society originating in New York and focused on evangelising young men. More importantly to Susannah, he was a veteran who understood something of the restorative nature of the *Album*. He had served as an Ordinary Seaman in the Royal Naval Division on *HMS Tiger* at the Battle of Jutland in 1916. He wrote:

> As a survivor of the Battle of Jutland, living overseas, I have been asked to give a short message to the English people. What shall I say? To my mind the only thing now in order must be something about the maintenance of peace, and so I urge that a strong friendship come to maturity between the American and British nation. Without their help, no major war can be fought; with their help, a favourable balance in fighting for peace will deter any militaristic activity. This unofficial and tacit alliance, at least under the present unsettled conditions, should be sought now, for to-morrow may be too late. At any moment, the spark may come which will set the world alight. God grant that saner counsels prevail. [*sic*]

Despite the excitement of her American adventure, Susannah still recalled the suffering war had inflicted on society and shared Riach's hope for the future. As a Catholic Priest, a veteran, and associated with an academic institution, Riach embodied many of the qualities that Susannah believed were needed for the rebuilding of society in the recovery years.

It was also at this time that Susannah was in contact with Charles C. Betts, the State Service Officer for Texas, based in Austin. This is almost certainly one of those contributions who was sought by letter, as he typed his extended contribution directly onto one of Susannah's sheets. It also confirms that she carried loose sheets to bind later. The role of the State Service Officer, in Betts' words, was to "work for the rehabilitation of the disabled veterans, their widows, orphans, mothers and fathers . . . 198, 238 men and nurses from Texas served during the World War in the Army, Navy and Marine Corps." Betts included a summary of his own active service in France between October 1917 and January 1919, and he had seen action at Toulon, Aisne, and Chateau-Thierry. He had qualified as a sharpshooter and had been awarded a Good Conduct Medal. He was clearly a soldier of ability and courage whose experience of war was typical of many men approaching middle age in the mid-1930s. John W. Brown of the State Health Office and Herbert N. Barnett of the State Health Department were both veterans of the Army Medical Corps and ensured that veterans were given the attention and care that they deserved. Susannah's interest must have triggered so many memories for men who were active, like Susannah herself, in making sure that the plight of ex-servicemen was not forgotten.

Just as in the earlier pages of the *Album*, Susannah wanted to include those with authority in government. With the assistance of Bob Barker, she was able to gain the signature of the Governor of Texas, James V. Allred, and other key individuals. Allred's signature is featured on two occasions, on consecutive pages. R. B. Stanford, his Secretary of State, appears beneath his second entry. These men were probably introduced to Susannah's project, personally or by proxy, at the turn of the year. Wilbourne B. Collie, the Acting Governor of Texas, gave signatures on both 31 December and 1 January. These help to give a context of time and place to the signatures of this part of the *Album*. Walter F. Woodul, the Acting Governor of Texas, gave his signature on 28 April. This collection of pages has been magnificently illustrated with arrays of flags and gold seals, making these the most vibrant pages to be found in the whole *Album*. The flags of the United States and the Lone Star of Texas feature in brilliant watercolour. There are also the four other flags which had flown over Texas: those of Mexico, Spain, the Confederacy, and France. To complete her reckoning of those who had directed Texas through to the years of the recovery, Susannah secured the signatures of all thirty members of the Texas Senate of the 44th Legislature and over 100 members of the state's Legislative Assembly.

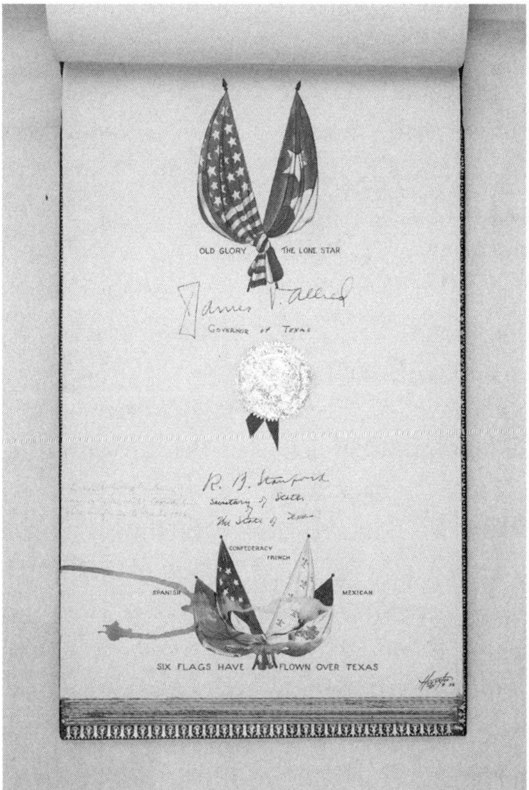

Governor of Texas Allred's page (Courtesy: Astley Hall Museum and Art Gallery).

There is the barest evidence of a fleeting visit back to New York in February 1936, through the inclusion of the signature of Alonzo F. Whyert of New York University, his name edged towards the centre fold of the volume as if an afterthought. New York offered a cold contrast to Texas at this time of year, and she might have struggled with her weakened leg. If she did travel she did not linger, for by 26 February the dated signature of Earnest O. Thompson, the Chairman of the Railroad Commission of Texas, appeared, two days after Susannah's 68th birthday. He was listed with other men of influence in the state. The page was headed by William C. McCraw, the Attorney General of Texas. The page included two other members of Thompson's Railroad Commission: Charles Vernon Terrell and the Secretary, C. F. Petet. The growing dominance of motor transport was represented in the *Album* by Mark Marshal, the Director of Motor Transportation. To emphasise the growing dominance of the automobile, Petet can be rediscovered in August 1942 presiding over a hearing in Austin, Texas to discontinue a passenger railroad service.[9] It is clear from his testimony in the 1940s that the age of rail had given way to roads soon after he had met Susannah. The Centennial Exposition had played its part in this change by extolling a state economy based on the new black gold and the automobile.

Susannah was intensely active in the late spring of 1936. On 2 April Susannah was back in Austin and asked Guiton Morgan, the City Manager, to sign the *Album*. She must have held this signature in high regard, as she kept it clear of any other autographs until 31 August, when she offered the page to George D. Fairtrace, the City Manager of Fort Worth. Morgan's office was in the same building as that of the mayor and other representatives of the Austin civic infrastructure. It is no surprise that Susannah moved around the building, presenting the story of the *Album* to all she met and, of course, Mayor Tom Miller placed his name alongside two City of Austin seals. Accompanying pages include the signatures of George Sheppard, the State Comptroller, as well as representatives from the Industrial Accident Board and the Commissions of Life Insurance, Casualty Insurance, and Fire Insurance. Susannah even managed to convince John J. Buchan, Executive Secretary of the Game, Fish and Oyster Commission, to include two gold seals with his signature. The wonderfully named Zeta Gossett, the Banking Commissioner of Texas, was also allocated a page to himself with a gold Texas seal next to his signature.

The Police Department was also housed in Austin's City Hall, and the city's Chief of Police, R. D. Thorpe, shares two pages of the *Album* with eleven of the officers and men of his department. The names and ranks given range from Roy L. Smith, Captain of Police, to J. B. Taylor, the desk clerk. Susannah even asked a traffic engineer and the police photographer to sign the pages. The two crews of the Austin Fire Department fill two pages of the *Album*, too, and an image of the State Capitol Building has been pasted alongside.

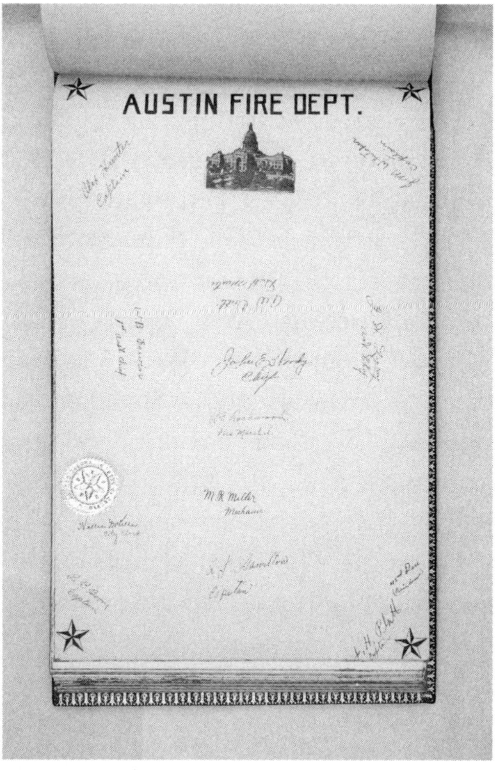

Austin Fire Department page (Courtesy: Astley Hall Museum and Art Gallery).

Even in these conversations with men who were giving service to their city, Susannah was able to ask them about their service to their country, and Captain Platt of the Fire Department added details of his time in the 42nd "Rainbow" Division. This, of course, had been the division in which Father Patrick Duffy had been so prominent. Susannah gained signatures of law enforcement officers from around the state, including Lee O. Allen, Sheriff of Travis County, with his assisting officer.

May 1936 is a period where Susanna's activity is difficult to trace. It is, perhaps, worth considering that she had originally planned to stay in the United States for six months. This was something which the passenger records for November 1935 had made clear. However this was not to be the case, as for whatever reasons, Susannah decided to remain in America.

An extended entry in the *Album* around this time is from the State Reclamation Engineer, Ralph J. McMahon, who offers his signature in Austin on two consecutive pages on 11 April. Susannah had a rather more serious conversation than might be imagined on this occasion. McMahon gave a good deal of detail to his two pages, including a typed outline of his responsibility for the management of the vast waterways of Texas and the importance drainage had for its agriculture. It reads as a statement prepared for all enquirers, and the four-paragraph account gives a great deal of technical and legal detail which seems out of place. What is surprising, however, is that it was typed directly onto one of Susannah's blank leaves. A degree of purpose and effort had gone into this contribution when a simple signature might have sufficed.

The second of his sheets displays two photographs. The first is of the Trinity River at Dallas before the reclamation and improvement of the margin at its banks. The second photograph was taken during the deluge of May 1935, demonstrating the effectiveness of the improvements that he had made to the flood defences. This page is punctuated with one of the most colourful of the Texas seals and striking gothic script above McMahon's name to describe his post. The Texas Board of Water Engineers takes up the entire following page, listing C. S. Clark (Chair), A. N. W. McDonald (Secretary),

A. H. Dunlap, and John W. Prichard as members. There is a rather incongruous collection of inserted material—a model of an "Engineers Transit," an etching entitled "stream measurement," and a map of Texas river watersheds. These men were succeeding against natural forces, moulding the world for the benefit of communities along the Trinity, Brazos, and [Texas] Colorado Rivers. Susannah recognized the importance of their work later in the year when she witnessed floods like no other she had seen.

Susannah travelled northwards in June 1936, and was in Washington D.C. by the beginning at the month. Of all the correspondence that Susannah made in her lifetime, she was about to send her most audacious letter. On 4 June she sent a letter on headed paper from the Astor Hotel to the President's wife, Eleanor Roosevelt. Susannah was in a strident mood, having been told that she could not seek the President's signature as she had done successfully in 1921. She begged: "surely, if one man stands high above all others that man is President Roosevelt it grieves me to think that I shall have to go back to England without his" [*sic*].[10] She outlined the course of her project to underscore her plea, giving examples of the prestigious signatures she had previously secured:

> [In] 1921 I got President Harding's, the cabinet, Senators and Congressmen. In addition I had the officers of the land, sea and air forces . . . I have the autographs of the King and Queen of the Belgians, the King and Queen of Italy and hosts of Allied officers . . . The first book is for the War Period and contains distinguished people of that period . . . I thought I would call the second book the 'Recovery Period' and get the autographs of those who piloted their nations safely through the most terrible Period the world has ever known . . . As these books are to be a gift to the British nation in memory of the Allied friendships to keep them unique there can be no copies [*sic*].

As a form of consolation she asked that she might have the signature of the President's wife: "Perhaps you will give me your autograph and that will prove that I really have tried to get the President's." She implored: "I hope Mrs Roosevelt you will not refuse the request I make. And in anticipation I thank you most sincerely" [*sic*].

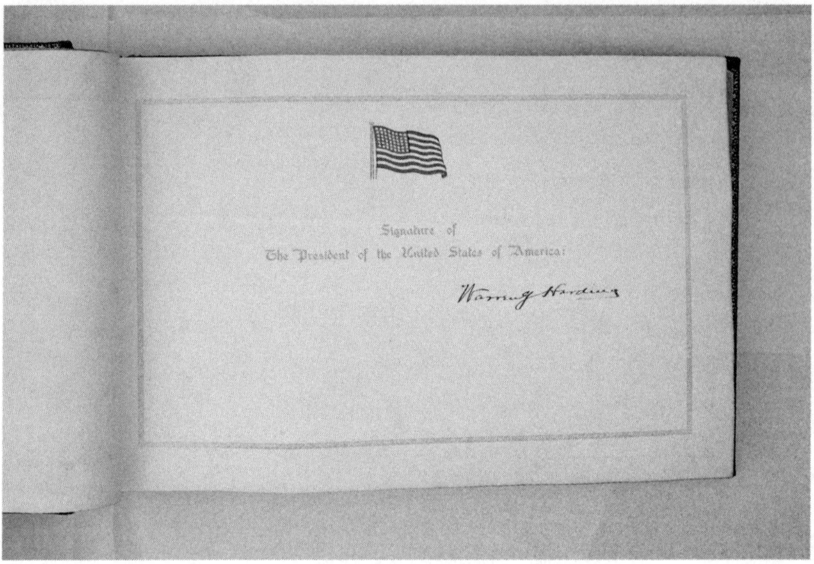

President Warren Harding's page (Courtesy: Astley Hall Museum and Art Gallery).

Unsurprisingly, Eleanor Roosevelt did not reply personally, and it was her secretary, Malvina T. Schreider, who returned her compliments on 6 June on behalf of the First Lady. There is, perhaps, a touch of irritation from Eleanor Roosevelt's staff, as there is a pencil note added saying, "I think this was done." Susannah acknowledged Schreider's reply on 10 June, this time writing from New York, to where she had suddenly removed to tend a sick cousin, Annie O'Connell. Susannah informed Schreider that she intended to return to Washington D.C. by 1 July. Eleanor Roosevelt's signature was to be sent on to the Astor Hotel.

Susannah was determined to add a Roosevelt signature to the volumes, and she succeeded with a signature dated 26 June 1936.

In the absence of the President's signature, Susannah resorted to pasting in a photograph offcut from Cunard's *Ocean Times* of 5 November 1936, on her homeward voyage aboard *RMS Samaria*. She ended her correspondence by promising to notify Eleanor Roosevelt when the books were to be handed over to the nation.

The Roosevelt correspondence is revealing for it tells, obliquely, that Susannah's 1921 visit to the United States was apparently funded by a wealthy but unnamed cousin. Susannah also claims that she gained contacts at government levels through the influence of Senator Boies Penrose. She gives an outline of the structure behind the volumes, now to be in two parts to represent the "War Period" and the "Recovery Period." Most importantly, the letter gives a sense of Susannah's own strength of purpose. The "Golden Books were to be a gift to the British Nation in memory of the Allied Friendships to keep them unique there can be no Copies. They will be preserved in Astley Hall Chorley Lancashire" [*sic*]. Susannah even goes as far as to tell Eleanor Roosevelt of her lamed leg and how it had limited the pursuit of her project. The letters to the President's wife also reveal parts of Susannah's itinerary, as in them, she wrote that she intended to go on to Houston and Galveston in Texas.

Nevertheless, Susannah lingered in New York, where there was a particular event which may have been one of the anchor points for her tour of America later that month. On 28 June 1936, Susannah was at a memorial service for Father Francis P. Duffy, the 42nd Rainbow Division's celebrated senior chaplain, held at St. Raymond's Cemetery in the Bronx. Susannah recorded signatures of men who attended this memorial on the very last page of the third volume. At least three earlier signatures in the *Album* also note a connection with the division. Duffy had signed the *Album* when Susannah visited the USA in 1921. Susannah stood shoulder-to-shoulder with more than 100 veterans of the 69th Regiment of New York.[11] The *New York Times* reported on the memorial service and indicated that there was a veterans' association for Roman Catholics of the Rainbow Division.

While in New York, Susannah also secured the signature of a Rev. Bernard Walston, who had served with the British Army throughout the Great War in the Artist's Rifle Corps of London, converting to Catholicism after the war and eventually becoming ordained. Susannah had met Father Duffy on her visit to New York in 1921. Walston had known Duffy during the war years and it is possible that the latter may have had a hand in prompting his conversion. Walston succeeded Duffy at Holy Cross Church in New York on his death in 1932, and in the context of the memorial service on June 1936, he was the chaplain of "Fr Duffy, Post 54, Catholic War Veterans" [*sic*]. Susannah deliberately attended the memorial service at which Walston was present, taking the time and trouble to return to New York when the focus of her visit had been Texas.

Susannah returned to Texas and was in Dallas by 28 July. It is possible that she travelled to and from Fort Worth within the day, as the distance is just over thirty miles, but there was much to see and every reason to stay over a longer period to take in the full programme of events. She gained the stamp and signature of the city's Postmaster, Walter B. Lunar, on that day. The Assistant Postmaster, George C. Young, also gave his signature. The visit to Dallas must have been one of the most memorable parts of Susannah's year of travel, with the city's Centennial celebrations well in hand after opening on 6 June. Bob Barker had probably helped Susannah grasp a sense of the excitement at Fort Worth rival Frontier Centennial, which had opened at the beginning of July.[12] On 29 July, Susannah met Read Johnson, the manager of Veterans' Association in Dallas, and he subsequently added his stamp and signature. Even in the clamour and bustle of the Centennial's main attractions, she was attentive to the main purpose of her project and in all probability they spoke of Father Duffy's memorial service. It may have been at this time that Susannah was introduced to Fort Worth Chief of Police, Henry B. Lewis. She also made sure that George Sergeant, the mayor of the city, gave his civic ascent to the *Album*.

Whilst Fort Worth's exhibition focused on the "Old West" of the 19th century, it has been seen that the Fair Park Exposition in Dallas also promoted opportunities for economic progress. The presentations were based at a site already used for the regular State

Fair and it was lavishly re-modelled for the occasion at vast expense, with Dallas committing $10 million at the outset—twice the total expenditure of the Frontier Centennial. Susannah took the autographs of two representatives of the Centennial Commission of Control that released finance for many of the structures created for the celebrations. John A. Hulen was the representative from Fort Worth and Henry Hutchings was the Commission's secretary. The full sum of the Exposition at Fair Park amounted to a phenomenal $25 million, and in a recovering economy this was either a great expression of confidence or an incautious gamble.[13]

The exhibition halls, many of which still stand today, reflected the state's brazen spirit, pushing boundaries of "classic modern." Susannah is sure to have strolled across the Grand Plaza and along the Esplanade of State, seeing her reflection on the waters which mirrored, as the Texas State Almanac has it, the "multitude of beauties of the surrounding structures." The Hall of Transportation and the Hall of Varied Industries, Communications, and Electricity faced each other across a 700-foot reach of water which stretched to the Texas Hall of State. The Poultry, Agriculture and Livestock Buildings were given the same aesthetic consideration as the Hall of Natural History, Hall of Horticulture, Hall of Domestic Arts, Aquarium, and Hall of Fine Arts. The Art Deco architecture defined the Centennial as "Texanic in ideals, continental in proportions and international in scope."[14] George Dahl, the Centennial Exposition's architect, balanced beauty and function in every aspect of the associated buildings. Paul Foik, J. Frank Dobie, and Louis Wiltz Kemp, already mentioned above, gave the historical perspective that allowed the modern architecture to contrast the historical narrative of the Centennial.

Dallas had spared no expense on creating an exhibition and park to thrill. The Fair Park was extended to give a superb venue for many of the exhibits and entertainments. Having been held under the flags of United States, Mexico, Spain, the Confederacy and France, the Lone Star was the one banner that the state was devoted to. A parade of flags gave an opportunity for spectacle and a display of devotion. The pageant featured a staged "Cavalcade of

Texas," with standing ovation from the vast audience on each occasion that the Lone Star of Texas appeared. This was not just about the past and Texan nationhood, but also an opportunity to display to the world the material worth of the state. Gaining a foothold in the international market place was an underlying purpose of the Centennial. It is no coincidence that Susannah sought the signatures of the leaders of the Chambers of Commerce of Houston and Dallas, and these men may even have been manning official stands at the Fair Park.

One of the more extensive collections of autographs in this period is composed of members and veterans of the Texas Rangers, the force responsible for preserving law and order throughout the state. The Texas Rangers had a significant impact on Susannah and account for nearly a tenth of the tally of names in the final volume. Perhaps it was her association with Read Johnson at the Veterans' Association on 29 July 1936 that enabled Susannah to meet and speak with over twenty of the men who had been involved in the Frontier War of the 1890s. Their signatures, particularly of those in the lower ranks, are sometimes quite laboured and scratched, indicating the advanced age of these old soldiers as well as a different era when literacy was less easy to come by. The recollections that they record often refer to their company and their officer, giving a real sense of the comradeship that still held their memories together.

Susannah always managed to find people with interesting tales to tell. Texas Ranger B. M. "Manny" Gault certainly had notoriety. He was one of the six law enforcement officers who ambushed the bank robbing lovers Bonnie Parker and Clyde Barrow in May 1934. He had struggled to prevent the curious from gawping at the bodies in the hours afterwards. Above all, the name that inspired these veterans can be found standing alongside them. Captain John R. Hughes was a living legend to the Texas Rangers, the man who had embodied the spirit and grit of law enforcement in Texas, initially as a captain in the Frontier Battalion and, from 1901, in the same role in the State Rangers.

Memorial Album title page (Courtesy: Astley Hall Museum and Art Gallery).

Alongside these men are veterans of the more recent Great War, such as Captain Julian Gillespie and Lieutenant Leist, who had been part of the American Expeditionary Force. Major C. B. Fullerton took the trouble to make an extensive note with his signature, having already served in Company 'B' of the Frontier Battalion from 1893–1895, the Texas Rangers, and had been recalled to serve in the Great War in the 36th Division of the U.S. Army. His son, Hal B. Fullerton, had served in the 29th Division. Two generations had faced conflict over three decades, serving together at the same time in Europe. Susannah captured them as comrades together.

Susannah was treated with great hospitality by the Texas Rangers when she visited their exhibition stand. M. T. "Lone Wolf" Gonzaullas, as the senior captain of the Texas Rangers, was head of the Bureau of Intelligence. He added this message to the *Album* which read: "Welcome to the Department of Public Safety State of Texas Exhibit at the Texas Rangers [Building] Texas Centennial Central Exposition at Dallas Texas August 11th 1936." The Director of the committee for Public Safety himself, H. Carmichael, as well as his assistant, both give their autographs. Beneath the signature of the veterans is that of E. A. Muret, the Project Superintendent and builder of the Rangers Station, the Centennial Park, and the National Exhibition Building exhibiting "the best of the 48 states" in Dallas.

The Centennial featured celebratory entertainment as well as stalls to inform visitors or to sell the state. It included dramatized recreations of great moments in Texas history. These were performed on gigantic stage areas with full wagon trains and pursuits by horsemen. They captured the Wild Western ideal which had inspired a spirit of adventure in her youth. It must have been in the context of the Centennial exhibition performance that she met Tex Cooper on 25 August 1936. Cooper had performed in a show for some years as a skilled rider and marksman and had even had some small appearances in films.

Mistaking a connection with Buffalo Bill, for they looked alike, Susannah spent a good deal of time talking with Cooper and he passed a photograph of himself to her. He wrote a long passage about his adventures on the reverse of a page in the *Album* and his signature is accompanied by two other performers who recreated the adventures of the Wild West, "The Original Cheyenne Joe" and Dudley White Jr. It is clear that Susannah was recalling the Buffalo Bill show she had seen in Liverpool in 1891, and though Cooper was an actor who did feature in several "Western" films in the 1930s, he had never performed with Buffalo Bill. It is worth noting that the *Liverpool Mercury* refers to Fenimore Cooper, the novelist, in both articles on Buffalo Bill's visit in 1891. It may be that Susannah was grasping at an incomplete recollection of these very same articles four decades after the event.[15]

Susannah made some very unlikely associations while she was in Dallas. The fact that she recorded the signature of the Chief of Police, R. L. James, is something one might take for granted by this stage. To find the immaculately laid-out autographs of the management and staff of *The Dallas Morning News*, *The Dallas Journal*, *The Semi-Weekly Farming News*, and the *WFAA* radio station is rather more surprising. Each media organisation had arranged for its corporate masthead to be printed on each respective page of the *Album*. The signatures are neatly ranged across full pages. Though other newspapers are represented in the volumes, all four of these enterprises were part of the Belo business empire. Many of the signatures are repeated two or even three times across different pages for people that had overlapping roles. These pages appear to be a bespoken undertaking and the staff to have dedicated a great deal of time and care to the presentation.

Susannah returned to Fort Worth at the end of the month, probably to stay with Bob and Nora Barker, before pursuing her next adventure. On 31 August she offered the *Album* to George D. Fairtrace, the City Manager of Fort Worth. The City Manager of Austin had already signed this very page and, perhaps in an effort to outdo a rival, Fairtrace added: "The Frontier City where the West begins," promoting Fort Worth's own celebratory contribution to the Texas Frontier Centennial.

Susannah did not stay long and was in Dallas two weeks later. Gene Autry, the contemporary film star known as the "Singing Cowboy," was given a whole page of the *Album* to place his autograph. He was filming *The Big Show* in the city between 15 and 19 September, and the crew used the spectacular exhibition areas of the Centennial Exposition for the film's location. The buildings provided a stunning set on which to play out the Hollywood drama and the scenes give a great sense of the excitement of the Centennial itself. The storyline allowed Autry to pursue his trademark horsemanship, with romance and law enforcement thrown in for good measure. It may have been through her meeting with the Texas Rangers that Susannah was put in the company of Autry, and they indeed feature on parade and in action in the film's background.

From the wording of his contribution it seems that he must have spent some time in Susannah's company and warmed to her. The eye is caught by the signed photograph of Autry on horseback and his written contribution opens with the greeting: "To my friend from England, always wishing you the best of luck and success," signing his name, adding a list of eight of the songs that had made his name in Hollywood, and then scribing his name again. Beneath his signature are those of Audrey Davis and Frankie Marvin from the management of Republic Pictures. Susannah's curious relationship with culture of the Wild West may well have reached its zenith at this point. She had left America by the time *The Big Show* was released in mid-November, but the picture included the song "Ride, Ranger, Ride," which might well have been familiar to Susannah, as it also featured as the headline song to the eponymous Autry movie which was released on 30 September 1936.

Susannah had met the State Reclamation Engineer McMahon in April and had cause to recall him when September came. Texas suffered even more significant floods in July and September than it had in the previous May when the land reclamation systems had been put to the test at Dallas. Three bodies had already been recovered from the Colorado River between Austin and San Antonio in July and houses had been washed away. A train had been wrecked when it had attempted to cross a bridge that had been swept away, and there had been two further fatalities. The *Standard-Times* of 20 September 1936 reported "the Colorado River rose to the highest flood stage on record; lives and property were menaced in its wild sweep through several hundred miles of the richest farming country in Texas."[16]

This catastrophe made a huge impression on Susannah and she deliberately marked the *Album* on several occasions, annotating the smear that crossed the account of Cheyenne Joe with "the Colorado marked this page." This is not the only instance, as the Board of Water Engineers page has a similar note which has been slurred beyond recognition. Moreover, on the stunningly illustrated page on which Governor James Allred and his Secretary of State, R. B. Stamford, placed their names, there is a slew across the "six flags" of Texas and Susannah has written "The marks below have been caused by the Mighty Colorado River which overflowed its banks, 1936" [*sic*]. These were no souvenirs, but relics of remembrance for the devastation this natural disaster had wrought on the ordinary folk. The deliberate marking of the *Album* in this way cannot be fully explained.

In June, Susannah had told Eleanor Roosevelt that she was going to visit Houston and Galveston. She had been quite definite about this point. She set out on her final excursion on 9 October 1936. She had had a busy morning meeting Oscar Holcombe, the Mayor of Houston, bringing the *Album* and its story to his attention. Later that day Susannah spoke with Miss May in the city's Airway Ticket Office. It was a fleeting moment, a transaction and a chat, but Susannah obtained two photographs of aeroplanes which she pasted into the *Album*. The first photograph is of an American Airlines DC3, which flew out of Houston. Miss May's annotation beneath is inconclusive for establishing whether Susannah boarded a plane there: "Transcontinental and Western Service American Airlines 'Coast to Coast' 1936" is a frustratingly imprecise caption.

The second photograph is of a Pan American Airways flying boat, the *Caribbean Clipper*. The company flew out of Houston with routes heading towards the Pacific and across the Gulf of Mexico. Miss May's annotation for this photograph, too, is similarly brief, noting that the aeroplane was "used from San Francisco to the Orient." Susannah's cousin, Anne Crewes, was certainly a possible port of call as she neared the end of her year-long journey. Her cousin lived at 233 Olmstead Street in the city. The fact that Susannah includes the photographs may suggest that she did fly. It might even have been her first air flight, as she had only been a spectator at Croydon Aerodrome in 1924.

If Susannah travelled briefly to the West coast, it is possible that she visited California in a very short excursion which occasioned another curious happenstance. Susannah knew that she was reaching the end of her adventure and her associations became more outlandish. One unorthodox individual to place his name in the *Album*, incongruent, perhaps, with the purpose Susannah had set upon, was Peter Howard. He was sometimes known as "Peter the Hermit," but Susannah gives him the moniker the "Shakespeare of Hollywood," adding that he "came from the Emerald Isle and taught Shakespearean plays." Susannah's supplemental comments become almost mystical, fitting for such an ascetic individual who held sway amongst the more earthly stars of the movies. He was somewhat of a tourist attraction on Broadway and certainly made an impression on Susannah.[17] His entry in the *Album* is heavily annotated in Susannah's own words:

> He lived in a wood house and adopted the dress of a hermit so that he could preach to the drunkards and worldlings. He was not a religious by profession. He kept reminding sinners that they had an immortal soul for which they had to render an account.

The photograph of Howard pasted alongside the account makes him appear slightly ordinary in comparison with the text, and Susannah seems to have been much taken by him, perhaps feeling that his spiritual sensibilities were not too distant from her own. She had lived through war, austerity and depression, and Peter Howard's asceticism amongst the glitz and glamour of Hollywood may have struck a chord with the stern retired school mistress.

Within ten days of her visit to the Airway Ticket Office in Houston Susannah was in Oklahoma. The evidence of her route seems to suggest that she was travelling by train at this stage. Her contacts in Oklahoma were very different from those she had in Texas. Worthy as their roles were, the signature of L. D. Rikey, the Oklahoma State Game Warden, was hardly on a par with the signatures Susannah obtained in Texas to represent civic responsibilities. Rikey's signature is supported by his Assistant Game Warden, George Bailey, and a Game Ranger, M. G. Goodwin. There is no context to explain their inclusion, other than that they locate themselves in Oklahoma City. They probably signed the *Album* before 18 October.

The other Oklahoma signatures are more intriguing, indicating that Susannah was pursuing a rather specific line of interest. All seem to date from 19 October 1936. There are several members of the Choctaw, Cherokee, Sac, and Fox tribes who have given their names in the *Album*. Some were clearly in a position of authority, such as Andy Payne, the Chief of Supreme Court, George D.

Bushyhirch, the Assistant Chief of Supreme Court, and Mary Elizabeth Hammett, the Deputy Clerk of Supreme Court. Their civic roles seem less important than their own backgrounds, and they define themselves by their tribal roots. Payne does not even feel the need to mention that he had been winner of the Trans-American Footrace staged in 1928. He ran the 3,423.5-mile route from Los Angeles to New York City along the famous Route 66 in 573 hours, four minutes and 34 seconds, averaging six miles per hour over an 84-day staged run.

The emphasis on a common thread of Native American heritage continues in this phase of the *Album*. The Governor of the Chickasaw Nation, Douglas H. Johnston, is given a full page for his signature. On the preceding page his daughter, Juanita Johnston Smith, gives an extended account of the brave conduct of the tribe in warfare and its role in forging the American nation: "They made it possible for the English speaking race." The words written by the various members of the tribes are more strident than those of Two Eagles when he wrote at the Centennial, though there is still an aching sadness. They echo the words that Mary Jourdan Atkinson wrote earlier in the year to describe the experiences of the Comanche and Tiguas of Texas as they faced the wave of colonists in the 19th century. One of Susannah's Oklahoma contributors was Juanita Mahaffey, who was one quarter Sac and Fox, being the grand-daughter of Alex Connolly, who was once prominent in tribal affairs. She wrote: "The tribe is now mainly extinct, there only being 150 or 200 full bloods left." This history of brave resistance and the decline of a society fascinated Susannah.

Susannah's interest in the welfare of veterans continued to help her to connect with the people she met whilst she was in Oklahoma and in all her interactions it was foremost in her thoughts. The name of Lutie Hailey Walcote can be found on the same page as that of Juanita Mahaffey. Walcote was Secretary of the Confederate Pensions Department. She was well-placed to appreciate the welfare issues that had affected veterans of the American Civil War as the youngest of its veterans reached their final years. The department had then taken responsibility for men returning from more recent wars and had a particular role in the years of the Depression. Walcote celebrated her distant Choctaw heritage and wrote proudly that there were "More Choctaw Indians in the Confederate Army of the War Between the States than any other State according to population." Walcote seems to have been moved by a similar spirit as Susannah and was in a stronger financial position to make her purpose a reality.

Still to this day the Oklahoma Veterans Centre is at 1015 South Commerce in Southwest Ardmore, in the grounds of the former Oklahoma Confederate Home. Lutie donated the land for this Veterans Centre and there is still a plaque recalling her dedication to these ex-servicemen.[18] When Walcote retired in 1943, she had become the Commissioner for the Confederate Pensions. She clearly wished to preserve a record of the work of the Confederate Pensions Board and presented the Oklahoma Historical Society with minutes and memorabilia for the sake of preservation.[19] Susannah had much to share in conversation with her. This phase of the *Album* includes people with a civic role guiding society through the years of the Depression, and there is a broader issue of Susannah recalling the people that were responsible for the care of veterans as well as the veterans themselves.

There are two further explanations for the presence of so many Native Americans clustered in the Oklahoma pages. Dettie Galdsby Dickens provides one possibility in the *Album* itself: "We have in Oklahoma City an Indian Club called the India-Okla Club. It is comprised of the different Indians residing in Oklahoma City. Once a year, the Club invites other Indians, and Indian Clubs over the state to participate with them at a yearly banquet held at one of the city's leading Hostelries. The object is to promote all things cultural." Dickens was the Business Manager for the Club and also the Financial Secretary in Douglas H. Johnston's Office.

A more surprising and seemingly unlikely opportunity appears possible. Remarkably, Susannah was probably present at a singular, if obscure, moment of history on the previous day. On Sunday, 18 October 1936, an eight-foot memorial was dedicated to Will

Rogers at Oologah, in northwest Oklahoma. Rogers had been an actor, comedian, satirist and to some, a philosopher. He was killed in an airplane accident in August 1935. He had a significant place in the nation's popular culture. Moreover, the Texas Centennial had incorporated a Will Rogers Memorial Centre in Fort Worth. Rogers had Cherokee heritage on both sides of his family, and the October memorial ceremony attracted closer friends and family from the community in which he had been brought up. About 600 people were in attendance.

On that same day the *Rogers Flyer* brought a variously reported 3,000 to 8,000 people to the Frisco railway station in Claremore on its maiden trip. Claremore and Tulsa were the only stops from St. Louis to Oklahoma City. Susannah made a connection with this event and acquired associated signatures on this and the following day. On the page stamped with the gold seal of the Supreme Court of Oklahoma, underwritten by a Chief and Assistant Chief of the Court, is an unsigned statement:

> The Cherokee were the first Indians to have a written language, Saquoyah, a member of the tribe and inventor of the Cherokee alphabet is now honored with a statue in the Hall of Fame in Washington, Oklahoma's foremost citizen and America's most loved countryman the late Will Rogers was a Cherokee Indian, the Cherokee are a proud and stable people.

Will Rogers was clearly in the minds of those who signed the *Album*, too.[20]

Susannah moved on, probably by train again, to Missouri. By 21 October, she was in St. James. This was a particularly small community. It is not clear how she met Woodrow Byington, but it was a point of call on the railway. Byington, probably from farming stock as many of the Byingtons of Phleps and Sainte Genevieve Counties seem to have been, made a first-hand account of life in the West:

> The Cowboys are of several different nationalities & different in looks as well as ideas they often have rodeos where they all meet to match their skill in riding wild horses also to rope calves & tie them they differ now as 40 years ago they all carried guns & knew how to use them they had to be fast drawing a gun. [*sic*]

Susannah ended her American tour with the fast, furious and unpunctuated words of a man who lived the reality of the West that she had dreamed of as a child. Now 68 years old, she had made the journey of a lifetime, but time, physical necessity, and emotional exhaustion were bringing her project to an end.

Susannah boarded *Samaria* at New York on 2 November 1936, a stop on its route to Liverpool via Boston. She made some well-rehearsed approaches to the Master, J. McRostie and his First Officer, E. M. Fall. She does not appear to have engaged with her fellow passengers as she might have done in her earlier years, and she even recycled the navigation chart from San Francisco to record the liner's senior officers. This may have been a curiosity, a souvenir, or a deliberate plan to extend the capacity for signatures. "All paper was finished chart used," she added, presumably after McRostie and Fall had placed their autographs. She had reached the limit of her paper supply and had concluded her quest.

Despite her endeavours, she died lonely and rejected in August 1950. The local Soroptimists made efforts to rehabilitate her legacy; they sent an anonymous letter to the *Chorley Guardian*.[21] It noted: "Forgetfulness of past service is a common trait in human nature, but some of us are glad to have been amongst those who during her lifetime showed their appreciation of Miss Knight's work for the servicemen."[22]

Forgetfulness is indeed a common trait in human nature. There is little public remembrance of her quest for allied friendship, peaceful reconciliation, and dignity for the victims of war.

Theresa M. Hunter was a Texan poet whose work reflected the history and culture of her state. Susannah met her during the Texas

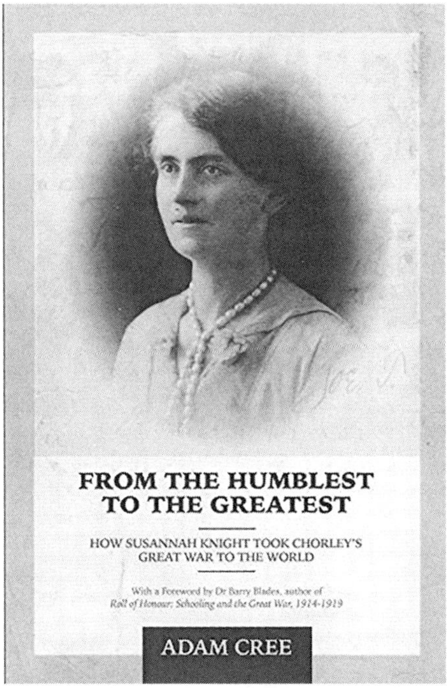

Cover of Adam Cree's book, From the Humblest to the Greatest.

Centennial in 1936. The poet inscribed "At Dusk" on a full page of the *Album*. Though not a literary marvel, it was chosen for Susannah. It is a fitting epitaph for a woman who gave so much of her life for others through faith, hope, and charity to the end of her life.

"At Dusk"
I saw three women enter a church
At dusk, one summer eve,
One was gold, and one was grey,
One wore a nun's black weave!
(What desire was in each heart
Thus from the world to draw apart?)
One begged her saint for a lover true,
One prayed for a soul's secret rest.
The nun, for all impartially
To her lips a crucifix pressed.

(So faint the gleam from the altar light
It could not make the place so bright!)
For lo! In the dusk of the summer eve
If here knelt these women three,
Like radiant stars, three virtues shone,
Faith, Hope, and Charity![23]

The *Chorley and District Memorial Album*, of which only one copy has ever been printed, is on display in Astley Hall, Chorley. If you see it, pause to recall the men it commemorates and the journeys the volumes have taken.

ENDNOTES

1. "Texas Centennial." *Handbook of Texas Online.* http://www.tshaonline.org/handbook/online/articles/lkt01, accessed September 26, 2013. Published by the Texas State Historical Association.
2. Chorley Memorial Album.
3. Correspondence with Mel Oakes, September 2013.
4. Texas War Records Collection, 1916–1919, 1940–1951. Dolph Briscoe Center for American History, The University of Texas at Austin.
5. Mayellen Bresie. "Foik, Paul Joseph." *Handbook of Texas Online* http://www.tshaonline.org/handbook/online/articles/ffo02, accessed October 11, 2013. Published by the Texas State Historical Association.
6. Francis E. Abernethy. "Dobie, James Frank." *Handbook of Texas Online* http://www.tshaonline.org/handbook/online/articles/fdo02, accessed October 11, 2013. Published by the Texas State Historical Association.
7. Quoted from the *Southwest Review*, Volume XXI, No. 1.
8. Mary Jourdan Atkinson. *The Texas Indians.* The Naylor Company: San Antonio, Texas, 1935.
9. Railroad Commission of Texas Docket No. 4824-R. 18th August 1942, Austin Texas. http://www.thehistorycenteronline.com/uploads/resources/tse_passenger_service_termination_testimony.pdf.
10. F. D. Roosevelt Library, Washington, letter from Susannah Knight to Eleanor Roosevelt, Eleanor Roosevelt Papers. Box 860, folder '110 ER Autographs 1936 I-L', 4 June 1936.
11. "Veterans Dip Flag for Father Duffy." *The New York Times,* 29 June 1936.

12. Texas Almanac and State Industrial Guide 1936, Book, 1936; digital images, http://texashistory.unt.edu/ark:/67531/metapth117161/ : accessed December 04, 2013, University of North Texas Libraries, The Portal to Texas History, http://texashistory.unt.edu; crediting Texas State Historical Association, Denton, Texas. 375.
13. Jim Parsons and David Bush. *Chicago Art Deco Magazine*, Fall 2011. 22.
14. Cullen F. Thomas, President, Texas Centennial Commission. 2 June 1935.
15. *Liverpool Mercury* (Liverpool, England), Tuesday, 7 July 1891, Issue 13572.
16. Dalrymple, Tate, etc. "Major Texas Floods of 1936." (Government Print Office: Washington D.C, USA, 1937), to be found at http://pubs.usgs.gov/wsp/0816/report.pdf.
17. "Peter the Hermit, Once Hollywood Attraction, Dies Unmourned at 90." *Gettysburg Times*, 20 March, 1969. 24.
18. http://www.oklahomahistory.net/CarterCountyHistoricalMarkers.htm.
19. *Minutes of the Board of Directors of the Oklahoma Historical Society*, 29 July 1943 at http://digital.library.okstate.edu/chronicles/v021/v021p315.pdf, accessed July 4, 2016.
20. Thanks to Carolyn Krumanocker, of the Oklahoma Historical Association, for her guidance on the Will Rogers connection to 18–19 October 1936.
21. Lancashire Records Office, Preston, Soroptimists of Chorley Minute Book—22 August 1950 DDX 1796/1.
22. *Chorley Guardian*. 25 August 1950. 5.
23. *Chorley Memorial Album*, III, p. 144, inscribed by Theresa M., Hunter in 1936 from *Panorama*. Austin, Texas, 1926.

Adam Cree.

Mody Coggin Boatright with his parents, Eldon and Frances (niece of Mody and Sam Coggin), in front, siblings John William, Claude Eldon, Ida Mae, Carl Daniel, Frances Rachel, Roy Roscoe, Frederick Eugene, Celina Madaline, Myrtle Elizabeth and Mody Coggin. Mody is looking down the line of his brothers and sisters.

THE FAMILY SAGA OF MODY BOATRIGHT

by James Mody Bridges

In the Texas Folklore Society publication *Madstones and Twisters*, Mody Boatright introduced the concept of "family-lore" to categorize the last four contributions in the volume. The family-lore referred to ". . . stories preserved by and told in a family."[1] The family saga was more formally conceptualized in a paper titled "The Family Saga as a Form of Folklore," published in *The Family Saga and Other Phases of American Folklore*.[2] Boatright stated, "I use the term mainly to denote a lore that tends to cluster around families, or often patriarchs or matriarchs of families, which is preserved and modified by oral transmission, and which is believed to be true."[3] He went on to state, ". . . (M)any a Texas family saga begins with a G.T.T.—gone to Texas—story."[4]

The Gone to Texas story on Mody Boatright's father's side begins with his grandfather, Daniel Thomas Boatright, who moved his family to Bell County in 1852. He had served as a deputy sheriff and jailer in Franklin County, Alabama, prior to coming to Texas. In 1862, he enrolled in the Confederate Army. Most of his regiment was captured in Arkansas on January 11, 1863, and he was imprisoned at Camp Chase in Ohio. Some of the prisoners were allowed to keep their African American slaves and servants, who were also kept in the prison, but a local outcry eventually freed the slaves and servants. The camp had been greatly overcrowded and rations were meager; both sides of the Civil War had trouble keeping their own troops fed, and prisoners were a secondary priority. D. T. Boatright was involved in a prisoner exchange and died on his way back home while convalescing at Catoosa Springs Confederate Hospital.

The Gone to Texas story on Mody Boatright's mother's side begins with Moses (Mody) J. Coggin and Sam R. Coggin, uncles of Frances McAulay, the mother of Mody Boatright. Mody and Sam

Coggin were brothers born seven years apart, Mody on January 14, 1824, and Sam on February 23, 1831. Both were born in North Carolina. The Coggin family eventually moved to Marshall County, Mississippi, when the brothers acquired "Texas Fever."[5] In 1855, they purchased their first lot of cattle on the Trinity River, in Houston County, and drove them to Bell County, where they kept the herd for two years, losing about half of the cattle during that time. This loss in their first cattle venture served to fix their determination to succeed as cattlemen. In 1857, the Coggin brothers moved what was left of the herd into Brown County.[6]

Sam Coggin had scouted Brown County before the move, and he liked what he saw. The land was on the edge of the frontier and Indians still inhabited the area. It was the controlled burns of the Indians that resulted in knee-high grass. The fires had burned away weeds and underbrush in the fall so that the native grasses would be available to the bison in the spring. Sam Coggin had looked out over the best ranching country he had ever seen, and acquisition of Texas frontier land in the 1850s did not require huge sums of money.[7] Also, the Indians who had created this high quality grass land did not have lawyers—or deeds—to the land recognized by the Texas government.

The Coggin brothers found themselves in the role of true pioneers, as the only activity that preceded their move had been Army maneuvers and surveying parties.[8] In all, about ten families had settled the area before the arrival of the Coggin brothers.[9] The majority of the new settlers lived east of the ninety-eighth meridian. The ninety-ninth meridian traverses Brown County, and it was along this line that the frontier vacillated for practically the entire last half of the nineteenth century. One reason is that the geographical region of the Great Plains bordered this area, where there was a scarcity of water and timber, and an abundance of Indians.[10] There was basically no "civilization" between Brownwood and New Mexico.

In April 1862, Mody and Sam Coggin left their cattle in the care of their neighbors, James and Frank Stiles, and enlisted for service in the Confederate Army.[11] At the eve of the outbreak of the Civil War approximately 2,700 federal troops occupied twenty-one different military posts along the Texas frontier. These union installations were evacuated under special terms. The Texas western frontier was left defenseless.

Seizing the opportunity, the Indians stepped up their depredations on the edges of the settlement. The Civil War, a form of reprieve for the Indians of the southern plains, perpetuated their life style for another fifteen years.[12] The Texans turned to the Confederate government for protection, but the Confederate government was taxed by the war, and frontier protection turned back to Texas. As the war progressed, designated companies of the Confederate Army were assigned "Indian duty." Sam Coggin served two years in the Confederate Army, but Mody Coggin evidently had a short term, as he was engaged in frontier service only in the summer of 1862.[13] Another threat posed to the settlers was deserters and lawless men who flocked to the unguarded frontier. After the war, both Mody and Sam Coggin remained active in frontier militia service.

Mody and Sam Coggin took part in several trailing parties to recover livestock stolen by Indians:

> Mody Coggin became involved in a successful episode on one occasion. One moonlit night some Indians had slipped in and stolen a horse herd. Coggin joined a group of men and tracked the Indians to their camp. The horse thieves were unaware of their pursuers. The settlers planned an attack at daylight and sent two men to watch the Indian camp. On approaching the camp, one of the horses' sudden movement rattled cups and pans, thus alarming the Indians. The surprised Indians fled the camp, leaving all behind—including their moccasins. The stolen horses were recovered, as well as the Indian ponies, and the Indians were left to make their way back to their main camp, barefooted and with no horses."[14]

In actuality, the Indians were probably gunned down.

In 1868, the Coggin brothers formed a partnership with W. C. Parks under the firm name of Coggin and Parks. The new firm, by buying, selling and raising cattle, increased the herd to over 31,000 head and did not owe a dollar.[15] A new danger rose to the cattle business around 1871. Prior to the time, the Indians had confined their livestock raids to horses and small bunches of cattle. But around this time, they changed their tactics.

In July of 1871, the Indians made a raid on the Colorado River, passing through Coggins and Parks' main cattle range. This was to be the largest cattle theft known in the United States. The lowest estimate placed on the number of cattle taken by them on this raid was 12,000 head. Coggins and Parks, being the largest owners of cattle in that section, lost between six and seven thousand head.[16] The rustlers were pursued by soldiers out of Fort Concho along with a posse of citizens gathered as quickly as possible. After a pursuit of three or four days the pursuit was abandoned, as the Indians had too much of a head start and were driving the cattle rapidly. The trail made on this occasion was the largest ever made by a single herd. The trail was covered by dead cattle that had been driven to death. Some had arrows in them, having been killed by the Indians when they could not be driven further.

A second raid occurred on Christmas day, 1871. Roughly 10,000 head of cattle were taken. This raid also passed through the heart of Coggin and Parks' range, and they estimated their losses at 6,000 to 7,000. Soldiers and citizens once again pursued the Indians, but they soon discovered that the Indians outnumbered them so badly that an attack would prove suicidal to the pursuers. Once again, hundreds of cattle were found dead on the trail, having been driven to death.[17]

J. W. Taber, a nephew of the Coggin brothers, said that his Uncle Mody told him that 24,000 head was the largest number they owned at any one time, and that the losses to the Indians were less than reported. He also quoted Mody Coggin as saying that it was impossible to handle a herd larger than about 3,000 at one time, and Indian raids could not have taken away many more than that.[18] Nevertheless, the larger estimates have persisted in historical records.

The Coggin brothers were among the first to erect a fence around their pastures. A fenced pasture allowed the ranchers to control the breeding of their stock and to hold the cattle ready for market. In addition, they could insure that it was their cattle that ate their grass and thereby maximize their profits.

On December 7, 1883, Sheriff W. N. Adams responded to an urgent request from the Coggins brothers. A large group had gathered at the Coggin Ranch southwest of Brownwood with the announced purpose of cutting the fences. The sheriff and thirty armed men brought the tense situation under control.[19] Numerous wire-cutters had threatened to burn property which belonged to county ranchmen with fenced pastures, and a flour mill partly owned by the Coggin brothers was destroyed by fire.

On January 3,1884, Sam Coggin married a twenty-five-year-old widow, Mrs. E. L. (Mattie) Smith of Alvarado, Texas. Sam was fifty-two years old when he married. After an illness of several months, Mody Coggin died on February 3, 1902. He had never married. His great-nephew, folklorist Mody Coggin Boatright, was born on October 16, 1896. Their lives overlapped just five years and four months.

Mody Boatright would have had several rich sources to feed the notion of the "family saga." Besides the original "Gone to Texas" pioneers in his family, his father was a cattle rancher who participated in Coggin cattle drives. Eldon Boatright, Mody's father, eventually built a ten-room house for his family, which also served as a school house. The ranch was on a wagon road between Sweetwater and San Angelo. Since San Angelo didn't have a railroad at the time, the ranch house was almost a "hotel"; people stopped on the way up for lunch and on the way back for lodging.

In one of the few writings about himself, Mody Boatright described his childhood in a letter to Hilton R. Greer, dated November 27,1935:

> My seventh birthday present was a Myres saddle. My pony was a sorrel and white pinto. . . . I began at this time to ride to Sanco, twelve miles away, for the mail. I also "helped" with the cattle, though I did not take to it as avidly perhaps as my father should have liked.
>
> The surviving traditions of the cattle country were never crowded out by what I learned from books. I had heard Sam Coggin tell about Indian raids and fence cutters. Bill McAulay, John Clampitt, Jim Rose, Fred Willard were my kinfolk, related by blood or marriage to my family.
>
> Inevitably I heard the songs, the legends, the tales of range. Now, wherever men live under pioneer conditions or semi-pioneer conditions, tall lying will develop. Among the liars will be some gifted artists whose tales will be repeated, passed on, disseminated until they become the property of the folk. Lore of this kind has always interested me; and the work of John Lomax and J. Frank Dobie convinced me that the tales were worth recording.[20]

Mody Boatright was the last of ten children born to Eldon Boatright and his wife, Frances McAulay Boatright, in 1896. Mody Coggin only had five more years to live. Perhaps it was because Frances's uncle Mody had never married that she named her last child Mody Coggin Boatright, so the elder would know that his name would live on. Mody Coggin Boatright's name stands out from the rest of his brothers and sisters. Perhaps this name gave a young Mody Boatright a special bond with his great-uncle Sam Coggin.

Perhaps young Mody may have held one of the moccasins from the surprised Indian party, a piece of wire from the first fence, or a weapon used in the Confederate Army. With the rich legacy, and the sources of history and folklore from and about his great-uncles, his father, his large childhood family, and the travelers passing through the Boatright house, it is perhaps inevitable that Mody Boatright would come up with the concept of the "family saga." Working on this project, it occurred to me that the concept of the "family saga" may be expanded to include family names as well. My middle name is Mody. My name carries the memory of a famed folklorist and a quintessential Texas pioneer, both of whom I carry a bond with, and my life is much richer now that I am aware of the saga of the family name.

[Acknowledgements: I wish to thank the Pecan Valley Genealogy Society for their assistance. After visiting them I was e-mailed references which were essential for the paper. They also supplied the photographs of the Coggin brothers. I also thank the staff of The Dolph Briscoe Center for American History, located on the University of Texas campus, where Mody Boatright's papers are archived—*Bridges.*]

ENDNOTES

1. *Madstones and Twisters.* Publications of the Texas Folklore Society, Volume XXVIII. Mody C. Boatright, Wilson Hudson, and Allen Maxwell, eds. Dallas: SMU Press, 1958. vii.
2. *The Family Saga and Other Phases of American Folklore.* Mody C. Boatright, Robert B. Downs, and John T. Flanagan. Champaign, IL: University of Illinois Press, 1958.
3. Ibid. 1.
4. Ibid. 5.
5. William Carroll Shive. The Coggin Brothers: A Thesis in History. December, 1974. Texas Tech University. 3.
6. James Cox. *Historical and Biographical Record of the Cattle Industry and the Cattlemen of Texas and Adjacent Territory.* St. Louis: Woodward & Tiernan Printing Co., 1895. 364.
7. Shive. 7.
8. Ibid. 9.
9. Cox. 364.

10. Shive. 9.
11. Ibid. 20.
12. Ibid. 24.
13. Ibid. 25.
14. J. W. Taber. "Reminiscences," dictated to his daughter, Mrs. Fielding Early. Manuscript copy in possession of Mrs. Early, Brownwood, Texas. Cited in William Carroll Shive's The Coggin Brothers: A Thesis in History.
15. Cox. 364.
16. Ibid. 364.
17. Ibid.
18. James C. White. "The Promised Land: A History of Brown County, Texas." *Brownwood Banner*, Brownwood, Texas, 1941.
19. Shive. 81.
20. Letter to Hilton R. Greer, dated November 27, 1935.

The author visiting the graves of his ancestors. Sam Coggin is to his right, and Mody Coggin to his left.

John O. West, Fellow of the Texas Folklore Society.

THE LEGACY OF JOHN O. WEST: MEXICAN-AMERICAN FOLKLORE FROM THE 20th TO THE 21st CENTURY

by Meredith E. Abarca and Lucy Fischer-West

So, here we are, at the 100th meeting of the Texas Folklore Society, gathered to celebrate. In one way or another, each of us expresses an interest in folklore and that's why we're here. But, even more significantly, *each* one of us has elements of folklore coursing in our veins through the *things we do, how* we say what we say, the *stories we tell, the songs we sing* and the *customs and traditions* we value. And *that's why*, as a Society, we have come to celebrate.

*****

There was much to go through after John's passing in 2010; file drawers still remain to be explored. Among his papers, I found an undated, yellowed, dittoed document entitled "Folklore in The Classroom," adapted by Diana Zacharias from Western Kentucky University. It is a guide for teaching, among which objectives are the following:

> The student will investigate and identify folklore as oral tradition.
>
> The student will recognize the universal likenesses of man as expressed through his customs.
>
> The student will observe the enduring nature of folklore through a study of beliefs and customs.

In *Why Teach Folklore*, it continues: Folklore says, "Let's pause for a while and take stock of who we are. Research of the beliefs, customs, stories and habits of Americans reveals that, in spite of rapid change, we do have a past. Placing ashes on the forehead on Ash Wednesday to symbolize a cleansing of the soul harks back to an ancient custom of cleansing the body with ashes. The hesitancy to give one's name to a stranger although serving a practical need today, is the logical behavior for one who believed in the magical relationship of one's name and soul. The paper money found in most newly purchased wallets is a survival of the belief that bad luck will come if one gives away an empty purse. To the adolescent [or person] searching for identity asking the question, 'Who am I?', folklore answers, 'I am the product of my past.' Modern America has a past; folklore brings us in touch with it. A knowledge of his roots better prepares all of us to cope with rapid change."

John O. West came to the Department of English at Texas Western College in 1963 to teach American Literature. Soon after, he began teaching American Folklore, using Jan Harold Brunvand's book, *The Study of American Folklore: An Introduction*, first published in 1968. As far as his classroom methods were concerned, being the English teacher he was, he had his students follow strict research project guidelines. He followed the collection formula set forth by other folklorists: the archive sheet, whether hand-written or typed. He had a basic research paper format for every folklore paper produced by his students. His next step was creating the first Mexican-American folklore course at Texas Western, still using Brunvand's book. It was natural, I think, because he'd grown up on the border, even though he spent his summers in Mississippi.

Since the Sixties he was faithful to both the American Folklore Society and the Texas Folklore Society. He and James M. Day traveled together in Mexico, chasing the trail of the tales told about Pancho Villa, throughout the summer of 1968. He came back with tapes of interviews done on a Wollensak reel-to-reel recorder, in Spanish, which is where our paths crossed. I had been James' work-study student my first year at Texas Western College, in his office down the hall from where John was department chair. Those tapes were my first job for John O.

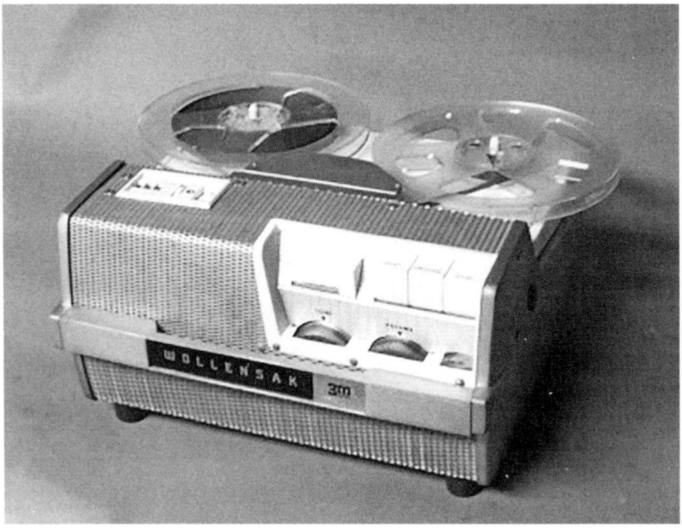

Wollensak reel-to-reel tape recorder.

I transcribed and *translated* every one by hand, then typed them, first using the Underwood typewriter in his office, then later, having a better Olivetti at home with a Spanish keyboard, switched to that one. I turned over to him, nice and neat, the transcripts—having cleaned up every "uh," "um," and "huh" throughout—which I *wasn't* supposed to do. I had inadvertently eliminated his sources' word-for-word storytelling style because John hadn't quite instructed me on how exactly things in folklore were done. Back to the tapes I went, and retyped every last page of those scripts before the summer was over.

Believing in the power of folklore to unite students in their exploration of their customs and traditions inspired many to do the research that later came together to become *Mexican-American Folklore*, published in 1988 by August House Press. It was the first book on Mexican-American folklore. Embracing his being a part of my very traditional Mexican family may have intensified his interest in capturing the folklore of the border. He dedicated the book to my mother and me, who had been his "guiding stars" through its production.

IBM Selectric typewriter.

By that time, I was no longer typing his every article on the IBM Selectric, purchased for putting together the *American Folklore Newsletter*, which we co-edited from 1972 to 1979. He did the work on a Tandy TRS 80, on floppy discs that, fortunately, someone at August House figured out how to read. His hunt-and-peck typing method had gotten a little more awkward after injuries sustained in a wreck in Scotland, but he managed to type everything he wrote on that trusty Radio Shack computer. Throughout the changes in technology, I served as editor, copy-editor, and consultant on anything related to what he was writing, if it was Mexican folklore-related.

Tandy TRS-80 computer from Radio Shack.

His folklore research often included photography, for which he used his Praktica 35mm camera, documenting adobe-making and construction for "Adobe: Earth, Straw, and Water," co-authored with his student Roberto Gonzalez and published in *Built in Texas.* He photographed house and church *grutas*, as well as grave decorations following the Rio Grande, later published in *Folk Art in Texas.* In his first foray into film-making, collaborating with Joe S. Graham in Alpine, he used black and white film in a hand-held Kodak 8mm camera and produced a short piece on the *candelilla* wax process.

Praktica 35mm camera and lenses.

More personally valuable for me, it is thanks to John that I have a film of my mother making tamales (during which I alternated between helping my mother cook and writing down our family's recipe). He did another short film on *Día de los Muertos* when our family went to the Juárez cemetery one November, as we had done all of my life.

John taught his Mexican-American Folklore course for decades, and we feared that when he retired, the course which he so loved would disappear from the English Department curriculum. Destiny—fate—serendipity—call it what you will, but it was Meredith Abarca's arrival in El Paso, hired the year before he retired, that has allowed that course not only to survive, but to flourish, going down roads that John could never have imagined.

*****

In 2001, when John and Lucy approached me about adding Mexican-American Folklore to my teaching repertoire, my first thought was: Folklore . . . what do I know about it? While I never took a course on folklore during my undergraduate or graduate literary studies, there was one thing that I felt I shared with John O. We both value common folks' stories, their talents, and their wisdom. At its core, this is what defines folklore.

Using John's *Mexican-American Folklore* book, I designed a "hands-on" course so that students learn to recognize and value the wealth of knowledge within their family's traditional practices. In 2003, as a result of the class's final project, one student found out the history of a *molcajete* (mortar and pestle) that had been passed down through five generations of women in his family. Showing interest in this piece of material folk culture made my student, Julian Piedra, the first male family member to officially own the *molcajete.* It was the central item in the exhibit I did featuring food folklore I knew, along with that of my students, titled "Mamá's Molcajete: The Mestizaje of Mexican Cuisines."

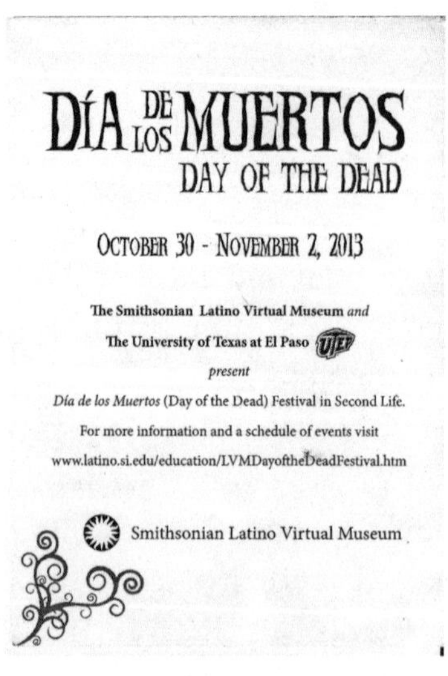

Poster for the Día de los Muertos exhibit for the Smithsonian Latino Center's Virtual Museum, 2013.

By request, I teach Mexican-American Folklore in the fall semester so that as a class we can create an altar for the Day of the Dead. Over the years, the number of students for whom this altar is the first one they have participated in creating increases. Yet, as we learn about the significance of honoring and remembering the lives of those who have passed away—and learn about the religious and spiritual symbolism of the altar's structure, about the required items such as *pan de muerto*, grains of salt, a glass of water, candles, and incense—it is not unusual for students to create an altar in their own homes and begin a "new" tradition in their families.

Image of the virtual placita, a cemetery.

The opportunity to create a virtual altar using Second Life's islands, a 3D immersive world, came in 2013. I was invited to participate in The Smithsonian Latino Center's Virtual Museum "Day of the Dead" celebration. The Smithsonian Latino Center has created a virtual *placita*, a cemetery, and a park-like section for displaying altars. For the last three years, we have engaged in translating aspects of our folklore into this environment, sharing stories of our loved ones with a global audience in the thousands. As our skills increase using Second Life's technologies, so have the altars. Because of his influence on me and my interest in folklore, the first one was dedicated to John O. West.

*****

Long before I did my first paper of the 21st century for the Texas Folklore Society, entitled "Folklore by Osmosis: Three Decades with John O.," most of you knew me solely as someone who tagged along to meetings. Thanks to my mentors in this beloved Society—Ab Abernethy, Joyce Gibson Roach, Lou Rodenberger, and Mary Harris—I was encouraged to find my voice and write about my folklore and culture firsthand, and I have, in every way I could think of, also encouraged my high school students to value and write about the customs and traditions that we share. More formally and substantially, Meredith has—with new methods and technology, and by incorporating her own special food studies field—breathed fresh life into the exploration and preservation of Mexican-American folklore. John's legacy lives on.

[This article was presented at the Austin meeting, April 2, 2016.]

Equipment used to record folklore research from the 20th Century.

A virtual altar, folklore research moving into the 21st Century.

STATE PENITENTIARY
HUNTSVILLE TEXAS

II. Texas Folk Song and Dance

Karen Reinartz Haile.

HERE A DITTY, THERE A DITTY, EVERYWHERE A LITTLE DITTY

by Karen Reinartz Haile

> Be kind to your web-footed friends, for a duck
> may be somebody's mother.
> Be good to your friends in the swamp, where
> the water is very damp.
> Be nice to the camel in the zoo, for his hump
> may be hiding your brother.
> Be good to the tiger and the monk, and we
> will let you smell our favorite pet skunk.

This song, "Web Footed Friends," was recorded in 1955 by Homer and Jethro, and sung at the end of every episode of the popular 1960s TV series *Sing Along with Mitch.* My aunt taught me the song when I was six. It is one of my favorite ditties.

What is a ditty, you ask? It is "an especially simple, unaffected, silly song," according to the Merriam Webster Dictionary. The word ditty originates from the Middle English word *ditee*, and the Anglo-French *ditè*, meaning "story song." The Latin word *dictare* means "to compose." The first known use of the word "ditty" was in the fourteenth century.

When I started researching them, I realized that there are hundreds of ditties, thousands of ditties, millions and billions and trillions of ditties. There are ancient ditties, modern ditties, echo, gecko, and retro ditties. There are micro ditties, psycho ditties, itty bitty, and kitty ditties. Ditties in rounds, ditties with sounds, pretty, witty, even do-wha-ditties!

But today, I am only going to tell you about 167 of them . . . or maybe less. Nursery rhymes are the most recognized form of ditties. Although the oral tradition of these songs is ancient, the earliest known published collection, *Tommy Thumb's Pretty Song*

Book, dates back to 1744, and includes ditties such as "Little Tom Tucker" and "Sing a Song of Sixpence." Of course, *the* most influential collection of ditties was the book *Mother Goose's Melody, or, Sonnets for the Cradle* (originally published circa 1781, and published widely in 1791), which contained "Jack & Jill" and "Hush-a-By-Baby," just to name a few. "Little Bo Peep" appeared for the first time in 1805, and "Mary Had a Little Lamb," in 1830.

A collection called *Our Young Folks: An Illustrated Magazine for Boys and Girls*, published in 1865, introduced a ditty that my husband Lee and I taught our kids. It goes like this:

Little fishy in the brook,
Daddy catch 'em with a hook,
Mommy cook 'em in the pan,
Baby eats 'em fast as she can.

That may have been the first song the girls learned . . . besides "Rye Wiskey," thanks to Lee's dad. (Thanks Grandpa Haile!)

In 1877, a collection called *The Baby's Opera* brought people favorites like "Here We Go 'Round the Mulberry Bush," "Bah, Bah Black Sheep" ("Have you any wool?"), and "Three Blind Mice." Some nursery rhyme ditties have reference to historical events. Few are as interesting—or as haunting—as "Ring around the Rosie," which is about the great plague of 1665, the Bubonic Plague. You probably have all, at one time or another, joined hands in a circle, laughing with friends singing: "Ring around the rosies, pocket full of posies, Ashes, ashes, we all fall down." Let's dissect this charming little ditty, line by line:

1) "Ring around the rosies" refers to the rosy red sores around the victim's mouth. At this time, he is contagious and soon will be dead.
2) "pocket full of posies" refers to pouches of herbs and spices people carried—not only to disguise the smell of death, but to ward off evil spirits, since they did *not* know what caused the plague.

3) "Ashes, ashes" is about burning the bodies once the victims died.
4) "we all fall down" is self-explanatory; everybody fell down . . . DEAD!

Children probably recited this ditty for hundreds of years, not knowing what it meant. It first appeared in Kate Greenaway's *Mother Goose, or the Old Nursery Rhymes* in 1881. In 1961, James Leasor published a book called *The Plague and the Fire*, which was the first known interpretation of the ditty as it related to the plague. How many of you sang "Ring around the Rosie" to your kids at night to help them fall asleep? While we are on the subject of gritty ditties, how about this one?

> If you ever see a hearse go by, then you will be the next to die.
> They wrap you up in a bloody sheet, and then they bury you six feet deep.
> It all goes good for about a week, and then your coffin begins to leak.
> The worms crawl in, the worms crawl out, and they play pinochle on your snout.
> Your stomach turns a slimy green, and pus comes out like shaving cream.
> You spread it on a piece of bread. That's what you eat when you're dead. . . .
> Yum, yum!

This next 1959 camp song appeared on the Smithsonian's "Folkways Collection" record album entitled *A Fish That's a Song*. It goes like this:

> Boys are made of greasy, grimy gopher guts,
> mutilated monkey meat, stinky little birdy feet,
> French fried eye balls floating in a pan of grease,
> that's why I hate boys.

Of course, that all changes when you turn thirteen, right ladies? Since we are talking about camp ditties, I want to touch on some of my favorites. Most of their origins are unclear, but I know that my 85-year-old mother sang many of these songs when she was a camp counselor in her teens. You may recognize some of them.

> The cutest boy, I ever saw, was sipping soda through a straw,
> The cutest boy, I ever saw, was sipping soda through a straw. . . .

Or here is one that was copyrighted in 1919. In a 1920 interview with Carl Sandburg, he said that he learned this next song from a grade school friend when he was just a young boy:

> A boy and a girl in a little canoe, with the moon shining all around,
> And as they rowed their paddles, you couldn't even hear a sound. . . .

Or this ditty, written and performed in 1961 by folk singer Tom Glazer:

> On top of spaghetti, all covered with cheese,
> I lost my poor meatball when somebody sneezed.
> It rolled off the table, and onto the floor,
> And then my poor meatball, rolled out of the door.
> It rolled in the garden, and under a bush,
> And then my poor meatball, was nothing but mush.
> So if you're eating spaghetti, all covered with cheese,
> Hold onto your meatballs, and don't ever sneeze.

And what about this camp ditty inspired by an organization called the Junior Birdmen, formed in 1934 and made up of young boys who liked to build model airplanes. My daughter Acayla still knows all the gestures that go with it.

> Up in the air junior bird men, up in the air upside down,
> Up in the air junior bird men, with your noses to the ground.
> When you see them a flying, with their wings made of tin,
> Then you know junior bird men, have sent their boxtops in.
> Takes 5 box tops,
> 4 bottle caps,
> 3 coupons,
> 2 labels,
> And 1 thin dime ****** (machine gun noise) ******

Karen and Acayla Haile performing "Up in the Air, Junior Birdmen."

One of my favorite types of ditty is a "round," which is sung by two to three people. The most widely recognized round is "Row, Row, Row Your Boat." The first round was originally sung by Danny Kaye in 1952 for the movie *Hans Christian Anderson*. The second verse is sung in counter-part, overlapping. This ditty was later recorded by Ann Murry, Sir Paul McCartney, and was even featured on an episode of *The Muppets*.

This next ditty was made into a round in 1786 by W. Hayes and published in "Three Oxford Cries," featured in the *Glen Collection of Printed Music* (National Library of Scotland). Cries were used by chair menders, fishermen, and rag pickers as they called out for business on the streets of Oxford in the 1700s—much like the bells and music of an ice cream man.

> Chairs to mend, oh chairs to mend.
> Mackerel, fresh mackerel, any old rags, any old
> rags?

And now, my favorite, an Elizabethan round:

> Rose, rose, rose, rose, will I ever see thee wed?
> I will marry at thy will sire, at thy will.
> Inch worm, inch worm, measuring a marigold.

This next ditty appeared in grade school songbooks in the early '60s. It was actually translated into English from a Mexican folk ditty. This silly song was introduced to me by Nannett Goyer, a fellow entomology student with Lee at Texas A&M. Some might label this as a "kitty ditty." Others would categorize it as a "mega ditty," since it has so many stanzas. You can decide for yourself, if you know enough stanzas.

I now present to you . . . "Señor Don Gato":

> Se*ñ*or Don Gato was a cat.
> On a high red roof, Don Gato sat.

He went there to read a letter, (meow-meow-
meow)
Where the reading light was better. (meow-
meow-meow)
Was love letter for Don Gato.

In this letter from his true love, he learns that she *will*, indeed, marry him. In his excitement, listen what happens:

Oh Don Gato jumped so happily
He fell off the roof and broke his knee.
Broke his ribs and all his whiskers, (meow-
meow-meow)
And his little solar plexus, (meow-meow-
meow)
Ay Caramba, cried Don Gato.

Don Gato is hurt very badly. The doctors try and try, but they are unable to save him, and poor Don Gato dies. Now, you might think that this is a depressing ditty, but listen what happens in the end:

Karen Haile dressed up and singing "Señor Gato."

When the funeral passed the market square,
Such a smell of fish was in the air.
Though the burial was slated, (meow-meow-
meow)
He became re-animated, (meow-meow-
meow)
He came back to life . . . Don Gato.

Don't you just love happy endings?

And now, the most amazing and oldest ditty that I found in my research: "Little Bunny Foo Foo." The earliest reference to this ditty is found in Chaucer's *Canterbury Tales*, believed to have been written between 1387 and 1400. Here is an excerpt:

And in the grove, at tyme and place set,
This bunnie few few and his field maus be met,
To chaugen gan (shawn-gen) the colour in
heir face.

The next reference to the bunny is from a sonnet written by William Shakespeare sometime between 1609 and 1613. This is another excerpt:

Clear wells spring not, sweet birds sing not,
Green plants bring not forth their dye.
Herds stand weeping, flocks all sleeping,
Nymphs back peeping fearfully,
For Rabbit Foofoo hath killed a mouse.

Any of these references can be hoaxes, as much of the information is vague and misinformation—especially that transmitted via the Internet—can be mistaken for fact. However, H. L. Mencken's book *The American Language* (circa 1919) cites yet another reference in a 1623 manuscript from the Plymouth Colony, documenting that a John Alders sang a "lullabye about bunnie foo foo" to his children.

Like all folk songs, passed from generation to generation, some change—or evolution, if you will—occurs over the years. This "modern" version is the one I learned when I was about eight years old:

> Little Bunnie Foo Foo, hopping through the forest,
> Scooping up the field mice and bopping 'em on the head.
> Then down came the blue fairy . . . and she said:
> "Little Bunnie Foo Foo, I don't wanna see you
> Scooping up the field mice and bopping 'em on the head
> I'll give you three chances, and if you don't quit bopping
> Those field mice, I am gonna turn you into a goon."

Of course, Bunnie Foo Foo does *not* heed her warning. After she scolds him the third time, he disobeys again. Well POOF—she turns him into a goon! Like many early nursery rhymes, this ditty teaches a very valuable lesson: "Hare today, goon tomorrow."

I wish there was time to tell you about other really fun ditties like:

> First you take the peanuts and you pick 'em, pick 'em . . .
> Then you smash 'em, smash 'em, smash 'em . . .
> Then you spread 'em, spread 'em . . .
> Whoa! Peanut, peanut butter and jelly . . .

Or this one:

> Oh tomba toad, oh tomba toad, why did you hop up on the road?

Oh tomba toad, oh tomba toad, why did you hop up on the road?
You did not see the passing car, and now you're stretched out on the tar.
Oh tomba toad, oh tomba toad, why did you hop up on the road?

Or the "almost cussing" ditty, popular in the early 1930s:

Mary had a steamboat, the steamboat had a bell,
Mary went to heaven, the steamboat went to . . .
Hello operator, give me number 9,
And if you disconnect me, I'll kick you in the . . .
Behind the fridgerator, there was a piece of glass,
Mary didn't see it, and Mary cut her . . .
Ask me no more questions, I'll tell you no more lies.
The boys are in the bathroom, zipping up their flys . . .

Or how about endless ditties that drove parents crazy in the car on long road trips? A Wikipedia article for this song shows that it exists in many languages; the article lists several possible sources, including a possible original publication of the song in *The Norwalk Hour* in 1949, but it was also described in someone's family diary in 1942 as a song that was performed by their children in a school talent show:

Found a peanut, found a peanut, found a peanut just now.
Just now I found a peanut, found a peanut just now.
It was rotten . . . Ate it anyway . . . Got sick . . .
Threw up . . .

And it goes on and on with the victim going to the hospital, dying, going to heaven, going to hell, getting a job there selling peanuts, getting hungry—and then eating a peanut. This ditty repeats itself until the adult that is driving the car screeches to a stop and threatens to tan the kids' hides!

I do want to mention a ditty taught to me by my Grandmother, Lillie Belle Dean, when she was 98 years old. She learned it from a friend when she was quite young. I believe it refers to a World War I soldier.

> Chester have you heard about Hairy,
> He chest got back from the arm-ee.
> I ear he nose how to wear his clothes,
> Hip hip hurray for the arm-ee.

Obviously, there are just a plethora of ditties that I could not include here, but I don't think it would be right to end this paper without singing a ditty about our great state of Texas and the Texas scouts who live here! The only information I have about this ditty is that it's a camp song, probably written in the late '50s. It somewhat describes the outstanding qualities of a Texas scout. I leave you with this fun ditty, sung to the tune of "The Yellow Rose of Texas":

> You can tell a scout from Texas, you can tell
> him by his walk,
> You can tell a scout from Texas, you can tell
> him by his talk,
> You can tell him by his manners, his appetite
> and such,
> You can tell a scout from Texas, but you sure
> can't tell him much!

Ditties are passed down from generation to generation, sometimes from century to century. They can be entertaining and educational, but mostly they help keep our folkways alive through fun and oftentimes silly songs.

Carol and Herb Bolland.

COME ON-A MY HOUSE: A LOOK AT THE HOUSE AND RANCH DANCES OF TEXAS

by Carol Bolland

For most of our history, Texas has been an agricultural state and, during the early years, didn't have large population centers. Having a place to socialize with friends and neighbors was not always available, and homes were the primary spots for getting together. In many cases, dancing was a popular activity, and house or ranch dances were born.

Such get-togethers were not unheard of in other parts of the country from colonial times. One type in particular, the Barn Dance (or Hoedown or Breakdown), occurred in the fall when the harvest was in. The farmers laid down their hoes and broke down their equipment and had a dance in the barn. In Texas, folks came together for barn raisings or, in East Texas, log rollings.[1] Charles Williams, past-President of the Texas Folklore Society, recalls attending barn dances in his early years in New England, and I have found references to such events in the Carolinas and other areas as well.

Out of these Hoedowns or Breakdowns has come a type of fiddle tune called a breakdown. A typical breakdown is "Turkey in the Straw." "The fiddle was the ideal instrument for the ever-expanding, mobile frontiers and was, in fact, referred to in the 19th century as the 'royal instrument of the frontier.'"[2] The fiddler was the most important element of the dance, providing the beat and the tune, and he earned himself a place of prominence in the community, often getting a soft job on the ranch or more credit at the store. It mattered little that he might be shiftless and inclined toward the bottle; when he picked up the fiddle and started to play, he was the king, and the longer and louder he played the larger his crown.

"Turkey in the Straw," a commonly known fiddle breakdown.

According to noted folklorist J. Frank Dobie, the bears in south Louisiana liked fiddling so much that they frequently showed up at country dances, not such a terrible thing as there were never enough women around for partners. He said that it wasn't too bad to dance with a bear, but they were sort of hard to turn loose of, or so the story goes.[3]

The tunes played were the old jigs, reels, and hornpipes that were ancient in the British Isles when the settlers first came to the New World. Many of the tunes, like "Irish Washerwoman," "The Campbells Are Coming," and "Sailor's Hornpipe," stayed close to their original forms. Most underwent subtle and gradual changes as they were passed along from one fiddler and generation and area to another, and now only a hint of their Old World ancestry remains.

Much of the early dancing was group dancing, for which a leader called the steps and patterns while the music was being played. Sometimes fiddle tunes became songs when lyrics were thrown in between calls. In the evolution of some fiddle-dance songs—"Sally Goodin," "Cindy," "Cotton-Eyed Joe," and "Old Joe Clark," for instance—the calls were dropped and the words became almost as important as the tunes."[4]

"Old Joe Clark"

Old Joe Clark had a yellow cat
She would neither sing nor pray
Stuck her head in a buttermilk jar
And washed her sins away
Fare thee well, Old Joe Clark
Fare thee well I'm gone
Fare thee well, Old Joe Clark
Time you're movin' on.

These traditional lyrics could be substituted with many variations.

In southwestern Louisiana in the 1800s, the fiddle was the primary instrument in the music which we know as Cajun. As the German influences from Texas were felt, the accordion was added to the mix and, with the addition of the triangle iron, the music became known as "la la." La la was primarily rural in origin, and when played at house dances, the dances also were known as la las.[5]

Undoubtedly, these dances spilled over into southeastern Texas, as the Cajun influence is still quite strong, especially in the Beaumont/Port Arthur area. Particularly in Texas, but now also in Louisiana, Western Swing style was incorporated into the music, in large part due the popularity of Harry Choates' fiddle playing. One of his best known tunes is "Jolie Blon."

Another folk song-and-dance tradition is the play party, which is not unique to Texas, as I found references to play parties in Arkansas and Kansas. "Many early Texas settlers were religious fundamentalists who believed that dancing and fiddle music were sinful. They satisfied the universal urge to move to music with the play party, which was song-accompanied dance that allowed no instruments. They called their rhythmical group movements 'marches' or 'games.' They danced in rings or in long-ways formations but never in squares, and they swung each other by hand, never by the waist."[6]

Just an aside here, in the late '50s and early '60s at Baylor University, dancing was frowned upon. Clubs would hold "functions" off campus, which everyone knew were dances. In the women's physical education classes I took a semester of "folk rhythms," where I learned to do the schottische, the polka and the cha cha, among other "rhythms," but never with a male partner.

The play parties used many popular dance tunes—"Skip to My Lou," "Old Joe Clark," "Old Dan Tucker," "The Gal I Left Behind," "Willis in the Ballroom"—but because of the lack of instrumental music, the words became all-important:

"Skip to My Lou"

Fly's in the buttermilk, Shoo fly shoo,
Fly's in the buttermilk, Shoo fly shoo,
Fly's in the buttermilk, Shoo fly shoo,
Skip to my Lou my darling.

Skip, skip, skip to my Lou,
Skip, skip, skip to my Lou,
Skip, skip, skip to my Lou,
Skip to my Lou my darling.

Play-party songs have preserved many stanzas that were lost in the fiddle-dance tradition. A play party usually began with a choosing game such as "Needle's Eye," similar to "London Bridge," and then progressed to ring-game songs like "Saro Jane" or "Coffee Grows on White Oak Trees," in which couples would join hands and form a ring. The ladies would march around a single man and sing the first part of the song at a slow tempo. The man would choose a partner from the ring, and the dancers would skip around them singing at a faster clip. This would continue until all the men had partners. From there they progressed into long-ways dances like "Weevily Wheat," "Little Brass Wagon," and "Baltimore." Play parties were not only popular among fundamentalists, they were necessary when no musician was around. In spite of the reservations laid on the players by their elders, play-party songs and formations were "just as joyful and exuberant as their sinful fiddling square-dance counterparts."[7] Jean Schnitz of Boerne related that her grandfather quite often sang for the play parties. She still has a songbook containing many of these songs.

When someone decided to give a dance at his ranch or farm, word was passed from neighbor to neighbor, by people on the streets, or by telephone. On rare occasions, the dances were by special invitation, but most of the time all who met certain standards of conduct were invited. The dances brought people from such a broad geographical area that they could not return home the same night, and so the dancing would continue for several days. Entire families came, mainly by wagon or buggy, a few by car, and others on horseback.[8]

Though most West Texas dances were held at ranches, they were generally referred to as "country dances." Bob Wills, however, often referred to them as "ranch dances." Bob played his first dance at the age of ten. His father, John Wills, the fiddler, sent him ahead to a nearby ranch with the instruments to set things up for the event. When it was time for the dance, Papa had not appeared. Bob didn't know if high water had hindered his getting there of if he had simply forgotten. As the crowd began to get restless, wanting to dance, Bob asked permission to play to get things started. The cowboys and ladies were amused, but were soon dancing away, so Bob played the six selections he knew until two o'clock in the morning when Papa showed up, after having enjoyed too many stops at the corn liquor wagons and in no condition to play.[9]

The influence of ranch dances on Wills' music was very important. The Western Swing style that he was so instrumental in developing was an outgrowth of his years playing for such dances. The dancing usually took place in the home. In order to be heard, the musicians, generally a fiddle and a guitar, stood in the doorway between rooms or at some other spot where they could be heard in two or three rooms. It was not unheard of to have the fiddler stroll among the dancers in order to help them keep the beat.[10]

Particularly on the ranches, the men often outnumbered the women, so a system was set up of pinning a number on the men as they arrived, to keep track of who had a ticket, but also to control the dancing. Since there was not a large dancing area, a certain number of men would be allowed on the dance floor at one time with their partners. When their set time was up, the next group would be called. In some cases, some of the men were dubbed "heifer branded" or "lady fair" and would tie a kerchief on their arm and dance the woman's part. Rollie Burns, a cowboy on the "22" Ranch in Crosby County, recalled that at a dance in 1881 thirty cowboys showed up and only nine women. The dance lasted three nights and two days non-stop. When a cowboy got tired he'd head to the bunkhouse for a nap, but the women were not given a chance to rest. "It could have been worse, however," Burns said, "as the men swung them so lustily they didn't have to exert a lot of effort. Their feet did get tired and sore though."

The children and teenagers would congregate outside to play and socialize. On one occasion, a grownup recalled that while the children were playing outside, the mothers would bring the sleeping infants out and put them in their wagons to sleep in the relative quiet. The children took great delight in moving the babies to different buggies or wagons. When it was time to go home, which was quite late, no one noticed the changes and it took several days to get the children back with their rightful parents.

One elaborate affair on the 3D Ranch in 1903 lasted from Friday afternoon until midnight Saturday. A bandstand was constructed and a piano brought in to help with the music. The only break in the dancing was for three hours Friday night to let the piano cool off. No mention was made of the poor fiddler who had played all that time, or about time out for food or comfort stops for the musicians.

As mentioned earlier, some Protestant denominations forbade dancing. Bud Browning, a Matador Ranch cowboy and fiddler at the turn of the century, was "too religious to dance, but not too religious to fiddle the better part of two nights and one day while others danced." Some were known to have "danced themselves out of the church" and had to be saved at the next revival. There were those who chose to dance out of the church in the winter and be saved at the summer camp meeting when there were no dances anyway.[11]

Linda Wolff of Victoria told me of her grandfather, Earl Daniel Smith, a cabinet maker/carpenter in Gage, Oklahoma, right across the Red River from Texas, who also played fiddle at dances. Coming home from a dance one night, he managed to step on his fiddle and pretty well smash the top. Being a resourceful wood worker, he went into the wood shed, found a cedar shingle, and carved a new top and continued playing.

Earl Daniel Smith's fiddle, with the top replaced by a cedar shingle.

In Comal County, in South Central Texas in and around New Braunfels, a town with a strong German heritage, house dances were equally popular, with most persons I talked to noting that there was generally not a reason for such get-togethers. As Buddy Zimmerman of Solms said, "We just wanted to have fun." Again, a space was cleared for dancing and the music was generally accordion and/or fiddle. In later years, when most folks had radios, they might simply turn on the radio. Polkas, waltzes, the schottische and two-steps were the most popular tunes. One of the most popular was the "Texas Schottische."

"Ach, Du Liebe Augustin."

Milton Kaderli, a young ninety-four-year-old when I spoke to him (but who has since passed away), grew up about twenty-five miles west of New Braunfels near Spring Branch. His family had a ranch in the area and his grandparents' house was near his on the property. When he was quite young, he would go to visit his grandfather every afternoon after lunch, and his grandfather quite often got out his button accordion and entertained young Milton. His grandfather died when Milton was five and he was given the accordion. Apparently Milton was a quick study, because he said that by the time he was eight or nine they would sit him on a box in the middle of the room, and he would play and they would dance around him. When I asked about the music, he said it was pretty much whatever he knew, lots of old German tunes, primarily.

Milton Kaderli, with wife Mary, circa 1940s.

Gloria Laguna, a Hispanic woman from Seguin, recalled a neighbor having such a dance in conjunction with a baptism. Most folks I talked to seemed to think they didn't need a real reason to have a dance. According to Virgie Van Kleef, who grew up on the outskirts of Gonzales, when folks had the desire to get together they would gather at one another's farm, clear out the furniture from the largest room in the house (or at least move it to the side of the room), and have a dance. The children would run around outside and play while the old folks danced. Since Gonzales is located in one of the areas of Czech settlers, it was probably polka music that those neighbors with instruments played. She also fondly recalled the Wednesday night gospel sings that happened at a nearby farm.

As people began to move into towns, dance halls and honky-tonks began to pop up. There were fewer of the house dances, but there were exceptions. Margaret Rockaway, who grew up in Edna, remembers getting together at homes to dance to the radio as a newlywed in the 1950s. She says they were Baptist and their parents, who also lived in Edna, would not have approved of them going to the honkytonks because beer was served. When I asked if the parents approved of the dancing, she laughed and said, "We may have forgotten to tell them about that."

Steve Pepper of Knox City recalls that, growing up in Wichita Falls, his family and the neighbors would gather in the carport and play music and dance. He laughingly said that one man played the beer bottle opener, a reference to the popping sounds as he opened the bottles. Jim Winn, who grew up in the area around Corsicana, said that so many dances were held at the Bergins family house that the living room floor was bowed in as the foundation began sinking from all the dancing.

A house in New Braunfels that hosted house dances.

Today the practice of house dances has largely disappeared, but there is an occasional dance at some of the large ranches in West Texas. My friend Lee Barlow, who plays bass, told me that in Lipscomb, Texas, from 1995–2010 each summer, they had a reproduction of ranch dances called the Naturally Yours Platform Dance. They built a dance platform and had food prepared and a live band. He played there for fourteen out of the fifteen years. People came from all over the world to the platform dances.

Michael Martin Murphey, a singer of American cowboy music, has presented some of these dances in the past few years. I had the privilege of playing at one of his dances in San Marcos a few years ago, when he invited the Texas State University Orchestra, of which I was an honorary member, to join his band for a Christmas dance on campus. Perhaps, if you are lucky, you will have a chance to attend such a function someday and experience a taste of our cultural past.

Endnotes

1. Francis Edward Abernethy. *Singin' Texas.* Denton: University of North Texas Press, 1994. 33.
2. Charles Townsend. San Antonio Rose: The Life and Music of Bob Wills. Champaign: University of Illinois Press, 1976. 2.
3. Abernethy. 62.
4. "Folk Music." Texas State Historical Association, Handbook of Texas Online, https://tshaonline.org/handbook/online.
5. "Music of Louisiana." https://en.wikipedia.org/wiki/Music_of_Louisiana.
6. "Folk Music."
7. "Folk Music."
8. Townsend. 16.
9. Townsend. 12–13.
10. Joe Carr and Alan Munde. *Prairie Nights to Neon Lights: The Story of Country Music in West Texas.* Lubbock: Texas Tech University Press, 1995. 24.
11. Carr and Munde. 12–14.

Jean Schnitz performing at a Hootenanny with Carolyn Arrington.

YODELS, CATTLE CALLS, AND OTHER MELODIOUS SOUNDS

by Jean Granberry Schnitz

Ever since the first cave man learned he could get attention by making unusual noises, people have been making a variety of sounds. Speech evolved into communication while music evolved from simple sounds to becoming more melodious and more complicated as the years went by. Unfortunately, not all musical sounds have become more melodious. Some sounds other than musical ones have become more complicated! Think about the range of musical styles, from classical to country, blues, "gangsta rap," and beyond. It could be said that melodious sounds range from the sublime to the ridiculous—but there is something for everybody!

Much has been written about the various types of music that have been popular in Texas, but not much has been written about the earlier sounds of Indian chants and animal calls that preceded the sounds brought to Texas by the early Texans. Anyone who has read a history book—or has seen a Western movie—knows the Indians were skilled at imitating bird calls and other such sounds. They also had various other communications, including war whoops. The music of early Texas Indians features interesting drum cadences and rhythms, and the songs are more chant than melody. They tend to be modal, not unlike the early songs of mankind in other parts of the world where simple chants were the first forms of music.

When human beings imitate animal sounds, they sometimes look pretty strange—and sound even stranger. People routinely call their dogs and cats, which can result in some pretty weird sounds, but they also call horses, cows, pigs, turkeys, deer, ducks, and other animals. Hunters use their own voices or a variety of gadgets that produce sounds similar to those made by animals. An experienced duck hunter can call in a flock of ducks with ease. Deer respond to the sound of crashing horns, and turkeys respond to shrill calls of various sorts. Successfully calling animals is NOT a matter of buying a gadget somewhere and simply blowing into it. There is an art to knowing whether the best choice is the "feeding call" or the "mating call" or whatever. That leaves the achieving of a realistic sound as the next challenge.

Think about how people call their dogs and cats. Voices are sometimes elevated into falsetto ranges and few people simply call, "Kitty, kitty" without appropriate voice modifications. I tend to call my cats with a falsetto, "Here, kitty witty, witty." Animals *know* the sound to which they would respond. The neighbors also know the sound, whether they like it or not.

Calling children can get pretty weird, too. Most people call their children by name when they want a specific child to appear, but some have more creative sounds that achieve the same purpose. Among farm families that sound might be the clang of a dinner bell, announcing the serving of a meal. Or it might be a certain whistle or shout. In rural communities today, it could be the fire siren announcing the arrival of twelve o'clock noon.

I know people whose shrill whistle can call people to attention for announcements at meetings and other gatherings. I also know people who simply cannot figure out what moves need to be made in order to create a whistle of any sort. There really is an art to whistling. It *can* be beautiful and unique! One of my mother's sisters could whistle tunes that included bird calls and other trills and frills. Karen Haile's songs and stories are frequently enhanced by unique whistles.

My husband Lew calls the deer that reside in our woods by simply shaking some corn around in a coffee can. That works for dogs, too, sometimes. South Texas ranchers can get their cattle to respond to the sound made by blowing a truck horn. Actually, hungry cattle also respond simply to the sound of a vehicle delivering hay or other feed. One of the funniest cattle calls I ever heard came over the hill behind my house after a herd of cattle got into our subdivision a few years ago. The cows enjoyed eating the neighborhood's shrubbery for several days while local police conducted a mini-rodeo, using police cars. It didn't work. One afternoon I saw cows running toward someone who was coming over the hill. The owner of the cattle had been found! What was his cattle call? "Come on, girls—come on!"

Somewhere between calling animals and singing is a form of music called yodeling, which can be beautiful—OR, it can be deadly awful! There is "Alpine" yodeling (such as might have originated in Switzerland or Appalachia), blues yodeling, "country/western" yodeling, and other types. Good yodeling requires that the tone be exactly "on pitch." Few sounds are more awesome and beautiful than those produced by a good yodeler. Case in point: the 2011 winner of the Miss America talent contest won for her yodeling ability. Did you hear her performance?

One of the most popular tunes to be played at Texas rodeos during the 1940s and 1950s—and even now—was "Cattle Call," featuring a form of yodeling. This tune was written by Tex Owens and made famous by Eddy Arnold, but others such as Slim Whitman do a pretty awesome job of it. Multiple opportunities to hear various artists performing are as near as your computer.

Yodeling seems to be less popular than it once was, but in certain venues, one can actually obtain lessons. A fellow by the name of Ron Taylor from Mountain View, Arkansas, is a popular entertainer at Texas music festivals, and he also conducts classes on the nuances of yodeling. Another yodeling performer is Janet McBride, who has performed at the National Cowboy Symposium in Lubbock for several years. She learned to yodel when she was a child. She explained: "We walked a mile up a dirt road daily to meet the school bus and that was my favorite time and place to practice. My brothers and sister didn't always appreciate my practicing and usually made me walk by myself. It didn't matter to me. I'd just yodel louder. . . ."[1]

Janet has a set of two CDs called *Fifty Years of Yodeling*, which features various other vocals and tracks. I visited with her in Lubbock several years ago and she seemed to enjoy giving hints and suggestions to help novices learn to yodel. Many of her early recorded tunes were tributes to Patsy Montana, another well-known yodeler. My brother and I, along with some other Beeville,

Texas, teenagers, learned to yodel singing a tune called "She Taught Me How to Yodel" back in the early 1950s. Multiple opportunities to hear this tune are available on YouTube by simply searching for it by name.

The Internet has more interesting sites on the subject of yodeling than you can imagine! These include suggestions on "how to yodel" as well as information about all aspects of yodeling. Among the tips in an article titled "How to Yodel" is a suggestion to "find a secluded area where your neighbors/family/lovers/children won't interrupt or become annoyed with you . . ." and then you can "Just go for it! Let it rip!"[2] It also suggests several ways to keep from sounding like a choking cat while learning to yodel. Another website claims that everyone can learn how to yodel, but I think that is probably too good to be true.

My own way to yodel is to practice while driving alone on a long car trip when cruising outside of towns or cities and when there are no vehicles driving alongside. Close the windows, turn on the air conditioner and maybe the radio or a yodeling CD, and—as they say, "Let 'er rip!" I seriously doubt that my marriage would have lasted 63 seconds (let alone 63 years) had I practiced yodeling when I was not alone in the car. But yodeling can certainly enliven a long, lonely car trip if there are no passengers within earshot!

Seriously, though, yodeling can be a very beautiful art form. Many examples of yodeling can be found on YouTube, Wikipedia, and other sites on the Internet, but Jimmie Rodgers' unique 1920s-style of yodeling is still my favorite. Someone once told me that all of Rodgers' yodeling was the same. It definitely was not! I have some records and CDs which claim to contain all of the 118 songs he recorded, most of which he wrote himself. A few have no yodeling at all, some begin and end with a yodel, while others have extensive yodeling passages. Some have yodeling at the end of nearly every phrase. Some are the classic, "O lee oh lay hee O," but others vary depending on required musical beats and fill-in sounds. There are sad yodeling sounds, as well as happy ones. In my opinion, all Jimmie Rodgers' yodeling fits the style of the music in which it is performed. *That* is one of the many factors that make him so special.

An outgrowth of this study of Rodgers' songs was the realization that he didn't sing to or about the same girl in his songs. There was Thelma, Susie Jane, "little girl," Katy Brown, Sadie Mae, Carolina Sunshine Girl, Mama, Good Mama, and on and on. Jimmie Rodgers got around to naming names of women who allegedly "done him wrong." I guess all those experiences made him want to yodel more!

One last observation: good yodeling requires practice, skill, a good voice, and an ear for music. In my opinion, the notion that *anyone* can learn to yodel with sufficient practice is WRONG! The other, more important requirement for learning to yodel is the ability to "throw" one's voice into the falsetto range appropriately and well. I know from experience that is a skill that is difficult to attain. Then some people, such as my brother Bill, can just naturally yodel beautifully—on the first try!

This brings us to the mention of singing as a melodious sound. Singing *can* be beautiful, *or* it, too, can be deadly awful. Musical training usually creates a better result, but the primary necessity for producing good singing is a good clear, musical voice without too much vibrato. I remember hearing a woman who occasionally sang in church back in Refugio, Texas, whose voice had such a vibrato that it made me want to get up and run down the road to get away. A tone MUST be "on pitch" to sound good—no matter what style of music is being sung. Sometimes renditions of well-known melodies such as the national anthem may or may not be recognizable as the singer seeks to personalize the performance.

Certain types of music require more musical training than others. For example, classical music contains more musical nuances than are required for what we call "country" or "western" music. The musical scores are more complicated in that type of music, which requires more skill on the part of the singer to make it sound good. The voice quality has to be "right" for the type of music. Instrumental accompaniment is a crucial part of the entertainment experience. Good "back-up" enhances a singer's performance!

In singing all types of music, from classical to popular to folk and country, or to hip hop and rap, it takes skill to enunciate lyrics so that the words can be understood. (Actually, some modern lyrics might be better if NOT understood!) It takes skill to vary the volume of the music, changing as required from loud to soft or whatever. Some voices sound wonderful no matter what type of music is being sung, and some voices simply do not.

Perhaps the biggest change in the way performers make their musical sounds is the modern use of technology. No longer is it necessary that a singer or performer be skilled at "projecting" their music to the back of the auditorium. They just turn up the volume on amplifiers as big as houses! It takes true skill, however, to "project." Back in the 1950s, I remember seeing and hearing Mary Martin perform as "Peter Pan." Our seats were near the back of the huge auditorium, but *without* a microphone or other amplifying device, we heard every syllable and every note that Ms. Martin sang. THAT was skill and talent, in my opinion!

Many are the ballads and songs associated with people working on the railroad, on the sea, and in other places. Here is a passage "lifted" from the stories of Pat Reagan in the book we wrote called *Some Were Cowboys:*

> One of the most beautiful sights and sounds I have ever been blessed to observe happened when we were takin' a big herd of . . . calves across one pasture and maybe even across a second one . . . and after awhile one of the cowhands would start singin' in Spanish. He might be at the front of the herd, or he might be at the tail end of the herd. And then another picked up what they called "second" so it would harmonize with the one that started the song and then after awhile somebody picked up a "tercero" or third and the three of them would be harmonizin'. I have seen it where there would be two sets of singers—one in the

> front of the herd, one in the back of the herd, and the people ridin' along the middle of the herd, might have been listenin' to one singer out of one end or two singers on the other, but still the harmonizin' was pretty. . . .[3]

Melodious sounds are everywhere if we just look for them! This is definitely not a case of "one size fits all." There are festivals and concerts in all sorts of venues. Music fills our lives in all sorts of ways, and it is an integral part of the folklore of all groups. We in Texas are blessed with many ways to make good sounds and enjoy the results.

Endnotes

1. Janet McBride. Insert for CD. *50 Years of Yodeling with Janet McBride.* CD Baby, 2009.
2. "How to Yodel." http://www.wikihow.com/Yodel, accessed 02-27-2017.
3. Pat Reagan (as told to Jean G. Schnitz). *Some Were Cowboys.* Xlibris Corporation, 2009. 76.

Bulldog Pep Squad.

BOOSTING THE EDEN BULLDOGS

by Margaret A. Cox

Football mania is sure to strike most any small Texas town in early Autumn, and the good folks of Eden, Texas (pop. 2000) always tapped into that energy to celebrate their team—the Eden Bulldogs—during the 1950s of my memory. I'll never forget those cool evenings in October as the full moon rose over the horizon, and the aroma of burning leaves filled the air. It was a magical prelude. Everyone hoped the Bulldogs would defeat the rival team one more time.

The goal posts, festooned with crepe-paper streamers, stood ready at each end of the field. The blue and white for the Bulldogs flapped merrily in the breeze, and the rival team's colors waved back. These goal post streamers acted as magnets to youngsters who delighted in pulling and playing with them during lulls in the action on the field. The streamers were seldom in pristine condition by the end of the game, when many raced to see who could pull down and wrap themselves with the most crepe paper.

As game time was approaching, the team gathered in the Field House for last-minute instructions from the coach. Band members, resplendent in their royal blue military-style uniforms, took their places on the metal stadium seats. And twenty-four members of the girls' pep squad, of which I was a member, filed in and seated themselves next to the band. On the ground below, the three majorettes pranced and twirled their batons, and the four cheerleaders began leading the group in yells for victory. Meanwhile, local fans filled the rest of the seats in the grandstand, as the seats on the other side of the field were filling up with rival boosters. At last everyone was ready for the game to begin.

Now, I'd like to say something about pep squad uniforms, because that leads to an amusing story. We always traditionally wore royal blue skirts and white tops, until one year when some style-leaders convinced everyone that slim, grey wool jumpers with white blouses would be nice for a change. Many of our mothers rolled their eyes, knowing that the jumpers would not be flattering to many of our short, plump, tall, or skinny bodies. But the grey jumpers prevailed. So, we were wearing the jumpers when we took our usual place marching behind the band at halftime.

The Band Director, who always devised our intricate routines, outdid herself when Eden played against the Paint Rock Indians in 1955. She had the entire ensemble enter the field in Indian pow-wow fashion, patting our mouths and bobbing our heads while chanting: "Hi-ya Ya-ya, Beat 'em, Beat 'em!" Just picture this: first came the band, with tubas and drums, then the majorettes with batons, cheerleaders with megaphones, and twenty-four pep squad girls in grey jumpers with white loafers and triple-roll bobby sox. As we came bobbing onto the field a loud burst of laughter came from the stands. And a pep squad member wailed: "Ohhh no, that was my mo—ther!" Everyone got the giggles and wobbled in the middle of the field. It was only the steady beat of the drum that got us back in step and off the field with some dignity.

The surprise halftime entertainment was quickly forgotten as we watched the team return to the field. Since now was the time to sing our school anthem, everyone became serious and stood with their hands over their hearts. The team paused in mid-field, holding their helmets in respect, as we all sang:

> Ole Eden High, Ole Eden High.
> We'll stand as one in rain or shine.
> Each night and day we'll always say,
> You're the best school in this land,
> Ole Eden High!

Afterwards, we remained standing while the rival team sang their anthem, and then the shrill whistle of the referee signaled the kick-off and the second half of the game got under way.

If by chance the Bulldogs won their game, all pandemonium broke out afterwards. A spontaneous parade was formed, and everyone joined in the march to the downtown square. Following the beat of the drum, we chanted: "We won! We won! We won, by golly we won! We've done it before. We'll do it some more. We won, by golly we won!" At the tail end of the parade were the young children, many bedecked with remnants of the streamers yanked from the rival team's goal posts.

An exciting perk of being a Bulldog Booster was being allowed to ride the school bus to all the out-of-town games. In 1956, it took at least four buses to transport the team, the band with their instruments, and the entire pep squad. The Bulldogs vied against such teams as the Junction Eagles, the Melvin Bulldogs, the May Tigers, the Bangs Dragons, the Early High School Longhorns, as well as the Menard Yellowjackets, the Rochelle Hornets, the Blanket Tigers, the Richland Springs Coyotes, and Bronte. Most of these were small schools with a class B ranking, as were the Eden Bulldogs. The bus rides were jolly fun. We entertained each other and the patient driver by running through the entire gamut of our school yells, then broke into round after round of "Row Your Boat," "Are you Sleeping, Brother John?", and the "Stars and Stripes" parody: "Be kind to your web footed friends, for the duck may be somebody's mother." We might have even added "99 Bottles of Beer on the Wall," if we grew bored with the other options and it was a really long bus ride.

After three fun years with the pep squad, I was elected a cheerleader for the 1956 football season. Only senior girls were chosen in those years, and we didn't even have to try out or show off our athletic ability first. For that, I was very grateful. Our team of cheerleaders included long-time classmates, Margaret Rose Jesse, Clarene Lollar, and Lois McDonald, and we spent all summer getting ready for football season. After learning of the cheerleader camp at SMU taught by Lawrence Herkimer, only two of us chose to attend: the two Margarets, aka Meg and Margo.

Meg was 5′2″, and I, Margo, am 5′8″. At the camp we met people from all over Texas, and some of the ones from large cities looked as though they had been cheerleaders forever. There were teams of four, six, and eight, all in color-coordinated workout clothes. We learned so many new things from the esteemed Mr. Herkimer, but we really faced a challenge on the final day. Each team was required to stand in the middle of a huge gym, and lead a cheer for all the hundreds of other cheerleaders. Meg and I survived that challenge, and after that, the thought of facing the Eden Boosters would be a "piece of cake!"

SMU Cheerleading School, 1956.

Upon returning from the cheerleader camp, Meg and I shared many new yells and costume ideas with Clarene and Lois. For instance, we all agreed that having white corduroy circle skirts lined with blue and white polka dots would be grand. The skirts struck just below our knees as was the style of the period, but in our routines we twirled around often to show off those "wicked" blue polka dots. White sweaters and white shoes and socks completed our fashionable ensembles. We were all set to roar into the new season with knowledge and style.

Bulldog Cheerleaders.

We cheerleaders discovered that we were responsible for so much more than just leading yells. For instance, we strung the streamers on the goal posts before each home game, with a little help from some friends with a ladder. And, we planned the Thursday pep rallies to boost team spirit. Often the rallies were held in the school gym, with the band, plenty of yells, and speeches by the coaches, the team co-captains, Superintendent Sanders, and other boosters. Other rallies were held on the town square, where wood was piled up for bonfires. Once, we even placed an effigy of a rival team member on the bonfire, and after band music, speeches and yells, we joined hands and danced around the fire. Then we got serious and sang "Ole Eden High," our beloved school anthem. Now, that was a fun evening, but I'm not sure if the extra spirit prompted a win of the Friday night game or not.

Boy, did we have some great cheers! We learned them from previous generations of cheerleaders, and handed them down to others. Our team compiled at least forty familiar yells, and Meg typed them up to have for posterity. We passed out copies to all members of the pep squad. Here's an example of a cheer with a Texas flavor:

> Wild & Wooly, Wild & Wooly,
> Bust a bronc, Beat a Bully,

Hootin', Tootin', Cotton shootin',
We're the Team that does the Rootin'
Zip, Bang, Eden!

Another popular yell was a real tongue-twister. It sounds like it must have been handed down from the Flapper era of the 1920s. We repeated it three times, each time louder and faster than the last. Once I finally learned the rhythm, I haven't been able to get it out of my head these past sixty years.

Iddle-sca-diddle, Beat'n-Bot'n-Wo-do-sca
Deet'n-Dot'nWah-Dot'n Chew!
Bulldogs! Bulldogs! Go right through!

We had many other yells, but I have only the words for a few written down.

As football season of 1956 drew to a close, all the team members and the spirit boosters were honored at the traditional Football Awards Banquet, held in the school gym. Letter jackets were presented to the boys for a season well-played by the coaches and the school Superintendent, Howard Sanders. Of course, everyone had the opportunity to wear their fanciest duds: many of the girls chose ballerina-length strapless formals, and the boys wore suits and ties. The school Lunch Room ladies cooked and served our feast. After that night, we cheerleaders hung up our megaphones. We shifted our attention to other things, such as our school studies to prepare us for life beyond Eden High School. Sadly, the Bulldog Booster days were no more, but they live on in my memories, as well as through the stories told by those of us who experienced them.

Cheering on the crowd at a game.

The Walls penitentiary looks much the same today as it did in this 1947 photo. Located just two blocks from the Huntsville city square, the red brick fortress was meant to separate convicts from the townsfolk (City of Huntsville Walker County Treasures photo).

REFRAIN FROM PRISON: HOW THE TEXAS PRISON MUSIC PROGRAM CONNECTED THE INCARCERATED AND "THE FREE"

by Ruth Massingill, Mel Strait, and Emily Jones

For more than fifty years, music played a pivotal role in bridging the chasm between the worlds of the Texas incarcerated and "the free." Beginning in the 1930s, musicians in prison bands played on national radio, performed in front of live audiences at public events, and entertained dignitaries and community groups inside the prison walls in Huntsville.

The Texas Prison Music Program facilitated social exchanges between prisoners and the general public, provided creative outlets for the convicts, and was a public relations bonanza for the Texas Department of Criminal Justice (TDCJ). The program was created in response to a national social shift from a focus on punishment to an emphasis on rehabilitation for prisoners. In Texas, the Prison Music Program is a significant aspect of the state's history of incarceration, as well as an integral part of its lore. This paper summarizes highlights of the Texas Prison Music Program and explores how that music traversed the prison walls, connecting the inmates and the free world.

From Silence to Song in Texas Prisons

The Texas prison system was established in the mid-1800s, with Huntsville as the base. During those early years, no musical expression of any kind was allowed. Inmates were even prohibited from singing while working. After the Civil War, prison administrators began some rehabilitation initiatives, which included allowing prisoners interactions such as harmonizing while working in the prison farm fields. By the early 1900s, music was being used by many prisons across the country as a diversion for inmates. Military-style marching bands and classical orchestras were popular inside the prisons, and often performed for community events.[1]

Texas prison reform with a focus on rehabilitation began in the early 1930s. The prison's general manager, Lee Simmons, was tasked with improving the Texas Prison System's brutal public image. Although not adverse to punitive methods inside the walls, Simmons was an expert in public relations who saw the value in providing public entertainment as a way to shape the message the public received about prison life. One of his most successful efforts was the Texas Prison Rodeo, which initially included the existing prison orchestra (all white males), but expanded to include the "Cotton-pickers Glee Club," made up of African-American men, and was soon followed by female inmate bands.[2] Simmons saw the rodeo as a "tonic for hard times" in a community where economic hardship and long workdays were routine for members of the free community as well as for inmates.[3]

The popularity of talented inmates and celebrity prisoners expanded the prison music programs and assured public support. National radio broadcasts and public performances around the state generated public enthusiasm beyond Simmons' expectations. By 1940, the rodeo was attracting tens of thousands to the Sunday performances every fall, leading to construction of an arena that could accommodate about 30,000 fans.[4]

In the 1960s, George Beto, then director of the Texas Department of Corrections, advocated for a school district for inmates, and was also determined to build a strong music program in the prison. Beginning in 1962, the prison bands' new music director, Dr. Harley Rex, developed musical groups that thrived into the 1980s, with assistance from more than a dozen band and choir directors. Rex remembers he was instructed to quickly create bands and choirs on each of the sixteen prison units. "We had 5,000 inmates at the end of my second year in the music program—the largest in the world," Rex recalls.[5] The Wynne Unit in particular developed a reputation for having the best bands in the prison system.

Other states, such as California and New Jersey, also established inmate music programs, but the Texas program was more visible outside the prison walls due to the highly popular prison rodeo, where penitentiary bands entertained and put a positive public face on redemption for convicted felons.[6]

From Inmate Amusement to Public Spectacle

Beginning in the 1930s, the Texas Prison Rodeo offered spectators a chance to interact with inmates in a safe yet thrilling venue. At first, the rodeo was held on the prison baseball field to entertain inmates and employees, but the event quickly became a tourist attraction for free-world citizens.

An early rodeo news release promised, "The Texas Prison System will give to the public something just a little out of the ordinary in the area of amusement and entertainment."[7] The rodeo was held every Sunday in October, and by 1935 about 25,000 citizens came to see prisoners perform daring stunts and to hear convict bands perform. At the height of its popularity, the rodeo even travelled to Dallas for an eight-day run at the Texas State Fair in the summer of 1950.[8]

Not surprisingly, transporting the entire rodeo to Dallas for more than a week of performances was a controversial and complicated undertaking. With elaborate security measures—both during travel and while on the fairgrounds—200 guards, matrons, and convicts made the trek without incident. Advance ticket sales for the convict rodeo were a record-breaking $30,000.[9]

From its early days, popular free-world musical acts were booked for the rodeo in addition to inmate musicians. It was the rodeo that really brought the musical talents of the inmates to public acclaim. Prisoners were eager to participate in the rodeo. "It was one of the few ways to get positive feedback . . . and to feel like a free person for a few hours," comments prison rodeo historian Mitchel Roth.[10]

The fifty-member prison jazz band was an especially prestigious group that always had a prime spot at the rodeo. Other inmate musical acts played on a flatbed trailer at the entrance to the rodeo arena. Musical genres ran the gamut from gospel to Country and Western to Latino to popular tunes of the day. The featured free-world musicians performed on a revolving stage in the middle of the arena.[11]

The list of free-world musicians who performed at the rodeo is a litany of the most popular artists of the time, ranging from Eddy Arnold and Curly Fox to Jimmy Dean, Dolly Parton, Willie Nelson, George Strait, and Johnny Cash. Cash's experience at the Texas Prison rodeo in 1959 gave him the idea to perform in other prison settings, most notably San Quentin and Folsom. Many convicts believed Cash had served hard time, but in fact he had never been a prison inmate. However, his affinity with prison culture led him to become an advocate for inmate rights.[12]

Riding the Radio Waves Out of Prison

Music created by prison bands flowed across the penitentiary walls from 1938 until 1944 during weekly broadcasts of "Thirty Minutes Behind the Walls," a wildly successful radio show that boasted as many as seven million listeners at the height of its popularity. The initial broadcast of "Thirty Minutes" in March of 1938 was the first time a prisoner was heard on radio.[13]

"Thirty Minutes" was broadcast across North America by Clear-Channel Radio station WBAP in Ft. Worth from the all-male Walls penitentiary in downtown Huntsville. Programming included interviews with state and prison officials as well as music by inmates. The original music director for the program was Jack Purvis, a talented jazz trumpet player who lost his freedom due to a propensity for robbery. For "Thirty Minutes," Purvis wrote the show's theme song as well as other original compositions, led the musicians during on-air shows, and trained many of the performers. Inmates were completely in charge of the broadcast, including publicity, production, and performance.[14]

From the standpoint of the prison officials, the program had two purposes: 1) to entertain and inform inmates in the Texas prisons, and 2) to serve as a public relations tool to develop a more favourable public image of the prison system, which was beset by news reports of escapes, beatings, and gunfights in the prison.[15] The musical acts were interspersed with self-serving speeches by prison officials and interviews with inmates about prison making them better people. The public was fascinated—this early reality show was the first to present information about criminals after they were imprisoned. The popular reception of "Thirty Minutes," which aired Wednesday nights at 10:30, was a surprise to WBAP, which had simply been looking for a public-service program to fill its late-night schedule.

The early inmate performances were only male musicians, but in 1940 the show introduced The Goree All-Girl String Band, one of the first all-female Country and Western musical groups.[16] It is widely believed the idea for an all-girls string band was conjured up by inmate Reable Childs. Childs was convicted in 1936 in the fatal shooting of her husband and received a twenty-five-year sentence. Although it was a gory crime, Childs was respected inside the prison by her fellow inmates and those in authority. She is said to have come up with the idea for a female band after seeing how male musicians received special privileges and sometimes were granted early paroles. "We could sing our way out of prison," she said. "We could be better than those men."[17]

She was right on both counts. The Goree Girls, who taught themselves to play and sing, quickly became one of the most recognized bands in the prison system. Male admirers sent candy, money, flowers and marriage proposals. The number of fan letters to "Thirty Minutes" increased from 32,000 in 1939 to 100,000 the year after The Goree Girls joined the show.[18]

The band also travelled to perform outside the prison. Often they would play more shows than a professional free-world Country band. However, they were always in Huntsville every Wednesday to perform live and do a radio show on "Thirty Minutes." Shortly after their first appearance on the radio show, The Goree Girls were featured at the Texas Prison Rodeo, where they "stopped the show."[19] Their popularity helped accomplish their principal goal—early release from prison. The configuration of the band was constantly changing as members left to return to the free world.

The Goree Girls reached an appreciative local and national audience with "Thirty Minutes Behind the Walls" (TDCJ Media Services photo).

Broadcasting by WBAP continued until about 1948, and then the radio show moved to KPRC in Houston, which aired the program into the early 1950s. The Goree Girls continued to perform and the male groups expanded to include more African American and Latino inmates.[20]

Community Groups Interacted with Prisoners

"Thirty Minutes Behind the Walls" was a stage show as well as a radio broadcast. Each Wednesday, hundreds of outsiders entered The Walls prison to watch the inmates sing and play in person before the show was broadcast. Some travelled great distances to see the performers they had heard on the radio. Attendance typically averaged 300–400, with as many as 900 for especially popular shows.[21]

A long-running favourite for the radio show—and for the Prison Rodeo—was an inmate group called the Rhythmic Stringsters, which was formed years before the rodeo and provided vaudeville-style entertainment at special events inside the prison. The band was known for performing its own compositions as well as popular tunes.[22]

The prison and the community of Huntsville were inextricably linked. In a mid-century archival photo, local Kiwanis members dressed in zebra-striped prison garb pose before entering The Walls dining room for a luncheon meeting, where music was provided by the prison orchestra.[23]

From bankers to college professors, Kiwanis members dressed as prisoners in this 1953 photo to attend a meeting inside The Walls dining room where they were entertained by inmate musicians (TDCJ Media Services photo).

Recently, recordings by outsiders and inmates were found on old reel-to-reel tapes in the museum archives. Greg Gathright, a former choir director in the prison music program, identified a gospel quartet from the Greater Zion Baptist Church that requested instrumentation for several acapella songs the quartet had recorded. In a cooperative musical undertaking, Gathright worked with inmates in the Wynne Unit to provide the instrumental music for the final recording.[24]

Prison Bands Performed at Community Events

Not only did community groups traverse prison walls to interact with inmates, prison bands also took road trips to perform at various community events. In 1940, the Texas Prison Board agreed to allow some of the "Thirty Minutes" musical acts to perform at venues outside the prison. Popular bands such as the Rhythmic Stringsters and the Goree Girls began to play at festivals, state fairs, fiddle contests, homecoming celebrations, and local rodeos that frequently took them on the road. Music dissolved the barriers and humanized the prisoners in the public mind. For the prisoners, this was a chance to be admired, to eat better food, and to see the world beyond the walls.[25]

Despite some officials' concerns about taking prisoners on the road, inmates did not push their luck. "It was a privilege to be able to get out and play," Gathright explains. "The inmates didn't want to mess up that privilege."[26] The prison musicians were under guard at all times. A long-time Huntsville area resident remembers prison bands playing during festivals in her hometown of Trinity, Texas, a small settlement about twenty miles from Huntsville. "The bands were really good. We would take my mother, and she would sit and listen to them all day. Of course, there were guards everywhere."[27]

The prison board considered curtailing the travel schedule, but enthusiastic letters poured in from communities where the bands performed, so the trips were allowed until the beginning of U.S. involvement in WWII, when they were discontinued. After the war, however, this ban was lifted, and the Goree Girls and the Rhythmic

Stringsters again travelled to perform at various events until about 1968.[28]

Celebrity Sojourns Behind the Walls

Performing in Texas Music Program venues made inmates celebrities within the prison and earned them admiration from free-world audiences, but some convicts were well known as entertainers before they landed in prison. Huddie Ledbetter, better known as "Lead Belly," was already a popular professional musician when he went to prison for murder in 1918. In the Sugarland Unit, he was allowed on Sundays to perform for both inmates and officials. He is well known for composing and singing a song to Texas Governor Neff pleading for clemency, which Neff promised—and granted—before he left office.[29]

Another talented musician who sang his way out of prison—temporarily—was James "Iron Head" Baker, a habitual criminal who impressed John A. Lomax, curator of folk songs for the Library of Congress. In 1936, Lomax was traveling to Southern penitentiaries and remote communities to record African-American folk songs. He convinced Texas prison authorities to release Baker into his custody to be a driver and companion in Lomax's cross-country musical search. Unfortunately, Baker committed more crimes and ended his life in prison.[30]

Juanita Dale Phillips, the infamous stripper who used the show name of Candy Barr, was one of the Goree Girls during her stint in prison for drug possession in the early 1960s. During her three years at Goree, Barr became one of the most popular entertainers at the rodeo, out-performing most of the Hollywood and Nashville stars headlining the prison rodeo.[31]

Harley Rex remembers working with Candy Barr while she was a prisoner. "She asked me to teach her a song so she could go out to the rodeo and sing with the Goree Girls," Rex says. "She wanted to sing 'Fever.' She was a gem to work with—smart and good looking."[32] Barr was a model prisoner, working hard to accumulate points to be eligible for parole. "I worked in the sewing room, the library and commissary, and I performed in the prison rodeo," Barr is quoted as saying. "I even sang in both the Protestant and Catholic choirs."[33] After her early release in 1962, Barr became the first prison musician to return as a free-worlder to perform at the rodeo, where she was a star attraction throughout the 1960s.[34]

Rock star David Crosby served time at the Wynne Unit in 1986. Like many of the musicians who were in prison at that time, Crosby was busted on a drug charge. Gathright remembers Crosby, who was in the Wynne Unit band. "Like all prisoners, he was assigned to work. Crosby worked in the mattress unit in the mornings, and in the afternoons he was assigned to the band," Gathright says.

Crosby played in several concerts inside the prison. "We liked to play on the yard anytime there was a holiday—Fourth of July, Veteran's Day, Memorial Day," Gathright explains. "A chance to play for the inmates was a status thing."[35] Rex recalls that even though Crosby was a proficient guitar player, he wanted to play cymbals in the prison band. According to Rex, he was pretty good on the cymbals, but he never played in the prison rodeo. Crosby's attorneys beat the charges against the rock star, and he was released before the October rodeo. Crosby is said to have commented that playing with the prison band while he was behind bars made him "happy and fostered creativity."[36]

Music Transformed Both Inmates and Public Opinion

According to Dr. Harley Rex, many of the inmates in the music program used their practice time as a sort of therapy. Rex says that as the inmates began to feel at ease with him and the rest of the musicians, they started to talk about events in their lives that resulted in incarceration. It was this experience that led Rex to develop a music therapy program at Sam Houston State University, where he was a professor in the music department. Today the university program is accredited by the National Association of Schools of Music and approved by the American Music Therapy Association.[37]

The incentives inherent in the prison's music program had many positive results, Rex and Gathright agree. Inmates had to have and maintain "clean disciplinary records" to participate. Infractions were not tolerated. Gathright remembers a bass player, "Robert," who was caught with marijuana and was immediately dropped from the band the day before a scheduled performance. "There was no time to replace him, so we did the show without a bass player." But, most inmate musicians treasured their positions in the bands. Gathright says many of the band members were doing a lot of time for serious crimes such as murder. Those prisoners were serving life sentences and weren't expecting to be released. "Being in the music program was a means of escape—they could play music and feel a sense of normalcy," Gathright says.[38]

Without a doubt, playing music was a transformative experience for many inmates. Having the status and privilege of being band members allowed them to take pride in their abilities and to be seen by the public as human. The Goree Girls' performances at the rodeo and on "Thirty Minutes" not only transformed the way the public viewed female inmates, it changed the way the women were treated as prisoners. Their musical success changed their public image and often gave them a means to shorten their sentences.

The rodeo also proved to be a way for inmate musicians to generate money for the prisoners' E&R (education and recreation) Fund. In 1970, the bands started recording albums and selling autographed copies at the rodeo for $5 each. "We sold about 2,000 copies during every rodeo," Rex reports.[39] Copies of most of the albums are in the archives of the Texas Prison Museum and have been digitized to preserve the recordings.

From the standpoint of prison officials, the music program also had many external public relations advantages, transforming negative public opinion about prison operations and the value of rehabilitation. Occasional negative feedback such as pressure from church groups to not hold rodeo performances on Sundays and to bar notorious performers such as Candy Barr were outweighed by the general popularity of the shows.

Prisons Are Silent Once Again

However, despite these benefits, after more than five decades the prison rodeo was cancelled in 1986 due to decreasing revenues, lack of funds to refurbish the stadium in Huntsville, and legal concerns about injuries. At the same time, the music program was also dismantled as political and public support for such prisoner privileges waned and the criminal justice system moved once again toward a punishment mentality and "rehabilitation, the guiding principle of penology, [fell] into disrepute."[40] The music program's role as a rehabilitation tool was discounted, and the musical instruments and other equipment were donated or discarded.

The only sounds of live music in the prisons these days comes from the prison choirs singing during internal church services or graduation ceremonies. Opportunities for playing in the outside world are practically non-existent. Recently, though, some original recordings made by prisoner musicians have come to light and are being digitized and re-mastered by faculty at Sam Houston State University in cooperation with the Texas Prison Museum archivist to preserve the history of the days when refrains from prison were commonplace.

Conclusion

In Texas, the decades-long prison music program is a significant aspect of the state's history of incarceration. With each public success, music forged bridges across the great divide between community and prisoners, and made history while doing so. Various accounts of the Texas penal system make mention of the program. A movie dramatization about the all-women prison band, The Goree Girls, has been "in development" since 2008.[41] In 2013, a BBC producer went to Huntsville as part of her research for a feature radio program about the history of prison bands in several states.[42]

Those fifty-five years from 1931 to 1986 hold a lot of history and prison lore, not only for the town of Huntsville but also for the world of music. The Texas Prison Music Program was an integral part of the first prison rodeo, the first radio broadcast by a prison inmate, and the first all-female Country and Western band, just to name a few milestones. The story of the music program is a treasure trove of larger-than-life, bizarre events that reverberated across the prison walls, touching and transforming both the lives of inmates and "the free."

ENDNOTES

1. Caroline Gnagy. *Texas Jailhouse Music: A Prison Band History.* Charleston, SC: The History Press: 2016. 11–13.
2. Ibid. 15–22.
3. Mitchel P. Roth. Interview by Mel Strait and Ruth Massingill, October 29, 2016, Huntsville, Texas.
4. Mitchel P. Roth. *Convict Cowboys: The Untold History of the Texas Prison Rodeo.* Denton, Texas: University of North Texas Press, 2016. 45–52.
5. Harley Rex. Interview by Mel Strait and Emily Jones, November 8, 2016, Huntsville, Texas.
6. Gary Younge. "Prisoner Soul: The Huntsville Penitentiary Band." *The Guardian*, April 10, 2013. Available at: http://www.theguardian.com/music/2013/apr/10/prisoner-soul-huntsville-penitentiary-band.
7. Roth interview.
8. Roth. *Convict Cowboys.* 173–177.
9. Ibid.
10. Roth interview.
11. Gregory Gathright. Interview by Mel Strait and Ruth Massingill, November 18, 2016, Spring, Texas.
12. Roth. *Convict Cowboys.* 299–305.
13. Skip Hollandsworth. "O Sister, Where Art Thou?" *Texas Monthly,* 2003. Available at: http://www.texasmonthly.com/articles/o-sister-where-art-thou/.
14. Gnagy. 67–72.
15. Gary Brown. *Singin' a Lonesome Song: Texas Prison Tales.* Plano, Texas: Wordware Publishing, Inc., 2001. 200.
16. Hollandsworth.
17. Ibid.
18. Ibid.
19. Ibid.
20. Gnagy. 155–158.
21. Ibid. 77–80.
22. Ibid. 158–162.

23. Ruth Massingill, and Ardyth Sohn. *Prison City: Life with the Death Penalty in Huntsville, Texas.* New York: Peter Lang Publishing, Inc., 2007.
24. Gathright.
25. Gnagy. 126–130.
26. Gathright.
27. Susan Pynes. Interview by Ruth Massingill, December 23, 2016.
28. Gnagy. 160–162.
29. Ibid. 47–54.
30. Ibid. 54–58.
31. Brown. 49–61.
32. Rex.
33. Brown. 54.
34. Roth interview.
35. Gathright.
36. Gnagy. 167–169.
37. Rex.
38. Gathright.
39. Rex.
40. Lorna Rhodes. *Total Confinement: Madness and Reason in the Maximum Security Prison.* Berkley and Los Angeles, Calif.: University of California Press, 2004.
41. The Goree Girls. *Movie Insider*, (2008) Available at: http://www.movieinsider.com/m4304/goree-girls/.
42. Vivienne Perry (producer). *Prisoner Soul.* BBC Radio 4, Aired October 28, 2013. Accessed at: http://www.bbc.co.uk/programmes/b01rtzdx.

Huddie Ledbetter.

B

III. Life in Texas—As We Remember It

Melton Barker Productions Flyer.

OUR PRE-TEEN SILVER SCREEN DREAMS AND PIED-PIPER MELTON BARKER, AN ITINERANT FILMMAKER

by Robert J. (*Jack*) Duncan

In January of 1951, roving filmmaker Melton Barker came to McKinney to make a kiddie film. Barker, who lived in Texas, traveled from town to town making short films in more than half the states in the Union, films that were somewhat similar to the *Our Gang* comedies made by Hal Roach in Hollywood. Roach's films featured child actors George "Spanky" McFarland, Carl "Alfalfa" Switzer, and William "Buckwheat" Thomas; those films later were syndicated for television under the series title *The Little Rascals*. In about seventeen years of production, 140,000 children interviewed, or auditioned, for parts in Roach's Hollywood *Our Gang* films, while only 176 appeared in the films, and just forty-one were put under contract.[1] Melton Barker was quoted as saying, "It took Hal Roach about 10 days to shoot what I do in a day."[2]

Unlike Hal Roach, Barker made essentially the same film over and over, changing only the location and the child actors. The same script was used. Even the same title was used; it was *The Kidnappers Foil*. Barker didn't pay the child actors, of course; their parents paid *him*. Film archivist and historian Dwight Swanson says, "Melton Barker was the most widely traveled and long lasting of the itinerant film producers, returning again and again to his series *The Kidnappers Foil* for more than four decades."[3]

Melton Barker had been making films for almost two decades when he came to McKinney in January of 1951. (I now know that he had made a previous such film in McKinney in 1935.) I had celebrated my ninth birthday just a few weeks before Barker arrived that January. My mother probably had heard "through the grapevine" that a film would be made in McKinney and that the director would be recruiting local children for the cast. I suppose that she heard it "by word of mouth" because my family did not subscribe to the McKinney newspaper at that time.

In any event, at 4:00 P.M. on Friday, January 12, 1951, my mother and I, along with scores of other local kids and their parents, met with Melton Barker in the big room on the second floor of the McKinney firehouse, next door to the city hall on Kentucky Street, a block south of the downtown square. Barker spoke to the group for a few minutes, then he and one or two of his assistants registered kids to appear in the film that would be made a few weeks later. Mom paid the registration fee of one dollar, got a written agreement that also served as a receipt, and received a four-page flyer about the project that Barker gave everyone. I felt like I was Hollywood bound—figuratively speaking, of course.

Actually, I don't recall having any Hollywood aspirations, and as far as I know the other kids didn't either. I think we all realized from the start that there was a small fee for being cast in the film, that the film would be made strictly for local consumption, that it probably would be shown just a time or two in a local movie theater, and *that* would be that. But it was a fun thing to participate in, and it was something that was new and unheard of, at least by us. Remember, this was several years before families had their own movie cameras to film family vacations and holiday celebrations. In fact, it was *way* back—when almost no one had a television set. It is hardly an exaggeration to say that we lived in another world back then.

Dwight Swanson says that Melton Barker was "certainly one of the most prolific itinerant film producers."[4] He also says, "Itinerant filmmaking was largely a small-town phenomenon."[5] Barker occasionally made films in big cities; for example, he made films in Dallas, San Antonio, Little Rock, and Memphis. However, he was much more likely to select a small town than a big city. Fewer than ten percent of his films were made in big cities. No one knows exactly how he decided upon which towns to visit. He shot a great many of his films in Texas, and that probably was a matter of convenience and economics, since he lived in North Texas or East Texas throughout his long filmmaking career.

The McKinney film was shot in probably just a couple of days within the next few weeks; much of it was filmed next to the band-stand in McKinney's Finch Park. As I recall, there were still a few very large uprooted trees and also many still-standing trees that had been stripped of their branches by a terrible tornado that had hit McKinney in the spring of 1948. The trees made a grotesque backdrop that the cameraman probably tried to avoid. Scores of McKinney kids participated. Most kids were in many of the group scenes, and each one had at least one line of dialogue and at least one close-up. Just like in Hollywood films, the story-line was shot out of sequence, to be edited later. Before each brief scene was filmed, Barker told us our few words of dialogue.

Between takes in McKinney's Finch Park.

I remember wearing suspenders and a pair of blue jeans with conspicuous patches on the knees. My mother had painted freckles on my face and used a black grease pencil or crayon to make it appear that I was missing one or two front teeth. I wore a cheap dime-store black derby hat that I believe was left over from my homemade Halloween costume of a few months before.

Tommy Duff and Jack Duncan in costume.

Swanson says, "The life of an itinerant filmmaker was difficult and tedious, resembling the work of a traveling salesman more than a creative artist."[6] Mel Barker's procedure worked like this: he would place an ad in a town's local newspaper, and the ad often included a short application form. Frequently an article about the project would also appear in the paper. Then Barker would meet with parents and their kids to "sell" them on the project and get a small initial payment. Barker called it an interview or an audition, but rarely—if ever—was a child rejected if his parents were willing and able to pay the fee and if the child was cooperative. Barker would later collect a final payment of a few dollars when he started shooting the film.

The film was usually shot in a local park or some similar public place. Sometimes Barker developed the film in his hotel room, and sometimes he had a company in Dallas develop it for him. No copies were made. A few weeks later, after the film was developed and edited, it would be shown as a short-subject at a local movie theater, usually within a month or so after the filming. It was shown along with a regular feature-length film. Typically, virtually all of the kids who were in the film, their parents, and other family members would attend the premier showing. The film might be shown another time or two, and then the film reels were left with the theater. I suspect that Mel Barker had some kind of a beneficial financial arrangement with the local newspapers and theaters. Perhaps the theater paid for the newspaper ads in exchange for ownership of the finished film.

Usually about fifty to one hundred children appeared in a Barker film. Most of the kids were in many of the group scenes. Barker had two or three associates helping him during the filming. Swanson says: "The filmmaking process had been honed to maximum efficiency. The only impediment to this efficiency was the fact that Barker and his crew worked exclusively with children, many as young as three years old."[7]

Although more than sixty-five years have passed, I remember the experience fairly well. I still have the four-page flyer that was handed to my mother at that first meeting in the firehouse. I also

Rehearsing the London Bridge scene.

have the two receipts that together account for the $4.50 fee. And I have those few snapshots that my mother took during the filming in McKinney's Finch Park.

On very few occasions in a few towns, a parent would claim that Barker's activities amounted to nothing more than a money-making scheme. Of course, no one was forcing that parent to let her (or his) child participate; it was completely optional. In a newspaper interview, the scam question came up. Barker replied: "I get that sort of thing [sometimes]. It usually comes from ignorant people who don't know what's involved. . . . If people follow through on this, I think they'll see it's legitimate. The kids get a big kick out of being in a movie, and besides, I work too hard for this to be a fake."[8]

In 2013, in an Internet blog about Melton Barker and his films, a man named John Wood wrote that when he was about seven years old, he auditioned at the Sooner Theater in Norman, Oklahoma, for a 1942 Barker film. John Wood wrote: "I was not picked for the film and now I know why. We could not afford to pay to be in the film. I always thought it was my lack of acting talent."[9]

Barker made hundreds of such films for over four decades—from 1933 to 1975—in towns in twenty-nine states, and those are just the ones that we know of so far. Frequently, he would return to the same town about once each decade, after a new crop of kids had emerged.

Barker's full name was Ennis Melton Barker. He was born in Dallas on February 14, 1903, to Doran Barker and Eva McIver Barker.[10] His mother was a native of Mississippi, and his father was a native Texan.[11] Melton was the youngest of four children; his siblings were Carrie, Cora, and Ernest.[12] Their parents had married in 1895 in Elkhart, Anderson County, Texas, before moving to Dallas several years later.[13] Early in life, Barker used his first name, Ennis, but in his itinerant filmmaking career, he used his middle name, Melton, so I am referring to him here as Melton—or Mel—Barker.

It is ironic that, although there are hundreds of ads and short articles about Barker in local newspapers that have become readily accessible in online databases within just the past few years, a great many of those ads and articles are identical or nearly identical. So, despite the plethora of different publications, not a lot of detailed information is known about Melton Barker himself.

Dallas city directories show that as early as 1921, when Barker was just eighteen, he was employed as a photographer by the James P. Simpson Company, a Dallas company that made on-screen local advertisements that were shown in movie theaters throughout Texas and in some surrounding states. For about a decade—the decade of the 1920s—Barker is listed in the Dallas city directories at the James P. Simpson Company in various job titles that range from photographer, chemist, and cameraman to department manager. Sometime between 1925 and 1928, Melton Barker married a young woman named Marian or Mariann, who was three years his junior.[14] In April of 1930, in the first few months of the Great Depression, James P. Simpson, Melton's employer, committed suicide.[15] The company itself may not have survived the Depression. In any case, Melton left the company in the early 1930s. Soon he became involved with live theater in Dallas, especially with one play in which there was a short movie film incorporated into the play. By 1933, Barker began his forty-three year career as an itinerant filmmaker. I suspect that the idea of becoming a roving filmmaker and being his own boss, especially during the Depression, held a lot of appeal for him.

Mel Barker often claimed, in print, that he had "discovered" the young child actor George "Spanky" McFarland. McFarland was from Denison, Texas, and he starred in Hal Roach's *Our Gang* and *The Little Rascals* kid comedies in Hollywood. Barker probably knew Spanky McFarland from his (Barker's) work at the Simpson Company. Spanky had been born in October of 1928. Two or three years later, he modeled children's clothing for a Dallas department store and appeared on billboards around Dallas and in print advertisements for Wonder Bread. In a newspaper interview in 1972—Barker's only known interview, by the way—he said that Spanky "was a little kid I used for bread and ice cream commercials."[16] Since both Barker and McFarland worked in advertising in Dallas simultaneously, it is possible, and perhaps even likely, that they did work together some. Barker supplied many newspapers with a photograph of himself holding young Spanky in his arms while standing in front of a Hal Roach truck. Although Barker apparently never filmed McFarland in any of his *Kidnappers Foil* films, he made the most of this connection with Spanky in promoting his own films. As Swanson pointed out, Barker frequently claimed that he had discovered Spanky McFarland "and said so at nearly every possible opportunity, even long after most of America had forgotten who McFarland was."[17]

Barker and one or two of his associates played the parts of the kidnappers in the films. The little girl character who was kidnapped in each film was conveniently named Betty Davis. Although her first name was spelled B-E-T-T-Y, rather than B-E-T-T-E, orally it sounded identical to the name of the contemporary adult Hollywood star, and that probably added a bit of glamor to the Barker film projects.

Beth White Stapleton of McKinney still remembers being cast in the 1935 film there. She says that at the audition, they asked her if she could cry. She cried. They asked if she could cry again. Beth replied that she could cry anytime. So they gave her the Betty Davis part—the role of the little kidnapped girl.[18]

Mel Barker shot a film in Newport, Arkansas, in 1938. The author of a 2011 history journal article about that film interviewed Ms. Metta Lynn Castleberry Crank in May of 2011. Little Metta Lynn, the daughter of a local dentist, was quite photogenic. She auditioned for the starring role of Betty Davis. She said that her father coached her by saying:

> "When they pick you up to kidnap you, I want you to scream and cry just like you were really being kidnapped. It doesn't hurt if you kick them, and hurt them or scratch them, I want you to just really do it." [She said,] So I did whatever my daddy told me to do. In fact, the man stopped. . . . and said, "Are you really all right or are you really afraid?" [The little girl very] calmly replied, "Oh, no, I'm fine."[19]

She told the interviewer in 2011 that she thought that her (method) acting had helped her get the part.

A few days later, young Metta Lynn Castleberry was in bed with the measles. When the word came that she had landed a starring role in the film, her mother got her out of bed and told her that she didn't have the measles anymore. In 2011, Metta Lynn recalled: "I still had a fever, and I was itching, oh, terribly so. If you ever see that movie and you see this little kid that is twitching all the time, that is what I was doing. She [her mother] told me absolutely not to scratch."[20] After the film was made, Metta Lynn suffered a relapse and was probably again confined to her bed. One wonders if any other kids contracted measles from being exposed to Metta Lynn during the shooting of the film.

In e-mail correspondence with Dwight Swanson in 2009, Laura Smith Legge said that she and her younger brother, Lance Smith, were in Barker's film in Cleveland, Mississippi, in 1972. She recalled:

> I remember Mr. Barker asking where the little red-headed curly haired girl was and someone

> said, "Here she is, right here," and he asked me to come over to him. So I walked over to where he was standing and he told me that he wanted me to introduce the movie! Well, I was ecstatic! Then he went on to say that he also wanted me to say "That's all folks" at the end of the movie. So I was in the very beginning by myself introducing the movie . . . during the movie I said the Mae West line ["Why don't you come up sometime and see me?"]. . . and I was at the very end closing the movie. Well, I was looking for an Oscar after all that![21]

Melton Barker was married and divorced at least four times.[22] On November 14, 1956, he married Carmon Ercell Ponder in Kaufman County, Texas, and that marriage lasted for nineteen years before ending in divorce.[23] The couple resided in Ennis, Texas, south of Dallas. There they owned and operated Punkin's Drive-In, a fast food restaurant, for two or three years, and probably lived in a house or trailer house either behind or beside the drive-in. Later the couple lived in a number of small towns in East Texas and North Central Texas: Athens, Atlanta, Pittsburg, Winnsboro, Lewisville, and Keller. In at least a couple of those towns, the couple operated, and perhaps owned—or owned an interest in—a movie theater. But fairly often Mel Barker would go back on the road to make films and leave Carmon to run the theater.

Barker had two trusted senior associates that worked with him. He also apparently allowed them to separately make some of *The Kidnappers Foil* films under the auspices of his company. They were William Dorsey Patton and George Wilt Sanderson, Jr. Most of their solo films were made in the early 1950s. Perhaps Barker was experimenting with making films in multiple towns simultaneously, or perhaps he was just trying to personally get "off the road."

Mel Barker may have been an alcoholic. If so, that may have some connection with his preference for a somewhat nomadic lifestyle. Of course, even if that is true, we don't know whether alcoholism was a contributing *reason for* why he liked being on the road or was a *result of* his being often on the road. We do know of one instance in 1940 in which Barker was convicted of driving while intoxicated in Mason City, Iowa, where he was making a film.[24] "Back in the day," as we now say, alcoholism was not considered a disease, as it is today; it was looked upon simply as a character flaw or personal weakness. In an Internet blog dated in early 2013, William Tienken recalled that he was in a Barker film that was made in Ottawa, Kansas, in the late 1960s. He said: "My most permanent memory is that I got a line wrong and the director cursing me. And I wasn't the only kid cursed at!"[25] Could this have been a drunken Barker?

As I mentioned earlier, Melton Barker made films in at least twenty-nine states. We know of just over a hundred of Barker's films that were made in Texas, and almost two hundred that were made in other states. There were likely a great many more than that. Only about twenty versions of *The Kidnappers Foil* are known to have survived. Some have been restored and can be viewed on the Internet.

The Social Security Death Index shows Keller, Texas, as Melton Barker's last residence. We know that he died in Meridian, Mississippi, in March of 1977, at 74 years of age. Some have speculated that Barker was on the road to make another film at the time of his death, and that may—or may not—have been the case. We do know that he made at least six films as late as 1975.

My friend Caroline Frick is an associate professor in the Radio-Television-Film Department at the University of Texas in Austin. Caroline has spent more than a decade doing research on Melton Barker and his unusual occupation of making the same film over and over. She has established a website on Barker and his films. Caroline has worked in film preservation at Warner Brothers, the Library of Congress, and the National Archives. She once said:

> I will always remember when I first saw a *Kidnappers Foil* film directed by Melton Barker. Although the original 35mm film had been transferred poorly to a VHS tape, I was

> immediately enamored by the chaotic exuberance of hordes of children performing for the camera—and, just as importantly, by the concerted effort to connect a so-called "amateur" production with Hollywood glamour. . . . The film's aesthetics? Quite rudimentary with a very difficult to understand soundtrack, but, at the same time, wholly reminiscent of the dozens and dozens of Hollywood produced children's short subjects that I had worked to preserve during my time in the Warner Bros. preservation department.[26]

Caroline restored a copy of Barker's *Kidnappers Foil.* It has been named to the National Film Registry, a high honor. Caroline said: "I don't know what Melton Barker would make of his films becoming a formal part of American film heritage, preserved by the Library of Congress and publicly shared with the world. But Barker's former stepson, Jim Ponder, wrote to say that he thinks 'Mel would have been very amused' by it all—and I believe that is high praise indeed!"[27]

Now back to early 1951 in McKinney. On March 13, the Ritz Theatre mailed out penny postcards saying that the kiddie movie would be shown (as a short-subject) on Tuesday, March 20, and Wednesday, March 21. Lots of McKinney folks went to the movies those two nights. My parents and I went. I think that my grandparents might have come to McKinney to go to the theater with us, but I really don't remember. I understand that the McKinney film has been lost to posterity. And that's too bad; it would have been fun to watch it again—at this late date.

One of the most telling and ironic facts about Melton Barker's life is that—despite the fact that he was married at least four times—as far as we know, he had no biological children. Some have said that he had no children because he had come to hate them! Maybe that aversion to kids was an occupational hazard.

Looking back from the twenty-first century, Barker's nomadic filmmaking career seems a rather quaint endeavor. However, for the tens of thousands of young participants, it was a folk practice that they undoubtedly shared with others for generations. The experience almost certainly affected them in a way that many of them probably will (or did) recall for the rest of their lives.

Endnotes

1. Caroline Frick. "Making Movies Here: The Legacy of Itinerant Filmmaker Melton Barker." *Communiqué*, Issue 04, 2009, p. 15, available online at: http://rtf.utexas.edu/sites/rtf.utexas.edu/files/attachments/alumni/communique-04.pdf. Accessed on October 27, 2013.
2. Owen Taylor. "Quiet on the Set!" *Delta Democrat-Times* (Greenville, Mississippi), Monday, May 15, 1972. 2.
3. Dwight Swanson. "'Wasn't That a Funny Thing That We Did?': Oral Histories of Itinerant Filmmaking." *The Moving Image*, Vol. 10, No. 1 (Spring 2010). 105.
4. Ibid. 102.
5. Ibid.
6. Ibid.
7. Ibid. 106.
8. Taylor. 2.
9. A message posted by John Wood on the Melton Barker and the Kidnappers Foil website, Community section, posted on March 1, 2013, available online at: http://www.meltonbarker.org/community/. Accessed on October 27, 2013.
10. Ennis Melton Barker's Application for a Social Security Account Number 461-32-1516; Issue State: Texas; Application Date: October 26, 1942; Melton spelled his father's first name as "Doran" on this document, while other documents have spelled it (or appear to have spelled it) as "Dorian," "Dorion," "Dorien," "Donon," or "Dorn."
11. United States Federal Census for 1930, Census Place: Dallas, Dallas County, Texas; Roll: 2319; Page: 20B; Enumeration District: 0083; Image: 898.0; FHL microfilm: 2342053.
12. United States Federal Census for 1900, Census Place: Elkhart, Anderson County, Texas; Roll: 1607; Page: 3A; Enumeration District: 0008; FHL microfilm: 1241607.
13. Texas, Select County Marriage Index, 1837–1965; Names: Dorion Barker and Eva McIver; Marriage Date: 12 Feb 1895; FHL Film Number 987144.

14. U.S. City Directories for Dallas, Texas, 1921, 1922, 1924, 1925, 1928, 1929, and 1930. She is also listed as Barker's wife on the 1930 U.S. Census.
15. "Dallas Man Found Shot Died Friday." *Corsicana Daily Sun* (Corsicana, Texas), Friday, April 11, 1930. 8.
16. Taylor. 2.
17. Swanson. 107.
18. Facebook posting by Beth White Stapleton's daughter, Anne Stapleton Skrabanek, on December 15, 2013, in response to Elizabeth Ann Duncan's posting on December 1, 2013.
19. All the information in this paragraph is from Robert D. Craig, "Melton Barker and 'The Kidnappers Foil'," *Stream of History* (Arkansas Historical Society), May, 2011, p. 17, available online at: http://www.meltonbarker.org/wp-content/uploads/2012/10/Melton-Barker-Newport-AR-7-6-11.pdf. Accessed on October 27, 2013.
20. Ibid.
21. Swanson. 108.
22. Besides Marian [or Mariann] (married between 1925 and 1928), Barker married Ruth Fitzgerald in 1936, Majel Penney in 1946 and Carmon Ercell Ponder in 1956.
23. Marriage license initially issued by Kaufman County, Texas, to Ennis Melton Barker and Carmon Ercell Ponder on November 11, 1956, and also showing that the marriage ceremony was conducted by C. E. Kelly, Justice of the Peace of Precinct # 1, on November 16, 1956; and Texas Divorce Index, 1968-2011, showing that Ennis M. Barker and Carmon E. Barker were granted a divorce in Tarrant County, Texas, on December 12, 1975.
24. "Melton Barker Fined on Drunk Driving Charge." *Mason City Globe-Gazette* (Mason City, Iowa), August 29, 1940. 8.
25. A message posted by William Tienken on the Melton Barker and the Kidnappers Foil website, Community section, posted on March 1, 2013, available online at: http://www.meltonbarker.org/community/. Accessed on October 27, 2013.
26. Caroline Frick. "In Search of Melton." December 12, 2012, Texas Archive of the Moving Image website, available online at: http://www.texasarchive.org/library/index.php?title=News:Caroline_Frick_Reflects_2012. Accessed on October 26, 2013.
27. Ibid.

THURSDAY AFTERNOON, SEPTEMBER 26, 1935

MELTON BARKER
Arrives on Coast to Produce a Kid Comedy in Gulfport and Biloxi.

Visiting relatives deep in the country sometimes called for rather rustic picnics.

VISITING IN THE 1930s

by W. Floyd Elliott

Now, looking back at my childhood growing up in the East Texas oil field, some of my fondest memories are those of my family and some aunts, uncles, and cousins loading up in cars and "going visiting." My maternal grandmother was the usual ringleader, deciding when, where and how. Her big Buick would be the lead car, and then probably ours and maybe another one—determined by whom all were going. Grandma never learned to drive, so after Grandpa Jernigan passed away in 1931, someone in the family always drove her—in *her* car—where she wanted to go. My dad was her favorite driver, as well as son-in-law, but if he wasn't going then Mother or Auntie would be her choice of driver. These visits were normally to see relatives, and for three or four days at a time. We took a lot of special food, gifts and other things, especially bedding for the kids to sleep on, what we called a pallet on the floor.

One of my favorite trips was to see the Hinkels. They lived a little way out of Carthage on a very rustic farm. The visits I remember extended from when I was a small boy of four or five and lasted until the last visit I remember when I was about twelve, at the beginning of World War II. Two or three times when we visited the Hinkels, he was operating his syrup mill. This was a special treat for the kids. I looked eye-to-eye with the old red mule that walked around in a circle that made the press squeeze the juice out of the ribbon cane. I wondered what the mule was thinking, but he or she never gave me a hint. It would be in the late fall, and the heat from the fire under the "cooking table vats" would feel very good.

I also enjoyed watching Mr. Hinkel work in his blacksmith shop. To me it was like watching an artist at work. He seemed so engrossed in the task at hand that you felt as if you needed to hold your breath while you watched. Each movement was so sure, precise, and accurate. As the result of the work emerged, you felt as if you had contributed. Mr. Hinkel also had a large woodworking shop where he made all of their furniture, as well as handles for tools and things like that. He also had a little sawmill where he cut timber into lumber, which he used to build things such as his house, barns, workshops, sheds, and pens. I think Mr. Hinkel must have made everything on that farm. When he was working on a project, you knew you were watching a master craftsman create a work of art.

Quilting was also a big thing at the Hinkels—she had a special room for sewing and quilting, with a quilting frame hanging from the ceiling which could be raised out of the way. Both of my grandmothers had a similar set-up in their homes, where the women sat around the frame, quilted, and talked (some might even call it gossiping). My Grandma Elliott had hers in her living room, while Grandma Jernigan had hers in her large master bedroom (with a small parlor for guests). All had a fireplace in the "quilting room," which made it cozy in cold weather. We kids would play under the quilting frame when bad weather forced us inside to the warmth of the snug space near the fireplace. Of course, occasionally we would get a little rowdy, but a quick kick from one of the women's feet down near us would usually quickly calm us down. Oh, those bygone days.

I'm sure the Hinkels had first names, but I never heard any. She always called him Mr. Hinkel and he always called her Mrs. Hinkel—as did our family. I always thought the Hinkels were related to the Jernigans, Elliotts or Griffins, since we visited them as other relatives of my mother and dad. In 1991, my mother passed away. The night before the service, we had a family visitation. Cecil (a Hinkel son—the one we were closest to), his wife, and a sister named Kathryn came through the receiving line. As I introduced them to my wife, I told her these were dear family members but that I really didn't know exactly how we were related. At this point Kathryn surprised me by saying that we were not related at all, but were closer than kin! She then proceeded to tell my wife and me how our families had become so entangled.

A few times we took Grandma Elliott (on the right) to see her sisters on a birthday.

My grandfather had a sawmill near Overton, and one day he was in town to get supplies for the mill and groceries to feed the hands. As he was coming out of the general store he was approached by a young man who had just gotten off the train and was still carrying a suitcase in one hand. The young man asked my grandfather if he could recommend a rooming house where he could stay while he was looking for work. My grandfather looked him up and down and said if it was work he was looking for, he had plenty of that at his sawmill. Grandpa told him he could help him put the supplies in the wagon and they would go to the mill, where there were living accommodations for the workers. Mr. Hinkel left with Grandpa and a strong bond was made. A few years later my grandpa died and Mr. Hinkel started his own family, as well as farm, and prospered—but the families always stayed in touch.

Another of my favorite trips was the one to Houston to visit my mother's uncle, Willis Jernigan, and his family. This was the only brother or sister of Grandpa Jernigan's that I remember ever seeing. Apparently, Uncle Willis and Grandpa had been very close and the families remained so, since Grandpa died in 1931 and the visits to see Uncle Willis that I remember were during the mid- and late-1930s. The Jernigan son and daughter's families from Houston continued the visits to the July 4th picnics at Grandma's farm until the end—about 2005.

Since Uncle Willis lived in the city of Houston, there wasn't the spread like at the Hinkels, but they had a large house and grounds with a very interesting garage and attached workshop. There was a good sized backyard fenced with a chain link fence, which they called a "hurricane fence." There were lots of trees, grass, and tables with benches and chairs.

Uncle Willis was a streetcar conductor/supervisor. The kids loved loading up in a streetcar on a Sunday and having Uncle Willis take us on a ride around town, checking routes, stops, etc. He would tell us stories about people and places as we discovered Houston. It would be hard to decide if the streetcar rides were the highlight of our trips to Houston or the trips to the Houston Ship Channel, where he taught us to "crab," as he called it. Back in the '30s, Houston was large, but nothing like today. It didn't take long to get to open spaces along the Ship Channel where kids could run wild.

Uncle Willis would load up his car with kids, tie the crab net to the passenger side door handles, and off we would go. He would find a place to park which would look like a bank on a lake, and there we would crab. He always had a big ball of twine, a large piece of dry salt pork, and of course, the crab net. He would cut several pieces of string about ten or twelve feet long, then cut off pieces of the pork. We always had to taste of it to be sure it was really salty. Then he tied the pork to the string and found a good place to tie the other end to a tree, rock, or bush. He would let one of us take the meat and throw it into the water. As the string got wet the line sank in the water.

After all the lines were in the water, he would get an old wooden box (like an apple crate) out of the car trunk and we were ready to run the lines. He showed us how to gently lift the line to see if a crab was attached and, if so, to continue raising the crab to just below the surface of the water—then ease the net under the crab and lift it up on the bank. What fun we had getting the crab into the box. Evidently, Uncle Willis knew where the crabs were since we could always fill our box in an hour or so, just before the youngest kids tired of the fun and we headed for his house.

In his backyard he had an old cast iron wash pot with a gas heating ring underneath. He would put water from the garden hose into the pot and then light the ring under the pot to heat the water. We all crowded around wanting to see the water boil but he would say that "a watched pot never boils," and then he'd take us into the workshop to wash up—he had a lavatory with the hottest water and big bars of smelly soap that we learned to use regularly. We would go into the house and report to our parents and tell everyone what had happened and soon someone would announce that the water in the pot was boiling and we would all rush into the backyard again. Uncle Willis would carefully rinse off each crab with water from the garden hose and drop it into the boiling water. Sometimes the squeamish would gag, but we enjoyed it in the main.

After a few minutes of boiling the crabs, Uncle Willis would announce that the crabs were ready and pass out plates. Then he would use a set of long metal tongs to carefully place a crab on each person's plate. After he placed the crab on our plate we would take it to the picnic tables, which were covered with oilcloth and set with silverware. There was an assortment of tools on the table for each person to crack the shells and pick out the meat; of course, the little ones were helped by their parents. We had salad and saltine crackers to go with the crabmeat. The older people would dip their crabmeat in bowls of melted butter and some would squeeze lemon juice on it, but most of us kids ate the meat plain and loved it. What fun! These crab feasts weren't our dinner, which usually came about dark and consisted of sandwiches, potato salad, and cookies. Instead of cold drinks, as we had with the crab, we had cold glasses of milk with this meal.

At least once during each visit, whatever the season, we had a fish fry. For this meal Uncle Willis would take the kids to a fish market a few blocks from his house where "we" would pick out a few large, whole fish from the display case where the fish were lying on a bed of cracked ice. Uncle Willis would point out why one fish would be better than another and not always dependent on the size. It usually took two or three of us boys to "tote" all the wrapped fish to the car and then to the backyard. Uncle Willis did all the preparation and cooking in the backyard. He would always explain that the lady of the house did not allow fish to be cooked in her kitchen since it smelled up the whole house.

Uncle Willis got his wash pot ready, but instead of water as he used for the crabs, he used cooking oil. We mostly just watched while he got things ready to prepare the fish for cooking, but he explained what he was doing and why. Believe me, he kept our attention as he used his cutting board and big knives. We watched him cut off the heads, cut up the fish, wash each piece, and flop it around in his pan of corn meal, in which he had sprinkled all kinds of seasoning to flavor the fish. Every few minutes he would drop some batter or a fish morsel into the pot to see if the oil was hot enough to begin cooking. Uncle Willis always cooked the fish out in the backyard in the spring, summer, fall, and winter. We ate there also, picnic style on the tables with their oilcloth coverings and the benches, much like our crab feasts.

When the weather was too bad to eat outdoors, we would eat our fish in the house. The older adults ate at the large dining room table, which must have seated about twelve. The rest ate at card tables in the living room, with the youngest ones in the kitchen. The host family women didn't sit much because they were busy serving food and seeing after the children. There was always a lot of talking and laughing—happy sounds, except maybe when an unsatisfied little kid would let out a cry every now and then.

Grandma Jernigan was always glad to see us.

Some years later, during World War II, my dad was serving in the Marine Corps and stationed at the Navy blimp base in Hitchcock (between Houston and Galveston) as the brig warden. In the summer of 1943, Mother worked on the Navy base as a secretary in the Administration Building filling in for people on vacation, while my brother Sonny and I spent the summer at Grandma's farm. Again in the summer of 1944, Mother worked on the base and I, between my junior and senior years in high school, worked there also as a clerk in the Public Works Warehouse. We didn't get to nearby Houston much due to the gas situation, but one time we were there and I noticed a road that looked familiar. I asked Mother if that wasn't the way to Uncle Willis's house. She said it was but it would be better if we didn't just drop in. She went on to explain that she had been told he was having trouble with his memory and it upset him to see people he should know but couldn't recognize. He also lived in the past and told long, boring stories. He could have been suffering from the then-unheard-of Alzheimer's.

And speaking of long, boring stories, as you read this one just remember I *am* related to Uncle Willis, and as I recount the many pleasant memories of our family's visiting in the thirties, more memories pop up. For instance, recalling the Hinkel "family" experience reminded me of our visits to my cousins W. A. and Kelly Elliott.

My dad had four surviving brothers (two were deceased, one in infancy and another by the flu epidemic while a teenager during the first World War) and two sisters (the older was third in order of the siblings, while the younger was the baby of the family). My dad was in the middle of the last three boys, who were each less than two years apart, so they were very close in age and in support and loyalty to each other. Our family and the family of the oldest of the three, my Uncle Allen, were especially close-knit so we visited them frequently and vice versa. Allen and his wife, Aunt Maggie, had two sons, as did my parents. W. A. was four months older than me, with Kelly almost two years younger than "Dub" (W. A.), while my brother Sonny was a couple of years younger than Kelly. We were a good mix, played well together, and were very close until about the time of World War II.

During the thirties and through World War II, Allen had a regular job at a lumber yard in Arp most of the time while working on his small farm on the side in his spare time, and following the war he became manager of the Wm. Cameron Co. in Overton, which handled a lot of the oil field business for the New London-based office of Humble Oil, as well as Shell and Gulf in the East Texas field. He built his family a new home in Overton, as you might say, "coming to town." During the thirties the Allen Elliott family lived on a few acres across the road from the Hill's large farm, about half way between Ma's (Grandma Elliott) farm and the town of

Overton. Ma was about seven miles east of Tyler and maybe twelve or so miles west of Overton. Maggie was a Hill daughter and had several married brothers and sisters living around, next to, or near to the Hill place. So when we visited W. A. and Kelly we also had a bunch of their cousins to play with and, in the summer, to share at least two or three great swimming holes. Sometimes when W. A. and Kelly came to visit us they would bring along two or three of these cousins to make us quite a pack of kids.

Also during the thirties, except for one year, we were living in the oil field at Leverett's Chapel or in the city of Tyler. Since Leverett's Chapel was on a very busy highway in the middle of the oil field and thickly settled with people, we had access to electricity (which helped provide running water) and even natural gas furnished by the oil company that had the oil production rights on our property; we used it to cook with, and to heat our water and house. So we lived uptown, so to speak, when it came to home comfort, as others did in our area (if a family could afford it). We had indoor toilets, baths, and kitchen sinks with hot and cold running water, and a refrigerator to keep our food cold. So when we visited many of our kin such as Allen's family, as well as some friends like the Hinkels, we experienced what I will call "country shock."

They did not have electricity, running water, indoor toilets, or even gas to heat their water, cook their food, or warm their house. They drew their water from a well (equipped with a rope and bucket) near the back door of the house. They bathed in a galvanized metal tub—outdoors next to the well in summer, and in winter in the kitchen next to the stove, which they used to heat some water. Their outdoor toilet, sometimes called a privy, was usually located a little farther from the back door than the water well, with no way to heat or cool it. The light in the house to see by after dark was supplied by kerosene lamps. Food was cooked on a wood burning stove at the Hinkels, and at my uncle's a kerosene burning stove was used. The house was heated at the Hinkels with fireplaces burning wood, while at Allen's house they used kerosene heaters.

What a difference we experienced in living conditions in some places we visited during the 1930s when compared to our own homes at Leverett's Chapel and Tyler. We could even repay our cousins for the pleasure we got from their swimming holes when we visited them by treating them to the municipal-type privately run swimming pool in nearby Sexton City or the one in Kilgore when they visited us. One result of World War II seems to me that it somewhat helped to equalize living conditions between city and country life for most places in our nation—most people say for the better, while some claim for the worse.

I need to give you a little more information about the Hill and Allen Elliott properties to complete my telling about the some comparisons between my memories of blacksmithing. The dirt road, as most in the rural areas were at that time, in front of Uncle Allen's house actually ran all the way from Tyler to Overton, east and west. Many other roads dissected or ran into it along the way, as did another smaller one that ran north from the main road bordering on the west side of Allen's property of a few acres, with a house, garage, and barn. Across the road, facing this side road where it intersected the main road, stood Grandpa Hill's blacksmith shop. It was a rustic, rundown looking barn-like affair with a wide, open entranceway on all four sides. These openings did not have doors, but rather rickety gates that could be opened and closed as needed. There were heavily fenced pens in the two back corners where horses and mules could be held, and maybe a bull or two every now and then in order to put a ring in his nose. A wagon, or sometimes even a "Model T" or similar vehicle like a tractor, could be driven through the building from one direction and out the other. The overall appearance was more of a dilapidated barn than a blacksmith shop, but above the front entranceway the letters—BLACKSMITHING—were crudely burned into a rough plank, followed by much smaller hand-painted letters, "By Hill."

About fifty yards east of the shop, facing north toward the road, stood the Hill house. Their home looked exactly the same as our Ma's, which was like most of the houses on farms in East Texas. It had a twelve-foot-wide porch running the length of the house front, with a matching one on the back side that contained the well housing where they drew their water. And, dividing the house right down the middle, connecting the front and back porches, was a twelve-foot-wide open hallway. This style of house inspired the term "dog run." In the middle of both exterior side walls was an attached chimney rising well above the roof line. The fireplaces in these walls extending inside the room, along with the kitchen stove, supplied the only heat for the house during cold East Texas winters. And the kitchen stove also supplied a lot of unwanted heat in the hot East Texas summers.

Oh, how well I remember a few times on a Saturday afternoon when I would be visiting my cousin Dub, gathering with the Hill clan on that nice front porch and "Aunt Idell," a Hill daughter, would be trimming all the men and boy's hair in preparation for church on Sunday. Later that evening she would style the women's hair also, but this was usually done out of sight in the kitchen near the water well. They thought nothing of treating us visitors as family, cutting our hair along with the family members. That was the way it was "way back yonder." When you visited you took part in all the "going-ons"—whether it was picking and shelling peas, picking cotton, gathering and shucking corn, feeding chickens, or slopping the hogs—you were part of it.

But, not counting the trips to the swimming holes, by far the most interesting and exciting part of these visits was spending time in the blacksmith shop watching Grandpa Hill work at his forge or hammering and prying on farm equipment he repaired for his large family and neighbors who brought animals and equipment for his expert attention. I had described Mr. Hinkel as an artist at his work in his blacksmith shop; the best description I could give of Grandpa Hill in his would be that of a showman, for he loved an audience to do his work before. One time I mentioned the fact that Grandpa Hill seemed to like to show off in front of us and I had noticed that it seemed to me he would wait until someone was there to do it. Dub said that might be the case, but he added that Grandma Hill was always getting on him not to do that dangerous work unless someone was there since he might get hurt and need help, or even sometimes things would develop where he needed some help moving, lifting, or holding things in place as he worked on them. I had to agree that a lot of his work was certainly dangerous and many times he needed help. One thing about it, though, was that most times he would let us kids assist him (even if he didn't need it) so we would feel like we were really helping.

Grandpa Hill was not a large man, just average size, but he was very, very strong—which he demonstrated countless times in the way he handled large animals, heavy farm equipment, and other stuff. I think, sometime or another, I remember someone referring to him as being "wiry." Again, in his own way, he was very much like Mr. Hinkel—he seemed to be able to make nearly anything needed by a farmer. As we were growing up, we learned to do many useful things by watching and helping him.

We visited many kinfolks in our East Texas area, some better off than the Allen Elliott family and the Hills, but also many more that were struggling to have enough to eat and keep a roof over their heads, since the times were very hard. My dad and Allen, being the two most financially successful in their family, each helped many of their relatives with food and some money when they could. Some were too proud to accept help, while others would not hesitate to ask for it.

They, my dad and Uncle Allen, also collaborated on trips visiting some of their uncles, aunts, and a lot of cousins on both sides of the river dividing Texas and Louisiana where the Toledo Bend Reservoir now spreads. Dad's grandfather was then gone, but he had many offspring and most of them still lived in that area. The grandfather's farm was covered by the reservoir, as was some of the offspring's land. Most had farms on or near the river which they got their main livelihood from, but they supplemented their food supply with fishing in the river. Dad and Allen, both in the lumber and building business, would coordinate their visits when their relatives needed some help with construction and mix in a week or so of fishing with their relatives. It seems to me they had two uncles in particular; my family would stay with one, while Dub's family would stay with the other. Sometimes all the kids would sleep at

Floyd Elliott's cousins, Robert and Richard Jernigan, pictured in Kilgore, Texas, 1932.

one place on pallets scattered out on the open-air porches and then play together all day. There was fun in numbers back in those days.

The kids didn't actually go fishing with the men folks, since they usually ran trotlines at night, but some of the older kids would take us to fish during the day along the river banks where it was safer. There also were some ponds formed by the river that made great swimming holes which we sampled two or three times a day. We had a lot of good times playing with many other children, eating together, and sleeping as a group. It was something like going to summer camp that some of our school mates had told us about.

I recall that on one trip our dads helped an uncle reroof his house; another time they helped another uncle tear down and build another barn. I remember once they helped a cousin, with others, completely build a house in one week and still get in a lot of fishing. Of course, back then houses weren't as large and complex as they are today. All told, these trips to the river area were great learning experiences, as well as much fun.

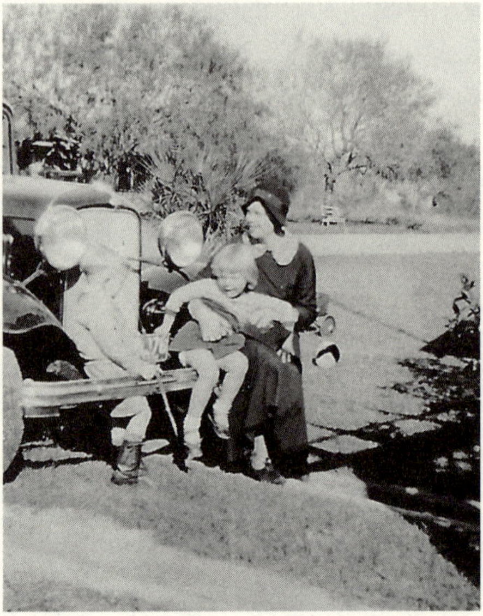

Rest areas were wherever you made them in the '30s.

I am sure the trip we took in the summer of 1939 to California in order to visit my Aunt Ruby was the longest, both in distance and time, of all the trips we made as a family. Ruby, her husband Carl Jeter, and their two children (Carl, Jr. and LaNell) had moved to the Oakland area a few months prior to our trip. I am sure Grandma Jernigan, and possibly some other family members, wanted someone from the family to go out to check on the Jeters and affirm that they were doing well. I guess Mother and Dad were selected for this job, so as summer neared Dad and Mother got things in order. Back then interstate travel was not as easy or so swift as in our modern day. One of Dad's first moves was to get us a new car and make sure it worked properly.

He selected a 1939 white four-door sedan from Holly Dodge Motor Co. in Tyler. It was a beauty, the recently introduced revolutionary new aerodynamic styling from Chrysler Motors that was very eye-catching; it would turn out to carry us all the way through World War II. Fond memories of this car (which I learned to drive at age twelve) have lasted me for a long lifetime. It certainly served my family very well.

Mother and Dad planned the trip around a schedule of three days going the southern route, five or six days visiting Ruby's family, and another three days coming back, taking a peek at the Grand Canyon on the return leg. Ruby had promised a few day-long and half-day sightseeing trips around their area of California, which they had become familiar with and enjoyed showing. We all were excited as the date of our trip neared. Originally, Grandma had planned to go with us, but due to some minor illness at the last minute, she backed out.

Dad had a Humble Oil Company map that pictured Texas on one side while the other side showed the whole United States. This map also showed a lot of wear, since we all wanted to see where we were going on this great adventure. Dad planned to pick up a California state map when we crossed their border.

We were well out in West Texas ready to make our first stop for a night's lodging at a roadside inn about dusk. I think it had a name something like Sand Dunes Motel, and was very typical of that period of time in the U.S. There was one room with two full-size beds and not much else except a small chest of drawers, a very small shelf-type dressing table with a little mirror hanging on the wall, and two straight chairs. In a small "shed room" off the back of this room was a bathroom—with the bare essentials. This unit was connected with the next one with a roof (as each in the three or four rows of units were), which provided each unit with a covered parking space. We decided each unit must be just like ours.

After unloading our luggage and testing the bathroom, we walked about a block down the street to a Mexican restaurant and had a nice meal. We had left home after a very early and good breakfast, stopping at noon for a picnic from Mother's straw basket filled with fried chicken and other goodies she had packed very, very early that morning so we would have a meal or two as well as some snacks along the way. Sonny and I were hoping for hamburgers, but Mother and Dad had assured us of having them several times later.

The next morning we ate at a little café next door to the motel and were on our way by eight o'clock. We did get our hamburgers for lunch, and Dad told us we were getting near to the desert we would be crossing and we must prepare for it. Back in those days cars were not air conditioned as most are now-a-days, so crossing the desert in the heat of the summer could be deadly. The alternative, night driving, was very dangerous also. Dad had learned of a service that was available where you could use special ice to cool your car as you crossed the desert. He decided to go that route, so after lunch he looked and found a service station that prepared your car, driver, and the passengers for this method.

Basically, this method used dry ice formed by freezing carbon dioxide rather than water. As the dry ice melted it released carbon dioxide into the atmosphere instead of water. Of course, the accumulation of carbon dioxide could be deadly in a closed car, so you had to ventilate the car enough to let the gas escape. Most cars in those days had vents in the body just forward of the front doors which could be opened from the front seat and would "scoop" in fresh air as you moved forward. The system required that the released carbon dioxide be forced out of the car so it could not accumulate in the car. This was achieved by opening the forward vents, having the dry ice in a position where the fresh air would be chilled by passing over the dry ice, and letting it escape out of the car through partially open windows in the back area. Our car was designed where this system should work well and safely as long as the correct procedures were followed.

Dad felt we could do this, so he filled out the necessary forms and paid for the dry ice, the installation charge, and the deposit on the special "bucket" that held the dry ice on the front floor on the passenger's side. If you did not return the bucket to a service center on the other side of the desert and wanted to keep the bucket, it was no big deal. If you checked it in at a service center you could get your deposit refunded.

This worked well for us as we crossed the desert, with Sonny and me sleeping most of the time while Mother was busy keeping an eye on us, the back windows, the front vents, and the dry ice bucket. Dad kept busy driving, checking Mother with a glance every minute or so, and tuning the radio to try to pick up stations as we followed the setting sun. About dusk we started seeing the foothills in front of the mountains and knew our day's travel was nearly done. As we came out of the desert we found a little town with motels; Dad selected one very similar to the one we had stayed at in Texas the night before and checked us in. Sonny and I had seen a motel based on an Indian motif where the units were styled somewhat like tepees and suggested we stay there, but Mother and Dad overruled us, saying we needed a more regular type.

We were tired and hungry by this time, since we had been driving several hours with only one stop. In the middle of the desert we came upon this place that must have been an oasis because of all the palm trees. We stopped at a service station to gas up and go to the restroom. Every business we saw seemed to be based on some form of dates. Next door to the service station was an ice cream parlor, so Dad suggested we have a milk shake—no one objected. Inside we found their specialty was date ice cream, so we all ordered a date milk shake. We all liked it except Sonny; he wanted some chocolate candy, which Dad got for him and then Dad finished Sonny's milk shake. We went to the next store which had souvenirs and such. Mother found packaged dates of different sorts, including candied ones, which she purchased in order to have them for baking.

We went back to the service station where Dad had parked our car and taken the dry ice bucket out and put it near our car, as we had been instructed, while we had our milk shakes and shopped. He replaced the bucket on the floor on the passenger side, we loaded up, and were on our way again. I don't know what happened to that dry ice bucket. I don't think we checked it in so maybe we left it at the Jeter's in California since we didn't use one on the return trip home.

The next morning we left early, crossed the mountains, and found our way to the coast. The Jeters were very happy to see us, as we were to see them, when we arrived at their new home in California. They had settled into a new way of life compared to East Texas, as Carl (the dad) had somewhat switched careers. Back in Tyler he and Mother's youngest brother, Fred, had operated a motorcycle shop where they sold and repaired a few Indian Motorcycles—but they devoted most of their time to their real interest, the racing activities they had carried on in conjunction with their business. Many times they had locked the doors of the business, taken off on their motorcycle rigs, and participated in the many races around the country. A big book should have been written about this part of their lives before they were forced to "settle down." Of course, another book should have been written about Fred's experiences just a few years later as a citizen soldier in the Marine's Pacific campaign of World War II. These two were certainly a pair of what we now proudly call America's "greatest generation." As a preteen youngster just prior to World War II, during the war and following it for the rest of my life, I had them and my dad as my "real life heroes."

It was an accident on the race track in Indianapolis that left Carl with a right leg broken in a few places, an injured back, and a great number of cuts and bruises that changed their lives. Fred permanently locked the doors to the motorcycle shop and went into the grocery and feed business until he was called up for the war. While recovering from his racing injuries, Carl became interested in aviation through some of his motorcycle racing friends, and with their help landed a good job when he was able to go to work. Since California was the center of much aviation activity at that time, this was where the Jeters ended up. Carl remained with the California aviation industry the rest of his working days, but he and Ruby drifted apart and following the war she and the kids moved back to Texas for a new life.

As for our visit to California in 1939, I still have many, many treasured memories. I have been to California quite a number of times in the intervening seventy-seven years, but none can compare to that visit. In fact, looking back over the nearly ninety years of my life and my travels to many parts of the world, I believe the visits in the 1930s were the greatest of all—especially those in Texas.

In the 30s people liked to dress up to travel.

Lee Haile.

WHISKEY STILLS IN THE HILLS

by Lee Haile

For me it all started when I was about a sophomore in high school down in Hondo, Texas. We were in the cow pen out back of the house one day when I asked my dad, "Why is that water trough made of copper?"

"It was part of our old still," he said.

Our still? I thought, "We had a still?" I was too dumbfounded to even think to ask anything else. See, we were raised Baptists and my mom did not drink. My dad only drank a beer every now and then, and on cold days during hunting season he had a little shot of whiskey, "for a sore throat." Over the years, I heard a couple of more references to "our" still, but it was never discussed and I got the feeling that I shouldn't ask.

Then when I moved back to the Hill Country I started doing nature tours. I was doing a weekly tour on the Detering Ranch in far north Uvalde County just south of Leakey, Texas, and Kit Detering, the wife of one of the owners, told me about a whiskey cave on the place. She said that it was up in the holler across the creek from the main house. She said that they would haul the whiskey out on mules. Well, one time when I was out there and I had finished a tour, I was telling the new exercise trainer about it. He was young and in shape, so I asked him if he wanted to go with me and see if we could find it.

We started up this real steep, short hollow that was half bowl-shaped, what we call a header holler. Now, I was expecting a big undercut that was open on one side, the kind you see where Indians sometimes lived. A lot of people call these caves. As we got about three quarters of the way up, I could tell we were getting near a cave because of the rocks. We topped out and didn't find anything. So we started back down, with him going down the right side and me going down the left side. This canyon was not more than a hundred yards across the top; it was really tight with lots of Spanish Oaks and cherry trees like you see in the heads of those hollers. It was really steep, almost sliding.

The header holler where the whiskey cave is.

About a third of the way down, there was a solid rock ledge that went all the way around that holler, kind of crescent moon shaped. It was only about three feet high, so I wasn't expecting anything. It was brushy around the base of this little bluff, and in the brush I noticed a piece of rusted iron over to the left side of the canyon, near the bluff. I called out to my buddy that I thought I saw a can or something metal. I dropped off the ledge and started following it around. When I came up on what turned out to be a gallon can, I started looking around and through the brush I could see a dark opening in the ledge. "I think I found something," I called. He worked his way over and we pushed on hands and knees through the Mountain Laurel bushes that were about four feet high. Sure enough, there was a cave!

The opening was only about two feet high and ten feet long, but we could see that it went back a ways. The roof stayed level but the floor sloped back from the entrance, so it got bigger the farther back you went. I was ready to go in, and I had brought a headlamp from the truck just in case. So I started in on my belly, going slow so my eyes could adjust, just to check it out. I had not even gotten my legs past the opening (so I was only about three feet in) when I heard the tell-tale buzz—a rattler! It was pretty steep going in, so it was not going to be easy to crawl backwards up the slope. My buddy wanted to pull me back out by my feet, but I didn't want to do that. Besides, it wasn't that big of a snake, only about three and a half feet. I also didn't want to lose sight of it, so I told him to hand me a stick about six feet long.

Now, this young guy did not know me that well, so it took a little talking to convince him, but he found one and handed it to me. I told him to get back in case that snake came out mad and I had to get out of there in a hurry. I couldn't see his face, but I could tell by his voice that he thought I was crazy. I just knew I wanted to go in that cave and I did not want that snake between me and the opening when I wanted to come back out. So I poked that snake until he got upset and decided to leave. He crawled over to the right side of the entrance and disappeared among the rocks. Now I could continue on.

After about ten feet, I could stand up. The floor kept descending and the roof stayed level. About forty feet in, the room ended in a wall. The room was now over twenty feet high and about forty by sixty feet. It was a nice sized room. Along the back wall was a spring that fell down into a pool about ten feet across and about three feet deep. The water was crystal clear, and there by the pool's side was what was left of the still! There was even a whiskey barrel in the pool. Everything above water was rotted and gone except for the rusty metal hoop, but everything below water level was in perfect shape, wood and all. There was even a set of metal rails used to haul the barrels from the still to the mouth of the cave to be loaded on mules. Later, I went back in with my daughters and we filmed and explored the whole thing.

Now, why would anyone go through that much trouble to put a still in a place like that? Well it all started with the 18th Amendment that put in place Prohibition, and the Volstead Act, which gave it legal teeth. Prohibition was supposed to reduce crime, robbery murder abuse . . . etc., and everyone was going to obey the law because it was "good for all of us." But like so much legislation with good intentions and forced on the majority by a few, the reality of the situation was far different. The reality was that it caused more crime, created vicious gangs, caused rampant corruption, and made criminals out of otherwise law abiding citizens. It was also vague. Did you realize that it was never illegal to have or consume alcohol, just to buy it or make it!

A whiskey jug.

Certain universities and businesses were exempt from the law "for scientific studies." Some farmers were allowed to make it for fuel. Doctors were allowed to have a certain quantity on hand to prescribe to their patients. I wonder if that is where the term drinking "for medicinal purposes only" came from. The doctors even petitioned Congress to take the ban off for them and allow them to prescribe whatever amount they wanted. Their reasoning was that lawmakers were not trained as doctors and couldn't know what amount would be beneficial for a patient. A lot of the "government men" that enforced the law were paid off by the gangster mobs in the big cities like Chicago, and most people felt like they were just trying to get rid of the competition so the mobs could control the market and charge what they wanted for their alcohol. People also felt like the government only wanted to control it so they could tax it. As a result, people mostly ignored it.

Since making alcohol was an illegal activity, there was a lot of folk vernacular, slang, or euphemisms associated with it, just like illegal drugs today. It was enforced through what is now the Internal Revenue Service, and so the people doing the enforcing were called "revenuers," "government men," or "the government." People who made and sold it illegally were called "moonshiners" or "bootleggers." The product was called "moonshine" (maybe because so much of the work was done at night). Wikipedia says the term derived from an old English term, "moonrakers." It was also called "shine," "branch water," "fire water" (from the Indian days), and "medicine" or "medicine water," "white lightning," "bootleg," "redeye," and "mountain dew."

Places where it could be bought and consumed were called "speakeasies," "blind pigs," and "blind tigers." Speakeasy comes from the practice of talking quietly and discreetly about it in public and/or talking quietly while inside to not attract the attention of the police. Blind pigs were a way of circumventing the law. Since it was not illegal to possess or consume liquor, just to make or sell it, you would pay a fee to see a "blind pig" and receive a complimentary drink. Blind tigers were set up to where you could not see who was serving you, due to a wall or drape so you could not identify the person you were getting the drinks from. All three terms preceded Prohibition, according to many sources.

Slang I heard from my parents and others for the act of consuming alcohol were "drinking," "taking a shot" or "snort" of whiskey, "getting a snoot full," "taking some medicine," "taking a drink 'for a cold,'" "bending an elbow," "having a nip," and "taking a hit off the bottle." Euphemisms for "having too much" are too many to mention. Wiktionary lists 303. *Roget's Thesaurus* lists 121 "official" terms, so I will limit them to ones I heard from my parents (mostly my mother) and others of their generation who were alive during Prohibition. They include "had too much," "had a snoot full," "feeling his oats," "being drunk as a skunk," "being off the wagon," "having too much medicine," and being "on a bender," "pie-eyed," "wall-eyed," or "three sheets to the wind."

Here in the Hill Country of Texas, with its strong ethnic German and Alsatian influences and being very rural, Prohibition was probably ignored even more so than in other places. I know that as I started asking for tales for this paper, it seemed everybody I talked to had a tale or two. Shan Kowert told me that when the government men (revenuers) came into Gillespie County and Fredericksburg, Sheriff Kimmell would call those who needed to know and tell them, "Hey . . . Otto, your cows are out, you hear me, you got that? Your cows are out!" This was confirmed by Evelin Weymeyer from the Pioneer Museum. Guich Kooch told me the cops in south Austin did a similar thing, only saying, "Your cows are on the road." I wonder if this was a common practice in rural Texas. Guich also told me there were three big stills with tanks about ten feet around in a stone building in the middle of the tannery in Fredericksburg. The smell of the tannery masked the smell of the stills cooking.

My cousin Robert Haile over at Sisterdale showed me big square beams, which are now holding up the water tank by the windmill at the old house, that used to be the roof of an underground still just back of that ranch house. They had a trolley system to bring supplies across the creek. Uncle Bill Whitworth, once the judge of Kendal County and Boerne, and who still lives there in that big stone two-story house, told how his mother served dinner once to the revenuers in the kitchen while the men were in the underground still working and the pantry was full of whiskey jugs. That took nerve!

Cousin Robert also told about Ira Soell. He said that the government men flew over his still and took pictures of him. Then they asked him, "Ira, are you cooking?" He said, "Well . . . I don't know . . ." Then they showed him the pictures and asked, "Is that you?" He said, "Why it sure is!" and they sent him to the pen for five years as an example to others. Afterwards, he always said, "That was the five easiest years of my life!" Another tale from Robert was about Booby Herbst. He drove a truck around hauling supplies. He thought he had been had when his suppliers said to him, "You sure are selling a lot of yeast and sugar up in the hills." He replied, "Well you know them old German women sure like to bake." They told him, "You keep that up and we will give you a break on the price." He said, "I thought it was over for me, but I come out pretty good!"

I asked Linda Kirkpatrick about a road just south of Leaky called Whiskey Mountain Road. It was just a few miles north of the whiskey cave that I had been in on the Detering Ranch I mentioned earlier. I was wondering if it was associated with that cave. Come to find out, it was not. It was a totally different cave that they made whiskey in during Prohibition. Anthony Sharp told me that when some of his kin tried to buy ninety acres back there and asked about the name Whiskey Mountain, they were told about the cave and the still in it.

Linda has an interesting tale associated with the cave from the 1860s. It goes that in 1867 a man named Tom Wall, who had moved to Texas from Canada in 1857, had a disagreement over business with his partner and brother-in-law of his second wife, a man named Reading Black, who was a Quaker and Union sympathizer. Tom Wall, who was a Confederate, shot and killed Black and then fled to Mexico until things cooled down. He then returned to the Frio canyon and his family hid him in the cave. They brought him food and supplies until he could be smuggled out, and he returned to

Canada and was never heard from again. But that side note to this paper is Linda's story, just one of many related to whiskey stills in the hills of Texas. You can ask her for the rest of the story.

Laura B. Garrison told me that there was another whiskey cave on the Patterson Ranch just south of Rio Frio on the east side of the canyon. Her brother had owned the ranch at one time and said there remained a still in that cave. The other two were on the west side. That makes three stills in a four-mile radius! Laura B. also said her brother was a bootlegger and used to haul whiskey to San Antonio. One time they got stuck in the river crossing just below Garner Park and the sheriff came along and helped them get unstuck, so they gave him a jug of whiskey. She said they told her that if they didn't sell it locally, the sheriff left them alone. She also told about her cousin who was a deputy sheriff and had a place on Bear Creek, just east of where her place is on Blanket Creek. He had a still there and was making whiskey. That makes four stills in a five-mile radius. His wife found it on the property and reported it to the sheriff, not knowing it was her husband's still. Oops!

A friend, Terry Theis, told me there was a still on their home place a few miles east of Harper, but he didn't know much about it. Mike Blakely, another friend of mine and a great Texas singer/songwriter and novelist from up in the Llano/Lake Buchanan area, told me that Longhorn Caverns, where they used to have dances in the cave, was a speakeasy during Prohibition. He said, "They would have dances on Saturday night and church on Sunday mornings, so on Saturday night it was whiskey and limestone and Sunday morning it was fire and brimstone!"

Now, what about "our" still? Ever notice how people like to talk about outlaw kin as long as it is far enough back to not be an embarrassment?

About ten years before my dad died we went to haul a load of pine logs from my wife's grandmother's place in northeast Georgia to use in our house we were building. On the way back, my dad got to reminiscing. I learned more about my family in the next thirty minutes than I had heard all my life. I found out that my Grandpa Haile, who died before I was born so I never knew him, at one time worked for my step-Grandpa Bierschwald (who was the grandpa I knew growing up) on a ranch in Sisterdale. It seems they were also partners in a still. He would bring sugar and supplies out and haul whiskey back to town. They all lived in San Antonio, but Mr. Bierschwald kept my grandpa at the ranch minding the still so that he could get friendly with my grandma. They had a boy who was sickly at this time, so they moved to the mountains in western New Mexico where some other kin had moved. My dad told me he now knew part of the reason Grandpa moved was to get his wife away from his boss. The child did not survive; neither did the marriage, and my grandma moved back to San Antonio and married Mr. Bierschwald. It was a contentious divorce and the two kids were caught in the middle. No wonder they never talked about it.

Was it all because of the "Devil Rum"? Quien sabe?

1906 Shotgun house kitchen, Dallas Old City Park.

COOKING WITH GAS: THE QUIET REVOLUTION

by Charles Williams

Jack Thorp, in his rambling autobiography *Pardner to the Wind,* tells the story of a highly regarded black cowboy in West Texas and Eastern New Mexico called Ad. Ad got married late in life. His ranching friends, wishing to send him and his wife a special present, told him to go to the railroad station in Roswell, New Mexico, to get their individual gifts. When Ad and his wife got there, they discovered nineteen cast iron stoves!

Besides highlighting the difficulty of communicating over the vast distances of West Texas and Eastern New Mexico in the late 1880s, this story also illustrates the high value placed on a seemingly prosaic appliance, the cast iron stove. The frontier wife who possessed one was fortunate indeed. Burning wood or coal or even prairie coal, they were a huge step up from open hearth cooking. As much as we romanticize Dutch oven-cooking over an open flame or a campfire, it was not exactly a housewife's dream—smoky, poorly controlled, laborious, and ashy. No wonder a cast iron stove was regarded as the housewife's best friend.

This paper will discuss the quiet revolution in kitchens, driven by new equipment, new methods of cooking, and new and more widely available foodstuffs. We will see how, compared to early settlers in Texas and elsewhere, we are now truly "Cooking with Gas."

Food preparation and menus for cooking on an open hearth, common in colonial kitchens, closely follows what we think of today as chuck wagon or camp cooking—extensive use of Dutch ovens, frying pans, and metal pots for boiling and soup/stew preparation. The food followed the general outline of soup, stew, fried meat (with or without a starch), breads and biscuits, mush and pone, preserves (strawberry was a particular favorite), and baked sweets—gingerbread, Indian pudding, and such.

A typical open hearth fireplace and kitchen is found in the Gano cabin, in Old City Park in Dallas. The cabin was built in 1845, and refinements were added in 1852. Besides the fireplace, there are a couple of tables. If there was a sink, it would have been a dry sink; water was brought into the kitchen by hand, either from a well or cistern, or a nearby stream. In the South, heat (and fear of fire) made the separate kitchen popular for early home construction.

Gano cabin kitchen fireplace, Dallas Old City Park.

Fireplaces got more sophisticated, with masonry construction and built-in oven compartments. Still, it was cooking over open flames and embers in a sooty, dirty, poorly controlled environment. Changes were on the way, however. By the mid-1800s, many urban middle class homes had cast iron stoves, burning either wood or coal. An important condition of this was access to a railroad, as cast iron stoves were very heavy, and the cost of freighting them was not negligible.

Cast iron stoves were a huge improvement over open hearths. This is not to say that the operation of a cast iron was (or is) all that easy. The fuel had to be laid and lit, and then the temperatures were controlled with a series of dampers and levers. Heat was checked by touch. They were finicky, and each one developed its own characteristics. The ash had to be emptied each day, and about fifty pounds of fuel was required to be added at various times. They had to be cleaned rigorously to prevent rust. On the plus side, the cooking was at waist level, was much more flexible, there was almost no smoke and, best of all, there was no ash in the food. They were well adapted to urban life.

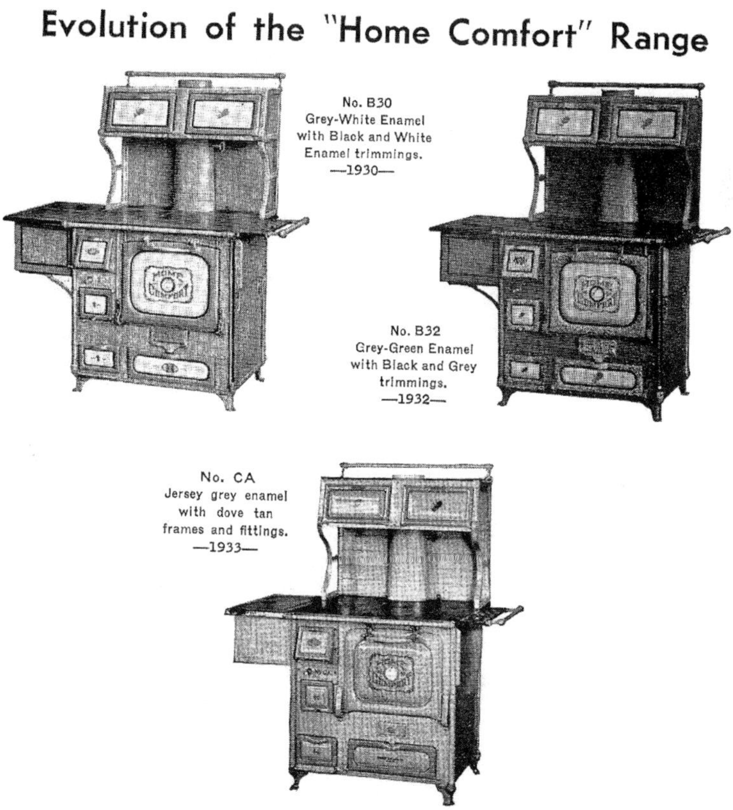

The latest and greatest Home Comfort ranges (1929–1933).

There were several significant changes in the availability of foodstuffs after the Civil War, as well. Sugar became generally available and the price dropped. Flour and spices other than nutmeg also became more generally available, with corresponding drops in cost. The biggest change was probably in meat, as refrigeration meant that beef became the meat of choice. The new factory cities demanded fresh meat, and Texans were glad to provide it. Swift and Armor were happy to refrigerate beef on the way from Ft. Worth to the local butcher shop. Refrigeration in most homes was an ice box or, in Texas, a root cellar. Other meats were also available, and canned meats (especially shellfish) were popular.

Another phenomenon became popular at this time: the cookbook. Prior to the mid-1890s, cookbooks tended to be compilations of household hints, kitchen lore, and general information (or misinformation, in some cases), as well as collections of general recipes—recipes full of "dashes," "pinches," and similar notations. Fannie Merritt Farmer, in 1896, published the first edition we would recognize as a cookbook. *The Boston Cooking School Cook Book* marked a revolution in cookbooks. For the first time, exact measurements were provided, and reproducible results were expected.[1] The Fannie Farmer cookbook started a revolution in cookbooks. Not only were cookbook recipes more exact, but manufactures of kitchen equipment (such as stoves) and foodstuffs (such as leavening agents), put out books that were guides to using their products as well as recipe collections.

Cover of Fannie Merritt Farmer's The Boston Cooking-School Cook Book.

The *Home Comfort Cook Book* from 1933 is an example of this kind of book. "Home Comfort" was the trade name for a series of iron ranges made by the Wrought Iron Range Company of St. Louis, Missouri. The cast iron ranges they offered evolved from 1870 to 1933. There are not many notable changes until 1924, when an enameled range became available. That was a real blessing for housewives who had to clean these ranges—and keep them from rusting! Their recipe books featured favorites such as "drop biscuits," which were typically called "gems" and were dropped into preheated cast iron biscuit pans.[2]

A big change in the fuel for stoves was already in sight by the 1830s. A naturally occurring phenomenon first made use of by the Greeks (at Delphi), flammable gas, was gradually coming into wide use. Actually, the first successful gases were manufactured gases, usually a coal product. Starting in England in 1812, by the late 1830s many big cities had gas distribution networks for illumination, both public and private. Texas was slower; the distribution system in Dallas was started in 1872, by the company that would (in 1906) become the Lone Star Gas Company. Amazingly, an effective mantle for efficient illumination from burning gas was not developed until the 1880s.

By the late 1890s, another source of illumination, without all the attendant problems of gas, became popular: electricity. Not all of the early installers of electric lights were ready to believe that electricity was more than a passing fad, however. Daniel Sullivan installed unique lights in his Dallas home around 1902. Sullivan, who was a water and gas fixture dealer, installed lights that were both gas and electrical! He was also the first person in Dallas to put indoor plumbing in his house, including a claw-foot tub supplied with hot water from his new gas water heater. His neighbors were scandalized! He did not let the availability of hot water spoil the family—bath night was still once a week, and the whole family bathed in the same water, as always.

Faced with decreased demand for their product, the gas manufacturing companies searched for another use; hence, the gas stove. Early models were unwieldy, but soon the oven was added under the burners as an integral part of the range, and the whole thing was made smaller. It was not until the gas companies themselves started making and selling ranges (and water heaters), however, that gas cooking started to take off. The new ranges offered some significant advantages. They were mostly smaller, simpler to use and more modern-looking than cast iron stoves. They had mostly cool surfaces, so touching them did not result in a burn. There was no ash associated with them, so you didn't have to haul fuel for them, and cleaning was much easier. Two huge advances came in 1915: the thermostat for the oven, and the introduction of natural gas to replace manufactured gas. By 1930, the new gas stoves outnumbered the old cast iron cookers by at least 2 to 1. It should be noted, that cast iron stoves modified for use with gas remained popular as well.

There were some disadvantages to the early gas ranges, primarily in ignition practices. Gas burners had to be lit with a match until the development of the standing pilot light. The pilot light could be blown out, so electronic ignitions have pretty much supplanted them recently, for safety reasons. Manufactured gas, primarily coal gas, was toxic, and natural gas was found to be safer. It was also piped at higher pressures, and so was more efficient. The availability of propane in pressurized tanks has meant that even rural locations not included in the gas distribution networks could have gas appliances.

"Cooking with Gas" had one more challenge to meet. As early as 1882, a Canadian named Thomas Ahern manufactured an oven heated by electricity. It was an idea ahead of its time, as electricity wasn't available many places, and the oven wasn't very successful. In 1896, Westinghouse came out with their first electrical appliance, a toaster/oven. By the 1920s and '30s, electricity became much more ubiquitous. The first use of electricity in the home (other than for light, of course) was probably not for a stove but a refrigerator. The development of Freon in the late 1920s made it possible—and popular—to replace the ice box with a more efficient food preservation tool. Meanwhile, electricity was becoming much cheaper and more readily available.

As more and more homes got electrical power, electrical stoves gradually became more popular. A likely competition (still going on today) sprang up between gas and electric stoves, partially carried out in cookbooks. Lone Star Gas published a typical gas company cookbook. Recipes highlighted the control possible with each company's particular oven, with emphasis on exact temperatures;[3] otherwise, these publications were quite similar to standard cookbooks, such as Fannie Farmer's. The cookbooks provided by the electric range manufacturers, on the other hand, spent a good deal of time talking about the features of the range and how to most efficiently cook with it.[4]

The electrical appliance revolution was about a lot more than ranges. Refrigerators were equipped not only with a cold box, but a small freezer as well. This allowed for a wider range of foods, especially desserts—and ice. In addition to coming with manuals to show how to use them,[5] refrigerators came with recipe books, or even tips for how housewives could help win WWII.[6] The real heyday of electrical appliances in the kitchen came just after WWII. Blenders, toaster ovens, electric skillets, and microwave ovens (based on technology developed for radar) changed how and when women cooked. Along about this time, another appliance, the TV, created a different frozen phenomenon—the TV dinner, and all that food item has brought upon mankind. There is no doubt that the freezer and these other appliances have all become as vital to kitchens as the range.

"Wartime Suggestions to help you get the most out of your Refrigerator," Frigidaire Div, GM, Dayton, Ohio, 1943.

Of course, many pamphlets were produced explaining the advantages of each of these new electrical marvels and how to use them, and a few recipes were usually thrown in. I want to make special mention of one such appliance and the effect it had on me. The chest freezer became popular in the mid-1950s. Up until then, when we butchered on the farm, we had basically four ways to preserve the meat—pickling, smoking, canning, or freezing in a commercial packing plant. The last was a large walk-in freezer in a nearby town, where you rented a drawer and they generally cut and wrapped your meat for you. Some of them, by the way, are still in business today. Entering was a literal breath of cold air in the summer, but it got mighty cold awfully quick!

When we got our first chest freezer (a top-opening model that looked like a refrigerator lying on its side), we were able to cut up and freeze our own meat, along with fruits and vegetables. The smokehouse went cold, the pickling crocks gathered dust, and the canning gear was phased out. My mother loved it, and we ate better, with more variety.

Besides those produced by appliance manufacturers, cookbooks put out by food purveyors became popular as well. Flour companies, sugar manufacturers, chemical leavening agent manufacturers, and shortening makers put out their own cookbooks.[7] A booklet from Imperial Sugar showed how to freeze selected fruits and vegetables so they came out not only eatable but attractive.[8] The preserving properties of sugar were known as far back as ancient Egypt, and chefs know a tablespoon of sugar keeps vegetables on a steam table bright and fresh looking.

Roughly in the mid-1800s another family of products became available and popular: chemical leavening agents. Natural leavening agents (yeasts) have been known almost as long as man has known about ovens and baked bread. After various experimentations, it was found that when a byproduct of wine making, called cream of tartar (a strong acid) was combined with baking soda (a strong base), superior cakes and biscuits could be made that did not have to go through a period of time to "rise." Thus, quick breads. The new leavening agents produced a stream of cookbooks and booklets, teaching housewives how to use this wonderful new product. As gas ovens had yet to become popular just after the turn of the century, cookbooks of these type were still designed for users of cast iron stoves. Some sponsored baking contests, and winners would have their recipes included in the company's cookbooks.[9]

Marion Harris Neil's Ryzon Baking Book, 1918.

Any discussion of foodstuffs would be incomplete if it did not include lard and its next of kin, pure vegetable shortening. In the early 1900s, hydrogenated vegetable oils were developed, and in 1911 Proctor and Gamble started marketing a hydrogenated cottonseed oil called "Crisco." It was a great success, because it looked and handled like lard but didn't need to be refrigerated and had a higher flash point than lard. Not to be outdone, in 1938 Lever Bros. put out a competing product, "Spry." With Aunt Jenny hawking it on the radio, it was a great success.[10] Health concerns in the 1950s cut into the popularity of hydrogenated oils, and Lever Bros. stopped making "Spry," although you can still get "Crisco."

One more foodstuff needs to be mentioned—Carnation milk, which, of course, had a cookbook for recipes that made use of the product.[11] As the Texas story goes, the Carnation Milk Company sponsored a contest for an advertising slogan. A ranch wife, wishing to enter the contest, came up with what she thought might be the winning entry:

> Carnation Milk, best in the land,
> Comes to you in a little red can.

Since she lived on a ranch quite a ways from town, she gave her entry to a cowboy who was going into town to mail it for her. A month or later, she got a letter back from the Carnation Milk Company saying they were not able to use her entry because it was too profane. After puzzling over what in "Carnation Milk, best in the land, Comes to you in a little red can" was profane, she called in the cowboy who had mailed the letter. After some foot shuffling, he admitted he had changed it slightly. Knowing how badly she had wanted to win, he had taken the liberty of zipping up her rather bland couplet "to give a better chance of winning." The entry he sent in read:

> Carnation Milk, best in the land,
> Comes to you in a little red can,
> No tits to pull, no hay to pitch,
> Just punch a hole in the son-of-a-bitch.

No wonder it didn't win.

It has been an amazing revolution in a relatively short period of historical time. American housewives, and housewives all over the world, went from cooking over open flames to fully equipped clean kitchens with all sorts of labor-saving appliances and far healthier foods (as well as all sorts of convenience foods) in less than a century, or just about three generations of cooks. Cookbooks and pamphlets came of age, and reproducible results became the norm instead of happy accidents. Recipes became exact, measurements and cooking temperatures became standard, and nutritional information was made readily available. It has been a quiet revolution, yet it has freed women to escape the demands of literally keeping the home fires burning. The great debate about which is better, gas or electric to cook with, still rages. The real answer is, "Both are better than wood or coal!" We may enjoy a meal around a campfire or off a chuck wagon, but nothing beats "Cooking with Gas!"

Endnotes

1. Fannie Merritt Farmer. *The Boston Cooking School Cook Book.* Boston, MA, Date Unknown.
2. Wrought Iron Range Co. *Home Comfort Cook Book.* St. Louis, MO, 1933.
3. Lone Star Gas Company. *Flame Favorites.* Dallas, TX, (circa 1930s).
4. Virginia Frances. *Electric Cooking: The Key to Modern Living.* Hotpoint Institute, Chicago, ILL, (circa 1946).
5. Montgomery Ward. *Cold Cooking.* Chicago, ILL, 1949.
6. Frigidaire Div., GM. "Wartime Suggestions to Help You Get the Most Out of Your Refrigerator." Dayton, OH 1943.
7. Mrs. Lenore Standifer. *Practical Recipes for Using Light Crust Flour.* Burris Mills, Ft. Worth, TX, (circa 1933).
8. Imperial Sugar. *Home Freezing of Fruits and Vegetables.* Sugar Land, TX 1948.
9. Marion Harris Neil. *Ryzon Baking Book.* General Chemical Co., New York, NY, 1918.
10. Lever Bros. *Aunt Jenny's Favorite Recipes.* Cambridge, MA, 1940.
11. Mary Blake. *Carnation Cook Book.* The Carnation Company, Milwaukee, WI, 1942.

Getting ready to attach a horse to a plow.

HOMESTEAD HERITAGE FARMS: A STEP BACK IN TIME IN CENTRAL TEXAS

by Charles B. Martin

In Europe in the early 16th century a group of people called Anabaptists emerged as a nonviolent Protestant group which sought to remove itself from any connection to any governmental or religious body, preferring to live a life of Christian simplicity. This movement included Mennonites, Amish, and Brethren, many of them later coming to America.

One small group, basically Anabaptist in design, was organized in New York City in 1973 in the slum tenements of the Lower East side of Manhattan, under the leadership of Blair and Regina Adams. This small body of believers began to homeschool their children, birth their own babies, and look for ground where they could grow their own food, at first across the river in New Jersey. Then this group of closely knit people (about one hundred), decided in 1979 to move west, particularly to Colorado, where they rented a ten-acre plot and learned the skills of farming. This spot turned out to be much too small, so they decided to join another small group in Central Texas. Eventually, the new group acquired 510 acres near Elm Mott (northwest of Waco) and called it Homestead Heritage. According to one of its publications, the group is "an agriculturally- and craft-based intentional Christian community . . . which stresses simplicity, sustainability, self-sufficiency, cooperation, service and quality craftsmanship . . . and strives to live in peaceful coexistence with the land, other people and other faiths."[1]

A small area of the Homestead property is devoted to various buildings where particular craft activities take place or where members gather for business or worship. This area, called "Homestead Craft Village," is open to visitors throughout the year Monday through Saturday from 10:00 A.M. to 6:00 P.M., during which time they can take self guided or group tours to watch craftsmen at work. A Homestead Heritage "Fair" is held yearly on Thanksgiving weekend to showcase its many arts and crafts, and demonstrate how they are made. This three-day fair has attracted thousands of visitors each year, averaging an estimated 18,000 in 2010.[2]

Many of the crafts are shown in the Craft Pavilion. The fiber crafts section has quilts of various bright colors in both traditional and modern designs, delicate needle work, wool sweaters and silk scarves, as well as a spinning wheel being operated by someone pulling wool into fine strands which become the necessary thread for the loom. Handmade brooms are also on exhibit, as well as the machine for pressing and trimming them, and they are also for sale. Although expensive, they are sturdy and should last a lifetime.

A broom maker.

Woodcraft is another skill resurrected at Heritage Farms, as seen in both musical instruments like guitars and furniture (desks, chests, rocking chairs, and even small boats). Most are for sale.

Other crafts shown or demonstrated in the Pavilion include baskets of all shapes and sizes, pottery, and leather goods such as belts and handbags. These items, too, are for sale. Metal work is done at a nearby forge. Large items like bedsteads are made, as well as smaller objects like fireplace sets, table lamps, axes and smaller tools, and even key chains.

A man working at a forge.

In another building the process of making Brazos Valley cheese is demonstrated, with various cheeses for sale to local businesses and guests at the fair. Other milk products like ice cream are available to fairgoers. An old hand-crank ice cream freezer, a butter churn with paddle, and some old milk bottles add a nostalgic reminder of an earlier time. Bee-keeping and honey production are part of life at Heritage Farms, and this art is illustrated with a cross-section of a honeycomb encased within glass panels with instructions on how to gather and process the honey, which is also for sale.

A large ice cream freezer.

One large tent is dedicated to activities for children: printing one's name on a card on an old-fashioned hand-operated printing press, weaving a belt on a simple loom or on a larger loom, making baskets, making hand brooms, making a tool box, making small wooden boats, and making a jump rope, to name a few.

A child learning to work a loom.

Numerous outdoor demonstrations are given at assigned hours. A segment of a barn-raising takes place at certain designated hours; it involves assembling notched beams for cross pieces and enlisting onlookers to raise them up. A large sign nearby contains and explains all the different tools used in this kind of construction. Sheepherding is demonstrated on the nearby commons with one sheep dog and three or four sheep that the dog corners and corrals. Apples are washed and put into an apple press to be squeezed for making cider. Basic ploughing is demonstrated with a simple plough pulled by horses.

Traditional barn raising.

One area of the fairground is devoted to fragrances and herbs. A sign explains the process of distilling fragrances from herbs like rosemary, and two ladies demonstrate the process. Beds of various herbs can be seen nearby, and packets of various seeds are for sale. A grist mill built in the 1760s (and much later brought to the farm and restored) actually grinds corn and wheat with a stone grinder, powered by a waterwheel. Packaged meal is available for purchase in the nearby shop.

Beds of herbs.

Since so many people attend this yearly event, food and drinks are provided in "food courts," both in the open and in the woods. Different courts have different menus, like Mediterranean Cuisine, Sabor de Mexico, Corndogs and Funnel Cakes, Brick-Oven Pizza, Beef Wraps, BBQ Chicken, Taste of Asia, and Desserts and Ice Cream. The homemade sorghum-pecan ice cream is made in very large motorized freezers operated, ironically, by electricity. Tables and benches provide seating.

A large tent is erected each year to accommodate children's music in the afternoon and a 100-voice choir and 40-piece orchestra in the evening. A large storage tank nearby collects rainwater that is directed to surrounding gardens, in keeping with the conservation goals of the residents. One part of the fair is like a small zoo with its pens of various animals: sheep, llamas, chickens, and goats. A few pens become a petting zoo for kids.

A barn built in New Jersey in the early 1800s was later brought to Homestead, restored, and now serves as a kind of art gallery where selected handcraft items are placed in a silent auction with minimum bids listed on them. During the two years I attended, these items were for sale: a walnut desk, $15,000; a child's Windsor rocker, $1,500; a pair of alligator boots, $320; a quilt, $2,600; a mesquite chest of drawers, $6,900; an alpaca and Merino wool cardigan sweater, cochineal dye, $350; a silk scarf, imported silk, $850; a pair of Teju lizard and burgundy kangaroo boots, $2,600; a guitar, mesquite side panels, Sitka spruce front and back, $2,800; a mesquite desk with turquoise inlay, $4,800; a jack plane, bronze sides, steel base, rosewood infill, $795.

Handmade boots up for auction.

Another restored barn, now called the Ploughshare, is used for hourly lectures on diverse topics like the value of grass-fed beef, small-scale farming, energy conservation, food preservation, sustainable gardening, and small-scale family farming. I attended a talk by Dr. Kay Toombs, Associate Professor Emerita from Baylor

University, who explained why she moved to Heritage Farms and why she chose to live the simple life:

> I hope I have shown . . . that a community committed to the goals of sustainability provides a context in which all members of the community, young and old, can live rich and meaningful lives that maintain a sense of purpose, integrity and dignity. Such a context nurtures relationships between generations, within families and among neighbors in such a way that it becomes natural (and not burdensome) to focus on the essentials of living—giving birth, nurturing the lives of children and caring for the sick and elderly—and to make these a central aspect of daily life. Such a community provides an alternative culture with a radically different set of values to those of the mainstream. Participating in such a culture requires a shift in perspective, a turning away from the cultural emphasis on radical autonomy and individualism (with its commitment to "standing on your own two feet," "doing your own thing," being totally independent) to a recognition of the importance and value of relationship, cooperation and interdependence. At the same time, acquiring the knowledge and skills to meet essential needs provides a foundation for exercising personal responsibility and taking back control of many aspects of daily living that in the wider culture have been surrendered to strangers.[3]

While Homestead Heritage might seem to be the new Garden of Eden, there's a serpent in Paradise, which reared its ugly head in February of 2012, when reporter Alex Hannaford of the *Texas*

Observer of Austin revealed cases of physical and sexual child abuse.[4] Religious sects like these attempt to live a Bible-centered life and follow the admonition to physically punish their children and not spare the rod in breaking their willful disobedience. Yet some ex-members of the sect reported witnessing very severe beatings of children to discipline them. Any sexual abuse of children, according to Texas law, must be reported to police within forty-eight hours. Five men (three from one family) were convicted of sexual abuse of children, but it was a year before the first one went to jail because the Homestead sect ignores the law and tries to solve such problems among themselves by "counseling" any transgressors. Victims of sexual abuse evidently received no counseling, and justice for them was not served. According to Hannaford, the leaders of the community were able to downplay the problem to the press so that the reputation of the community was not damaged.

The group, Hannaford adds, is run by a very authoritative leader, Blair Adams, who dictates whatever decisions are made, even requiring an intensive investigation of prospective members and making them sign a form stating that they will not talk to anyone outside their group about controversial issues. In April of that year Brett Shipp, investigative reporter of WFAA Channel 8 in Dallas, gave a similar report with basically the same findings.[5]

In my two visits to the Homestead Fair I was most impressed with the quality of the crafts and the notion that people can live together in peace in a Christian community. The few people whom I talked to seemed very nice and also happy with their style of living. After reading about the crack in the varnish of the painting, I ask myself, "It's a nice place to visit, but do I really want to live there?" I highly recommend that you at least make that first visit and Come to the Fair.

ENDNOTES

1. *Homestead Heritage and Its Roots. An Introduction.* Colloquium Press, 2010. 1.
2. *Dallas Morning News,* November 14, 2010. 10E.

3. Kay Toombs. "The Human Dimension of Sustainable Culture." Colloquium Press, 2010. 22–23.
4. "Heritage of Abuse." *Texas Observer,* Feb. 10, 2012, April 23, 2012.
5. "Waco Religious Commune Accused of Masking Abuse." WFAA Channel 8, April 26, 2012.

Handmade guitars come with lessons.

Fine Arts Show

John Meadows.

OLD CARS DRIVING AROUND AUSTIN: BOYHOOD ADVENTURES BEHIND THE WHEEL

by John Meadows

I grew up listening to my Dad's yarns about his teenage adventures with automobiles in the 1920s. Austin was a much smaller and simpler place then. He and his friends could scrape together fifteen dollars or so and buy an old heap—maybe just a frame and an engine—and get it running. There were no inspection laws. They'd use crates for seats, find some wheels, and away they'd go. Dad became a really good mechanic and driver.

The automobile industry was new and unrestricted. Anyone who could cobble together something self-powered could offer it for sale. By the 1920s well over *1,500* makes had been offered—36 in Texas alone![1] There were steamers, all-electrics, gasoline fueled, and even a couple of spring-wound models. One little car had just one cylinder. When it began to move the driver could feel it being yanked along, one piston stroke at a time.

Most cars had just four cylinders, though some had more. The sounds of traffic included squealing brakes, gears grinding during shifting, and all sorts of horns, including oo-gah horns, beepers, and even bells. Very old cars had big rubber squeeze bulbs that made their horns <u>HONK</u>! Pedestrians crossing at an intersection could hear the rhythmic tapping of waiting engines and the putt-putting of the exhausts.

Cars had smells, too, of horsehair upholstery, hot lubricating oil, and exhaust fumes. Wheel bearings and other parts had to be lubricated regularly. When's the last time your car had to have a lube job?

Automobiles had real bumpers. One car could carefully push another without damage to either one. Fenders were strong enough to stand on. Once Dad and some friends were driving down a country road in one of their jalopies and had to slow down behind a poky truck full of watermelons. They pulled up close and one of the guys clambered over a front fender to the bumper of their moving car and handed back a couple of melons to the others without ever being seen by the truck's driver.

Unpaved roads could become so deeply rutted that a car's wheels, narrower in those days, would stay down in the ruts and guide the car. A driver approaching a closed farm gate could set the throttle low, jump out of the car, run to the gate and open it, let the car go through, close the gate behind it, and catch up with the car again. A car could even be driven down railroad tracks if enough air was let out of the tires. The extra-soft tires would bulge down on each side of a rail, which tended to keep the car from veering to the left or right.

My Dad's buddy Irving once "walked" his four-cylinder Hupmobile down Austin's main street just for fun. He strolled along beside it reading a newspaper as the car idled slowly along in low gear. Irving said that the Hupmobile's engine was saying, "Chick-en Hock-ey, Chick-en Hock-ey." Gas-thirsty Cadillac engines said, "Cup-and-a-half, cup-and-a-half."

Once Dad was riding with Irving as they raced along a raised road through cotton fields outside the city. There was a sharp turn ahead, but Dad was bound by their unspoken rule never to question one another's driving. Irving gasped—and the Hupmobile flew off the embankment, flipping over in the air. Dad was thrown through the cloth top, and the car fell heavily, right side up, against the far side of a stout post in the field. The wooden spokes of all four wheels were broken. Fortunately, both Dad and Irving escaped serious injury. Dad still had a photograph of the Hupmobile beside the post.

Austin's steep hill at 19th and North Lamar was a challenge. The weak little electric cars of the day, powered by heavy storage batteries, had no choice but to find an easier way up. Model T Fords that had their gas tank up behind the driver relied on gravity to make the gasoline flow forward to the engine. At the steepest part of the hill the tank became lower than the engine, which then ran out of fuel. Drivers handled the problem by backing up the hill. A steam car would climb up as far as it could, stop for a minute to let the steam pressure increase, then chuff easily over the top. Steamers were major competitors with gas cars. It's even possible that if the quick-pressurizing flash boiler had been perfected before the gas-driven cars' electric starter that some steamers might still be on the market.

When he was in the National Guard Dad drove trucks with mechanical governors that limited how fast they could be driven. The drivers discovered how to disable them: as they started down a steep grade they would put the truck in low gear and hold down the clutch pedal. Once the truck was coasting downhill really fast, the clutch pedal would be released and the low gear would make the engine spin really fast—faster than the governor was designed to go—and Bang! The governor would fly apart. After that, the drivers could go as fast as they wanted.

The first car I remember in our family was a black Ford sedan, probably made in about 1940. It was a V-8, with one of the peculiar-looking distributors of that model mounted on the front of the engine. There was lots of space under the hood, allowing fairly easy access to most of the engine's exterior components: generator, starter, carburetor, and so forth. The ground beneath the car was visible between the engine and the insides of the front fenders. The car had running boards, like most cars then.

One of the cars we had when I was growing up was a Kaiser Vagabond. The guy who sold them was a family friend. We combined a driving vacation with a trip to Ypsilanti, Michigan, to pick up our car spanking new at the plant. It was so new that it had to be run back through the paint-drying process again. I got to tour the plant and see giant machines stamping out hoods and body panels.

It was a good car, one of the earliest hatchbacks. The upper part of the trunk lid, including the rear window, could be raised out of the way, and the lower half of the lid folded out level to form a substantial shelf. The back seat folded down to form a flat space from the rear of the car all the way to the back of the front seat, large enough for a mattress even with the trunk lids closed. The car's engine was a Red Seal Continental Straight Six, made by a company that manufactured engines for heavy equipment.

We continued our vacation by driving into Canada for a few days. In an antique store there I found a pair of kerosene-burning cowl lamps that had flanked the windshield of a Model T Ford. They aren't headlights; they're more like what we call "parking lights." One of these hardy little lanterns will cast an image of its lens on the far wall of a dark room. Later, I acquired a kerosene tail lamp with a big red lens, as well as a smaller lens on one side to illuminate the license plate.

For years there was a grand old touring car, tall and bony, visible at the end of a street in North Austin. The car was a Dodge Brothers touring car built around 1920, still in pretty good condition. It was open sided except for a raised cloth top. Touring cars then weren't equipped with built-in side windows. The wheels, though narrow, were quite tall and held the old Dodge high off the ground, which was an asset on the bad roads of the day. The lady who lived there said it belonged to her son and that she was keeping it for him. By then the car had been sitting there for thirty years.

When I was in college I heard that someone had a Peerless automobile for sale, so I went to have a look. It was parked behind a filling station in East Austin. Made in the late 1920s, it had front and back seats and a folding top, which was down. I liked its wedge-shaped radiator, which looked like it was parting the wind even when the car was standing still. I didn't buy it, partly because I didn't have the money and partly because I was suspicious of how the guys selling it had acquired it.

One teenage birthday when I was barely old enough to drive Dad presented me with my first car. I looked out the front door, and there at the curb sat a 4-cylinder '27 Chevrolet, a car much like a Ford Model A. It was an open-topped roadster painted with orange and white house paint. The trunk had been cut away clear to the back of the front seat, exposing the insides of the rear fenders, the rear axle, and the road below it. It looked awful.

I came to love it. We put wider, more modern wheels and tires on it, and I drove it everywhere. The frame was made of wood like those of many cars then. Even the steering wheel was made of wooden sections nicely joined together. Old wooden steering wheels with exhausted glue could pull apart in your hands, which could be scary. Once in a while I had to start it by cranking the engine, which takes some caution and experience. I had acquired some wary cranking skill starting the old monster Farmall F-20 tractor at my Dad's farm.

I had my first automobile accident in the Chevy on a rainy day in downtown Austin. The light had turned green and I had started across the intersection when the car ahead suddenly halted. I stepped on the brake, which was made to stop only the rear wheels, and skidded helplessly about twenty feet. I had almost come to a stop when I lightly collided with the rear bumper of the car that had stopped ahead of me. A frowning middle-aged man got out of the car to see if any damage had been done. He looked at his bumper, scowled at me, and got back in his car without a word. I probably looked pretty scared.

One night when some of us teenagers were out running around in our (and our parents') cars, we stopped on the roadside to get out and chat. Bobby left his Model A idling, but didn't set the brake. He heard the crunch of tires on gravel and spun around to see his little coupe gently rolling backwards toward the brushy dropoff beside the road. He yelled to the boy nearest the car, "Murphy! Murphy! Stop my mill!" Murphy looked just as the car started over the edge and whooped with laughter as it crushed through the brush and rumbled down backwards out of sight. We all ran to look—and there was the little car, caught among the juniper branches, shining its headlights back up at us and still idling happily. The next day Bobby had a wrecker pull it back up. It was just fine except for some scratches from the juniper.

My second car was a Graham, a small top-heavy sedan. It was a bulbous little car made in about 1940. I drove it to high school and to out-of-town football games as far away from Austin as Alice, Texas. When the brakes began to get bad I shamelessly slowed it down by gratingly forcing the transmission into lower gears. Though the Graham wasn't anything special for a high school kid,

I was really glad we hadn't gotten the old Nash that Dad found for sale. It was a big rounded white sedan that looked like an upside-down bathtub: very uncool. Years later, I had a Nash Rambler Station Wagon that was a good car. One of my favorite later cars was a two-door '54 Chevy Bel Air Straight Six. I drove it around Austin, around Texas, and even to California, where it broke down. I managed to fix it up and drive it back to Austin.

My folks were friends with some people who had a grand old cream-colored Jaguar which they let me drive occasionally. It was made in the late 1930s and had a stand-up chrome radiator and a jaguar on top of the big chrome radiator cap. There were swooping front fenders with large headlights. It was a right-side steering car, interesting to drive on American streets. It had turn signals—the first I had seen. An illuminated pointer would flick up outside of the doorpost on the side you were going to turn toward.

Jaguars of its vintage were heavy cars. Its transmission sounded truck-like as it was put through the gears. The folding top had three positions: all the way up, part-way down (exposing the driver but not the rear seat), and all the way down. A shiny, elongated S-shaped brace flanked each side of the top when it was up. This feature was thought elegant by some American car makers, who later used it as nonfunctional decoration on some of their models. The Jaguar's heavy trunk lid folded out into a substantial shelf. In that position the inside of the trunk lid could be raised to reveal baize-lined recesses for a complete set of mechanic's tools—missing, alas, on that vehicle.

In 1957, I drove my Aunt Lora's little Nash Metropolitan from Austin to Houston. It was an unusually small design for an American car at that time. Made in the mid-1950s and smaller than today's Mazda Miata, it was quite stylish—even cute—and was marketed with women in mind.[2] I enjoyed the trip, breezing down the highway in the little car with the top down.

I was working at an Austin hotel when it was visited by a club of Cord and Auburn automobile owners. They were driving especially handsome models manufactured in the 1930s. It was really nice to be able to stroll among the old classics and see them up close. The

Cord's hoods were fairly tall and rectangular, with several broad louvers that extended unbroken along the sides and across the bluntish nose. Because of their rectangular shape, Cords with these hoods were commonly known as "coffin-nosed." Another Cord model sported two sexy chrome flex-pipes emerging from each side of the hood. The Cords were front-wheel drive, with big rounded front fenders extending forward beyond the hood and containing hidden headlights.

The Auburn Roadster was also a beautiful car, with its "boat-tail" body tapering together at the back of the vehicle. Both Cord and Auburn made a series of exceptionally good-looking models beginning in 1929 and maturing through the 1930s. Photos of several models may be found on both Wikipedia and YouTube.

Just a few years ago I was in a Wal-Mart parking lot in Navasota, Texas, and noticed an old couple loading their stuff into an auto I couldn't immediately identify. It wasn't out of place among the other parked cars. I looked and discovered that it was a Studebaker, well-cared for and still stylish. It was probably manufactured in the 1960s as one of the last models the company produced.

I love antique cars, which for me means those made before 1940, and especially those made before 1930. It saddens me and makes me a little mad when I see some grand old car left out in the weather to deteriorate. Lots of cars have gone extinct just in my lifetime: Mercury, Packard, Oldsmobile, and Plymouth, to name a very few.

Since I've been driving I've had a VW van, a pickup, a Cadillac, and various other cars made in Japan and Korea. They've all been satisfactory in their way, and some were really fun. I still miss the '27 Chevy, though.

Endnotes

1. Beverly Rae Kimes, and Henry Austin Clark, Jr. *Standard Catalog of American Cars 1805–1942*. 3rd Edition. Iola, WI: Krause Publications, Inc., 1996. 5.
2. Patrick R. Foster. *The Metropolitan Story*. Iola, WI: Krause Publications, Inc., 1996. 41–53.

Elizabeth Ann Harris, 1947.

BEFORE I WAS FIVE

by Elizabeth Harris Duncan

Their voices echo in my heart in the quiet moments. Your people, the people you were born to and loved first, never leave you. I hear them often, with their peculiar mixture of Texas-Tennessee-Kentucky-Virginia cadence and pronunciation, their good common sense and strict ideals. It's a time long gone. Perhaps you will get the flavor of some of that time as I try to slip into young 'Lisputh Ann's skin and tell you something about my view of life then.

Any house Grandmother lived in had a water well, a bucket and dipper by the back door, a Jersey cow, chickens, guineas, a garden, number two tubs, a churn, and a toilet (which is a whole 'nuther story). Grandmother sang hymns all day—"In the Sweet Bye and Bye" and "I Won't Have to Cross Jordan Alone." Sometimes when she wasn't drawing or heating water, washing, starching, ironing, sweeping, mopping, scrubbing, gardening, canning, feeding, milking, making butter, frying up a meal, baking biscuits or making pie, Grandmother used a shiny black and silver machine on a little table in her bedroom. The table had graceful, curvy, wrought-iron side panels for legs, and a little wrought-iron see-saw platform underneath. Sometimes she would let me rock on the platform—and I could go fast! Once I crept under the table when she was in the kitchen and rocked back and forth a while. Humble, sweet-natured, kindly Grandmother came as close to pinching my head off as I ever saw. Rocking a Singer back and forth when there is material under the needle is a shamey-shamey thing to do, just as bad as being stingy or tacky.

The kitchen was the center of the house, and Grandmother was the center of the kitchen. The old wooden table was stained from years of use, but always scrubbed clean. Granddaddy had stretched rawhide over the seats of the ladderback chairs, and some of the hide still had hair on it. Sometimes I worried that Granddaddy would make seats out of the old Jersey cow.

Gentle old Great-Granddaddy Rackley lived with us for a while, and he sat in the kitchen, cocked back in one of those chairs. He'd drum his fingernails in rhythms on the table while Grandmother cooked. He always seemed to have a soft three-day growth of whiskers and a funny, musty old-man smell. He would hold me in his lap and we'd play "This Little Piggy" and "Patty Cake."

Sometimes Great-Grandmother and Great-Grandfather Jones lived with us, or maybe we lived with them. They didn't tolerate children well. Red-headed "Papa" Jones was "touchous," and my job was to stay out of his way. It didn't take much to make him faunch and rare. Tiny little Mama Jones, however, did the most magical thing. She sat in the kitchen rocking chair, quiet as a mouse, making lace in thin air, from a string and a little bone stick. I wasn't allowed to bother her, but could watch from the doorway. If I got too close I might annoy her or knock over her snuff can. But, oh, how I wanted to crochet!

There was a pretty little white bowl with roses painted on it in the middle of the table. Prettier than the bowl was the spoon. It had delicate curved edges and was called a "sugar shell." It didn't take me long after I started walking to discover that I could pull out a chair all by myself, climb up onto it, balance, and then climb up onto the table. I'd make myself comfortable on the table, then use the lovely sugar shell to steal a taste (or two, or three). I didn't know about rationing. The tasting, of course, happened only when nobody was looking. Then somebody (usually Grandmother) would catch me, warn that climbing would make me "go boom" onto the floor, and lift me out of harm's way back to my own natural level. Grandmother would always say, "Ye gonna git sugar diabetes jist as shore as ye're a-livin.'" Then she would shamey-shamey me.

Some people were real, like Mama, Grandmother, Granddaddy, Aunt Elaine and Uncle Jack; but Daddy was on the dresser, a black and white picture in a frame. In the picture, he had on a Marine uniform. When we went to town, every time I saw a man in any kind of uniform I would point and ask Mama, "Is that my Daddy?" just in case he had got out of the frame. Thirteen-year-old Aunt Elaine got into a hair-pulling, eye-gouging, ear-biting tussle with a neighbor girl because she said I didn't have a daddy. Aunt Elaine came out on top, literally, and convinced her that my daddy was away fighting the war, and she better keep her bull-corn mouth shut if she wanted to live another day.

Always shadowing my peaceful little world were the darkness of war and the boogerman. I knew the boogerman would get me if I strayed out of our yard or didn't "be-have." We went to the show once in a while, and I saw newsreels about the war. I heard about the cold, heat, snow, rain, bombs, torture, disease, fire, flood, maiming, blood, bullets, and death. I halfway understood that my Daddy was fighting something, maybe the boogerman. I heard talk about how all four of Daddy's younger brothers might have to go to war, and how Uncle Jack might have to go to war.

None of the women drove. Most often, we walked when we went to town or to the Nazarene church or visiting. I always liked going to town to see so many people and colors. I really liked the old men who lounged around the courthouse in their overalls, spitting and whittling. Well, I didn't like the spitting, but I liked the old men. I liked to watch them sharpening little pocket knives on a whetrock and shaving slivers from sticks. One of the whittlers made a tiny basket for me out of a black walnut shell after he dug the "goodie" out, and I kept it for years with my other play-pretties.

One day we were fixing to go to town, and of course, I was raring to go. Grandmother told me, "Hold ye tater, honey, we'll go dreckly." We finally set off, Mama holding my hand so I wouldn't stumble in my white shoes. I was bald as an egg until I was two, so I had on a starched white bonnet, too. Grandmother carried her trusty black parasol. She always carried her parasol outdoors when she wasn't wearing a sunbonnet. When we got to town, there was something wrong with the flags at the courthouse and the post office. I loved the flags, the bright colors and the way they floated out in the tiniest breeze. This day they weren't right; they were low on the pole, not at the top like they were supposed to be. I asked Mama why the flags were funny and she said, "The president died." I didn't know what a president was, but everybody was solemn and scared-looking. There was talk everywhere about the war and what would happen next. It felt like an even darker cloud was casting its shadow on our people.

Most days were peaceful, though, and I spent a lot of them with Grandmother. Sometimes she was just "give out" and her hands were "sore as a risin" after a long day of work. She would fill a white dishpan with water from the bucket, dip a rag into the water, and "rench off" before she went to bed. She'd put on a white cotton gown, take down her long gray hair, and brush it before "hitting the hay." Then in the morning she re-braided her hair and wound the braids around her head again. She started the day fully dressed (no robe or slippers in those little houses), heading out to milk in her sunbonnet and apron.

Uncle Jack was just about my favorite person in the whole world. He always called me "sugar." Everybody else called me 'Lisputh Ann. I found out decades later that Granddaddy had advised him to call all young females "sugar" so he wouldn't get in trouble with whatever sweetheart he might be with. Uncle Jack loved tamales and sometimes bought them from stringy little old Mr. Carpenter. Mr. Carpenter pushed a cart down our street (on his way to the jockey lot) calling out "Hot tamales, red hot!" Uncle Jack and I would sneak out by the cowshed and eat them right out of the cornhusks. Grandmother and Mama didn't want us eating those tamales—said they were made out of cat meat. We did it anyway, red grease running off our elbows, lip smacking good. If we weren't caught red-handed, we were surely caught red-elbowed. Sometimes Uncle Jack hired out for a week or two to do farm work when he wasn't in school. I always missed him and waited for him to come back.

James Jackson (Jack) Jones and Elizabeth.

About the time the president died, seventeen-year-old Uncle Jack came home with a Navy uniform. He was going to war. My heart was broken. You see, in my little mind when a man wore a uniform and went away, he turned into a picture in a frame. I bawled and squalled and threw wall-eyed fits, rolling fits, and hissy fits, but it didn't do any good. Grandmother was stoic, Mama was crying, Aunt Elaine was crying, and I was screaming when he walked west from our house to catch the bus. Aunt Elaine says I got away from them and chased him down the road, screaming "Uncle Jack, come back, Uncle Jack, come back," but I don't remember doing that. She may have mixed in the scene from the movie *Shane,* or I may have forgotten that part. I learned the song "Bell Bottom Trousers" and sang it all the time, hoping my Uncle Jack would come back.

In December, 1945, Daddy *did* come home. I was going on three, and Mama was renting a room from the Rushings. I couldn't comprehend that a real person was going to come out of that picture in the frame. One morning a taxi pulled up out front, a tall man got out, and Mama went running out the screen door, letting it slam behind her (shamey-shamey). Billie Rushing grabbed me up into her arms to watch. Daddy seemed to me the tallest man I had ever seen (about six feet) with black hair (like in the picture) and blue eyes (which in the picture were gray) and big, strong hands. He was dark-tanned, blue veins stood out on his muscled arms, and he had a nice smile. He told me, "Hidey, 'Lisputh Ann," and picked me up so I was tall, too. He smelled like Granddaddy's cigarettes and hair tonic, but not like Granddaddy's whiskey. I was floored—he was real!

Everett Lee and Mary Elizabeth Harris.

Daddy got a job as an ice man after he got home, and I went with him one day. We walked up to the ice house, he put me in the truck, put on his brown leather shoulder vest, grabbed a huge set of tongs, and loaded block ice onto the back of the truck. Some blocks were big, and some were small. They were all so heavy that I couldn't push them by myself, so I knew Daddy was really big and strong to just pick them up and carry them over his shoulder. On his route, the housewives had signs in the windows that told him how much ice they wanted. He would hook a block of ice, sling it over his shoulder, and carry it into the house to put into the icebox for the customer.

I spent a few weeks about that time picking the "sprout" portion out of my pinto beans. There was a tiny scar on the little finger of my right hand in the shape of that sprout and I was convinced that if I ate that piece of a bean I would have another scar like that. None of the household could persuade me otherwise. I liked greens too, and Grandmother cooked poke sallat one day for dinner. It was a hot day, and I was running around without a dress or shoes, so Mama probably wasn't there. I climbed up on my chair, ready to eat my pintos, greens, and cornbread. The greens were larrupin', and I ate a lot, with the juice running down my chin and chest. By the time dinner was over, I was broken out from bottom lip to boley button from that juice. Never got to eat poke sallat again, because they figured if it was ruining me on the outside, it was probably ruining me on the inside.

The last place we lived before I was five was a duplex on Anthony Street. One day in the Spring of 1948, I was learning to use blunt-nosed scissors to cut out my first set of paper dolls—you know, the cardboard doll with different sets of clothes you can attach. In the middle of my work, Mama said we had to go over to Mrs. Sadler's house because it was coming up a cloud. Well, I didn't want to go. Mama grabbed up a flyswatter and cocked it, so I became ready to go. Sure enough, it was dark and gloomy outside, kind of yellow-green-black looking, still and sweaty. The potato wagon was turning over in long, low rumbles off to the southwest. We hoofed the two blocks to the Sadlers', whose house was attached to a concrete foundation instead of set on bois d'arc posts. I was looking out the window when the first quick little whiffs of wind came. Then all of a sudden stuff started hitting on all sides of the house at once. Leaves, sticks, branches, gravel, shingles, chicken houses, outhouses, everything that was the least bit loose was flying through the air. Mama was sitting in the middle of the room on a straight chair crying, and all the neighbor women (who had also come to Mrs. Sadler's) were praying and shouting, generally making nearly as much racket as the storm was. Mrs. Coleman said she was going to knock a knot on my head when I started toward the windowglass again. Well, the storm didn't last very long and the house didn't blow away, but there was a mess of trash all over. Mr. Reeder's onion fields had been beaten to a pulp by rain and hail, and the whole world smelled like onions.

The Mill Block got the worst of it. Great-Aunt Odessa and her friends at the cotton mill had to crawl out of the building under and over timbers, broken glass, machinery, and electric wires. My third cousin, Little Stella, and her mother (Nadine) lived close to the cotton mill. Nadine had gone out on her front porch to look at the cloud. She had baby Happy Jack in one arm and was holding Little Stella by the hand. That tornado hit so fast and so hard that it snatched Little Stella away from Nadine and sat her down in a field a hundred yards away. She didn't have a scratch. Little Stella was famous for years for surviving that ordeal.

Shortly after that, people started building storm cellars; but that's a whole 'nuther story, too.

Uncle Jack didn't turn into a picture in a frame; he came back for visits between duties. He was there when we spent the night at Grandmother's in July of 1948. It seemed like a normal evening—Grandmother cooked, we ate, and I still didn't understand why the grownups got to drink their sweet tea out of a pretty goblet and I had to drink out of a jelly glass. We listened to the radio, and I went to sleep on a pallet next to Mama and Daddy's bed. I woke up in the middle of the night and got up to check on Mama and Daddy. They weren't there and the boogerman came to mind, so I went to find Grandmother. She wasn't there. Granddaddy was sleeping hard in her bed and wouldn't wake up. Granddaddy was a high-strung hard-living, hard-drinking ring-tailed-tooter. When he wasn't barbering, he wore dress western shirts and pants, a fine gray Stetson, and hand-tooled cowboy boots. He had a big horse named Buck that he rode in the rodeo, and a shiny black Cadillac. Sometimes he didn't come home at night, and sometimes he came home lit up like a hoot-owl. I decided it would be smarter to wake up Uncle Jack. He pulled me up next to him on the couch and said, "Just go on back to sleep, sugar; your Mama and Daddy went to get a new baby for you, and Grandmother went with them."

Well, that was interesting. I had heard Mama was "expecting," but I didn't know what that meant; and why would anybody want to go out in the middle of the night when you could just as well wait until the sun was up? But I went back to sleep, snug against Uncle Jack's chest.

Grandmother was in the kitchen when I woke up the next morning, and breakfast smells were drifting through the little house and out the windows. Coffee, sausage, eggs, biscuits and gravy, and my little jelly glass of sweet tea were almost ready. I never could keep milk down, so I always drank sweet tea. I hiked my hiney up onto the chair with quilts stacked on it. I asked if Mama and Daddy were still out getting a baby, and Grandmother said they were going to bring a brother home in a day or two. I was pretty excited. I imagined that it would be like cousin Happy Jack, plump and cooing, and that I could dress it up and carry it around; I was really looking forward to getting that baby.

Boy howdy, was I wrong. Three days later, he came home with Mama. He was skinny and wrinkled, had a bad temper, and was rude and selfish. He acted like a little heathen. He tee-teed and doo-dooed whenever and wherever he wanted. He got fed whenever and wherever he wanted. Nobody but me seemed to mind that he was such a knucklehead. I didn't much like him and said so. Shamey-shamey.

Then I was five, and my world had changed, for sure and forever.

CONTRIBUTORS' VITAS

Meredith E. Abarca is from Nuevo Laredo, Tamaulipas, Mexico, and came to Laredo as a child knowing three phrases in English: "Excuse me," "How much?" and "Thank you." Shortly thereafter, she and her family moved to California, where in 2000 she received her Ph.D. in Comparative Literature from the University of California at Davis; soon after that, she landed a position in the English Department at the University of Texas at El Paso. Her first book, *Voices in the Kitchen,* published by Texas A&M Press in 2006, pays tribute to her mother, Duvi Vélez, and other Mexican-American working-class women whose philosophies are frequently overlooked. Her work is well-known internationally; she has lectured at the University of Gastronomical Sciences in Parma, Italy; the University of Technology in Sidney, Australia; the Sorbonne in Paris in 2015; and, in 2016 she was an invited participant in a food studies symposium at the University of Oslo, Norway. She is the Humanities Book Review Editor for *Food & Foodways,* the most important academic journal in Food Studies, in which she has published. Her latest endeavor included the mentoring of a Ph.D. student as they co-edited *Latinas' Presence in the Food Industry: Changing How We Think about Food.* In 2016 she was promoted to Full Professor. Meredith has been involved with the Texas Folklore Society since 2002, was Vice-President and Program Chair in 2016, and serves as President in 2017.

Lucy Fischer-West's first road trip with her husband John O. West was to the Texas Folklore Society's meeting in 1971. Her first presentation began the 21st century meetings in 2000, and since then she has participated on both TFS and TSHA panels; her pieces have been in five Texas Folklore Society publications, and she was the Society's President in 2010. Lucy's book *Child of Many Rivers,* published by Texas Tech University Press in 2005, garnered a Southwest Book Award, a Violet Crown Citation Award from the Writers' League of Texas, and was a WILLA Literary

Award Finalist. She is a lifetime educator, currently teaching high school world history to 140 hormone-ravaged boys at Cathedral High School. In 2013, Lucy received a Stanford University Certificate of Recognition for Exceptional Teaching, and she was named Teacher of the Year for the Diocese of El Paso in 2014. In 2015, she received an Outstanding Teaching of the Humanities Award from Humanities Texas, the state arm of the National Endowment for the Humanities.

Carol Bolland has been a member of Texas Folklore Society since 2003. A native Texan, growing up in Waco and Fort Worth, she received her B.M. and M.M. in music theory and literature—and a husband—at Baylor University. After spending 29 years in "exile" in western Pennsylvania while her husband was on the faculty at Clarion University of Pennsylvania, they returned to Texas in 2002 and currently are enjoying retirement in New Braunfels, making music as the founding members of Dusty Relics, a band that specializes in classic country music. Carol has enjoyed putting her musicological skills to use in her golden years, researching and writing papers for the TFS, and is grateful to her husband Herb for his assistance in these undertakings.

James Mody Bridges' association with the Texas Folklore Society began with the first meeting he attended as a youth with his family, when his grandfather was honored at the annual meeting in Alpine in 1968. Ernest Speck, his step-father, was a frequent contributor to the TFS and a former President. Jim attended many other meetings as a youth, and especially enjoyed watching the old folks' behavior during the Hootenanny. The project in this book has been a tremendous opportunity to gather insight into his family history and to more appreciate his family heritage. Jim contributes a weekly comic strip to the Marfa, Texas, newspaper, *The Big Bend Sentinel,* titled "The Adventures of Dick Decent." Currently, he is retired. After a long hiatus, he is happy to be reunited with the Texas Folklore Society.

Paul H. Carlson is Emeritus Professor of History at Texas Tech University. A member of the Texas Institute of Letters and the Philosophical Society of Texas, he is also a Fellow of the Texas State Historical Association. A former president of the West Texas Historical Association, he has published more than twenty books, including *The Plains Indians*, a History Book of the Month Club selection. He lives along the upper Brazos River in Lubbock County.

Michael Collins served Midwestern State University for twenty-seven years before retiring in 2012. He earned his B.A., M.A., and Ph.D. degrees in history from Texas Christian University. In 2006, the MSU Board of Regents selected Dr. Collins as a Regents Professor, and they named him the Hardin Distinguished Professor of American History in 2008. A Fellow of the Texas State Historical Association, he is a specialist in the American West and Texas, as well as twentieth-century U.S. political and diplomatic history. His publications include five books, among them: *Texas Devils: Rangers and Regulars on the Lower Rio Grande, 1846–1861; That Damned Cowboy: Theodore Roosevelt and the American West, 1883–1898;* and, *Profiles in Power: Twentieth Century Texans in Washington.* In 2008, the Minnie Stevens Piper Foundation of San Antonio honored him for his lifetime commitment to teaching excellence. He is now an independent scholar living in New Braunfels, Texas.

Margaret Anna Cox of Austin grew up in the small town of Eden, Texas, fourth generation of Concho County pioneers. She majored in Library Service at North Texas State College (now UNT) in 1961, worked thirty-five years in the University of Texas Library, and presented papers at three TFS meetings. Her stories have appeared in *The Family Saga, Death Lore,* and *Tales of Texas Cooking.*

Adam Cree is a History Teacher at Saint Michael's High School, Chorley, Great Britain. He studied History and History of Science at the University of Lancaster. He has been cataloguing and researching the *Chorley Memorial Album of Astley Hall* and its compiler, Susannah Knight, since 2006. As a consequence, he has published *From the Humblest to the Greatest—How Susannah Knight Took Chorley's Great War to the World*. He has a wonderful daughter called Martha.

Elizabeth Harris Duncan is a native of McKinney, Texas, where she still lives with her husband, Robert J. (Jack). She has served the Texas Folklore Society by providing local meeting arrangements and as a member of the Board, as Vice-President and as President. Retirement from Raytheon's Space and Airborne Systems provided the opportunity to pursue a "bucket list" of aspirations. Completing a B.A. was one of those items, and that occurred in 2012 at Texas Woman's University in Denton. Things like volunteering, going parasailing, swimming with dolphins, touching a glacier, growing tomatoes, and making quilts for Project Linus are others. When her sister, Linda, suggested she write about some of the memories of early childhood and a little family during World War II, "Before I Was Five" was added to that bucket list.

Robert J. (*Jack*) Duncan has taught at Collin College and Grayson County College. He is a life member of the Texas State Historical Association and a member of the East Texas Historical Association. Jack's articles have been published in many popular and scholarly periodicals. For more than sixteen years, he has worked as a writer/editor/researcher for Retractable Technologies, Inc., a medical device manufacturer in Little Elm. Jack often takes graduate history courses at UNT, in which he has written approximately thirty biographical entries for the *Handbook of Texas*. Jack has lived in McKinney most of his life. He is married to his high school sweetheart, the former Elizabeth Ann Harris; they have two sons and five grandsons. Jack is a former President of the Texas Folklore Society and a life member; he has been an active member for forty-seven years.

W. Floyd Elliott was born in 1928 near Tyler, Texas, and raised in the East Texas Oil Field. After attending college, he taught in the

Overton ISD Schools for twelve years (three years elementary, three years junior high, three years high school, and three years as high school principal), at Kilgore College for three years, and twenty-eight years at the university level. Currently retired from the Texas A&M University System, he resides at a retirement center in Tyler. The story "Visiting in the 1930s" comes in part from his book *Tangled Trails* (Outskirts Press, 2016).

Barbara Finlay is Professor Emerita in Sociology at Texas A&M University. She was born and raised in rural McCulloch County, Texas, where she has returned after her retirement. She has published several books and numerous articles based on her sociological research, focusing mainly on religion and gender. Dr. Finlay has also maintained an interest in Texas local history, having written numerous articles about the history and lore of rural Texas.

Matt Gibson and **Erin Marissa Russell** are recent graduates of Texas Woman's University in Denton, Texas. They met in Dr. Phyllis Bridges' Shakespeare class and credit Dr. Bridges not only for seating them next to each other at a showing of *King Lear,* which led to them falling in love, but also for instilling a love of folklore and introducing them to the Texas Folklore Society. They were married on New Year's Eve in 2015, and are working together on a novel based on the hermit's legend. Both are freelance writers. Erin is an editor, and Matt is a rapper and musician. The two are opening a content marketing agency in 2017.

Karen Reinartz Haile has five favorite things: dancing, singing, laughing, learning, and being with family and friends. By being a part of the Texas Folklore Society family, she has enjoyed all five of her favorite things at each and every TFS meeting for the past thirty-six years. Those of you who really know Karen and her husband Lee, know that they raised their two daughters, Acayla and Sierra, to live and love the old ways—and the tradition continues!

Lee Haile has been a TFS member since he gave a paper on folk toys while he was still a student at Texas A&M. He graduated with a degree in Entomology (bugs) in 1982. He has been active in the TFS ever since, with his family. Most people know him from the "hootenannies" at the annual meetings. He worked for years in the Ag world as a consulting entomologist checking crops. He has been the folk toy maker at the Texas Folklife Festival for thirty years. He lives in western Bandera County in the beautiful Texas Hill Country near a little town called Tarpley. He has a sawmill and a full woodshop where he builds furniture, and yes, he is still building on his house. These days you can catch him performing around the Hill Country at festivals, schools, wineries and other places, or giving birding and nature tours and river tours.

Mariann Fisk Laughlin holds a Master's degree from Southern Methodist University and a Master's degree in School Mid-Management from Texas Woman's University. She received her B.A. in Political Science and English from the University of Houston. Mariann has also done modeling and acting, and was listed with an agency in Dallas, Texas, for eleven years. She is a member of many genealogical organizations, but is most involved in the Daughters of the Republic of Texas, and served for seven years as a member of the French Legation Museum Committee. She currently serves on the Board of Management of the Daughters of the Republic of Texas. She is also a recipient of the Mamie Wynn Cox Award from the Daughters for her historic research. She grew up in Athens, Texas, but her mother's family roots were in the Austin area. She currently resides in Fort Worth, where she is a member of the First Methodist Church and Ridglea Country Club. She is the mother of Commander Erik Lohrke, USN, and Lindsay Lohrke Johnson. Mariann enjoys gardening, art, music, gold (sometimes), and her six perfect grandchildren.

Dr. Charles B. Martin has been an active member of the Texas Folklore Society since the mid-1960s, serving at various times as President, session chairman, and speaker. He has degrees from the University of New Mexico (B.A.), the University of Florida (M.A.), and the University of Missouri (Ph.D.). He taught English at the

University of Missouri (five years), East Central University, Oklahoma (five years), and the University of North Texas (thirty-five years, retiring in 1999). He taught abroad in Spain (two years) and Morocco (one semester). He has traveled extensively in Mexico and Guatemala.

Ruth Massingill, Ph.D. is associate department chair and associate professor of Mass Communication at Sam Houston State University. She is lead author of *Prison City: Life with the Death Penalty* (Peter Lang), and she produced an award-winning HIV/AIDS video series. Her doctorate in social marketing is from Teesside University in England.

Mel Strait, M.S. is a musician, a clinical associate professor in Mass Communication, and coordinator of the SHSU Broadcast Production Track. He has extensive experience as an announcer and writer, including an award-winning soundtrack for a video series. He recently completed a documentary about the Boeing B-17.

Emily Jones is a recent graduate of Sam Houston State University. Her undergraduate degree is in Mass Communication, with a concentration in Broadcast Production.

Charlie T. McCormick is serving as the 6th president of Schreiner University in Kerrville, Texas. Prior to this appointment, he served for 7½ years at Schreiner as the Provost and Vice-President for Academic Affairs. Charlie grew up in Snyder, Texas, where he learned that stories matter, and he chased this belief throughout his educational experiences at Abilene Christian University, Texas A&M University, and the University of Pennsylvania, where he earned a doctorate in folklore and folklife. He has researched and written about cruising on the strip, tunnel legends on college campuses, and eating rattlesnake at the Sweetwater, Texas, Rattlesnake Round-up. He is currently working on a book-length manuscript on American women bullfighters.

John Meadows is a born-and-raised native of Austin, Texas. He served a hitch in the U.S. Navy, after which he attended UT Austin via the G.I. Bill. John remains active as an actor and folk musician. He has done everything from driving dump trucks to serving as Reading Clerk before the Texas House of Representatives. The Texas Folklore Society is one of his favorite organizations.

After a varied career, **Vicky J. Rose** attended Sam Houston State University as a non-traditional student, obtaining a degree in journalism with a history minor from Angelo State University. Her articles have appeared in numerous magazines; she was a 2014 WWA Spur Finalist for her short fiction story, "A Promise Broken, A Promise Kept." Two of her novels are sold by Amazon, and a third—about a reluctant female town marshal in 1870s Texas—is to be published by Kensington in 2018. She lives with her son, Dan, two cats, and a dog in Central Texas, ten miles from where she grew up.

Jean Granberry Schnitz was born in Spur, Texas. She graduated from Raymondville High School in 1948, and from Texas College of Arts and Industries in Kingsville in 1952. She and Lew Schnitz were married in 1953; they have three sons, four grandchildren, and two great-grandchildren. A retired legal secretary, she lives near Boerne. As of 2017, she has presented thirteen papers to the Texas Folklore Society, most of which were published in TFS annual volumes. She has also written numerous other papers, articles, and books. Jean served more than ten years on the Board of the Texas Folklore Society, and was President in 2006–2007.

Jo Virgil, a fourth-generation Texas, recently retired from her job as the Community Outreach and Information Specialist for the Texas Governor's Committee on People with Disabilities. Before that, she did freelance reporting for the *Fort Worth Star-Telegram,* and then served as Community Relations Manager for Barnes & Noble for many years, learning much from the authors she worked with there. She has a Master of Journalism degree with a minor in Environmental Science, reflecting her love of writing and appreciation of nature. She has been a Texas Folklore Society member for many years, and loves telling and hearing tales (and tall tales) about Texas.

Charles Williams made the journey from a small farm in Upstate New York to being Executive Director of the Will Rogers Medallion Award Committee. Along the way, he was a Ceramic Engineer for several companies, most recently Texas Instruments, from which he retired. He holds fourteen U.S. patents and has published numerous scientific papers and other erudite articles. He became a professional storyteller over fifty years ago and, in 1991, a Cowboy Poet, making him one of the most accomplished Alternate Reality Expounders performing today. He has served the Texas Folklore Society as Board Member, and in 2016 he was President.

Jerry Young was a teacher, administrator, storyteller, and writer. He was very involved in all of these. According to Barbara, his widow, the Texas Folklore Society was one of his favorite organizations, and he was planning on being at the annual meeting in the spring of 2017. He was very excited about his article on Jacob Brodbeck being published.

INDEX

A

B

C

D

E

F

G

P

Q

R

S

T

U

V

W

Y

Z